D1338000

1965

Also by Christopher Bray

MICHAEL CAINE: A Class Act
SEAN CONNERY: The Measure of a Man.

1965

The Year Modern Britain Was Born

CHRISTOPHER BRAY

**SIMON &
SCHUSTER**

London · New York · Sydney · Toronto · New Delhi

A CBS COMPANY

First published in Great Britain by Simon & Schuster UK Ltd, 2014
A CBS COMPANY

1 3 5 7 9 10 8 6 4 2

Simon & Schuster UK Ltd
1st Floor
222 Gray's Inn Road
London WC1X 8HB

www.simonandschuster.co.uk

Simon & Schuster Australia, Sydney
Simon & Schuster India, New Delhi

A CIP catalogue record for this book
is available from the British Library

ISBN: 978-0-85720-278-9
ISBN: 978-0-85720-279-6 (ebook)

The author and publisher have made all reasonable efforts
to contact copyright holders for permission, and apologise
for any omissions or errors in the form of credits.
Corrections may be made to future printings.

Typeset in the UK by M Rules
Printed and bound by CPI Group (UK) Ltd, Croydon, CR0 4YY

CONTENTS

PICTURE CREDITS

For S.K., whose year this is.

1965 TIMELINE

1 January: Timothy Leary publishes *The Psychedelic Reader*.

4 January: T. S. Eliot dies.

7 January: The Kray twins are arrested.

9 January: *Not Only . . . But Also* begins on BBC television.

10 January: The *Observer* announces that George Melly is to be its pop culture critic.

24 January: Winston Churchill dies; his funeral takes place a week later on 30 January.

4 February: Confederation of British Industry founded.

6 February: Five days after his fiftieth birthday, Sir Stanley Matthews plays his last game of First Division football. He will be knighted later in the year.

14 February: The millionth Mini rolls off the production line.

16 February: The second Beeching Report suggests the closure of all but the most mainline train services in Britain.

20 February: *Ranger* lands on the moon.

23 February: Bridget Riley, Gerald Laing and Peter Phillips take the New York art world by storm.

24 February: Jennie Lee boosts government spending on the arts, saying she wants a 'gayer, more cultivated Britain'.

9 March:	After twelve years' work, John Fowles finally completes his second novel to be published, *The Magus*.
11 March:	Sylvia Plath's *Ariel* is published posthumously.
15 March:	Hugh Casson's new brutalist Elephant House opens at London Zoo.
18 March:	Aleksei Leonov, on board *Voskhod 2*, becomes the first man to walk in space.
1 April:	Ian Fleming's final James Bond novel, *The Man With the Golden Gun*, is published.
4 April:	Early Bird satellite, which allows Europeans instant contact with America, launched. (It becomes operational in June.)
9 April:	The Beatles' 'Ticket to Ride'/'Yes It Is' released.
23 April:	The Pennine Way opens.
1 May:	Albert Johanneson is the first black man to play in an FA Cup Final.
27 May:	Kingsley Amis publishes *The James Bond Dossier*.
May:	Ruth Rendell's second novel, *To Fear a Painted Devil*, serves notice she will be a serious writer.
May:	Bob Dylan, touring the UK and staying in London, invents the pop video with his *Subterranean Homesick Blues*.
June:	R. D. Laing turns Kingsley Hall in London's East End into a centre for radical experiments in therapy.
3 June:	Harold Pinter's *The Homecoming* opens at the Aldwych Theatre.
3 June:	Gemini 4 astronaut Edward Higgins White becomes the first American to walk in space.
16 June:	Richard Lester's *The Knack* premieres.
18 June:	John le Carré publishes *The Looking Glass War*.
June:	Drink-driving law inaugurated.

19 June: The Beat poets congregate at the Royal Albert Hall, marking the formal birth of the literary underground.

7 July: *Tomorrow's World*, which will be the BBC's long-running technological magazine show, airs for the first time.

12 July: Education Secretary Tony Crosland issues Circular 10/65 designed to 'eliminate separatism in secondary education'.

15 July: Leonard Bernstein's *Chichester Psalms* debuts.

20 July: Bob Dylan releases 'Like a Rolling Stone', the longest single yet heard.

22 July: Johnny Speight's *Till Death Us Do Part* debuts on the BBC.

25 July: Dylan goes electric.

27 July: Edward Heath, a grammar school educated MP, is elected leader of the Tory Party.

1 August: Television advertisements for cigarettes are banned.

12 August: Barrister Elizabeth Lane becomes the first woman to be appointed to the High Court.

20 August: The Rolling Stones release '(I Can't Get No) Satisfaction' in Britain.

23 August: *Doctor Who and the Daleks* opens at cinemas.

28 August: Robert Moog's electronic synthesiser is heard live for the first time in an afternoon concert of *musique concrete*.

August: The Confederation of British Industry is formally opened for business. The Wilson government immediately agrees to its plea for Britain to go metric. (Nothing much happens on this front until, well, nothing has happened, actually.)

11 September: Construction starts on the first Concorde airframe in Bristol.

September: Ralph Nader publishes *Unsafe at Any Speed*, a critique of the motor industry.

September: Evelyn Waugh publishes his *Sword of Honour* trilogy.

1 October: *Thunderbirds* begins on ITV.

2 October: Season 4 of *The Avengers* begins on ITV.

6 October: Ian Brady is arrested for murder.

8 October: The Post Office Tower opens to the public.

14 October: Muriel Spark's *The Mandelbaum Gate* is published.

16 October: The Beatles are awarded MBEs at Buckingham Palace.

3 November: Edward Bond's *Saved* opens at the Royal Court Theatre.

3 November: Ken Loach's original television version of *Up the Junction* is broadcast.

8 November: The death penalty is abolished.

13 November: Kenneth Tynan says 'fuck' on live television.

21 November: David Bailey's *Box of Pin-Ups* is published.

29 November: Mary Whitehouse founds the National Viewers and Listeners Association.

November: Allen Ginsberg publishes 'How to Make a March/
Spectacle', in which he argues for flower power.

3 December: The Beatles' *Rubber Soul* is released.

8 December: Dennis Potter's *Stand Up, Nigel Barton* is broadcast.

8 December: First Race Relations Act comes into force.

22 December: 70 mph speed limit introduced on British roads.

23 December: Harold Wilson appoints Roy Jenkins Home Secretary. He immediately bans the flogging of prisoners – the first of many pieces of legislation that will engender what is called the 'permissive society'.

INTRODUCTION

'Great cultural changes begin in affectation and end in routine.'

Jacques Barzun, The House of Intellect

It was the year that Britain got up to speed with the supersonic age (not to mention metrication), the year that we went car crazy – and the year in which craziness was held to be the only sane reaction to an insane society. It was the year comedians and television shows and rock bands imported the aesthetics of the avant garde into their work, and the year that pop culture came to be taken as seriously as high art. It was the year that communications across the Atlantic became instantaneous, and the year when, for the first time in a century, British artists took American galleries by storm. It was the year that the grandees of the political elite realised they were too grand for their own good, the year feminism went mainstream, the year censorship was sin-binned, the year taboos were both talked up and trashed. It was the year when everything changed – and the year that everyone knew it.

We are talking of 1965, the year the old Britain died and the new Britain was born. Because 1965 planted bomb after bomb under the hidebound, stick-in-the-mud, living-on-past-glories Britain that preceded it – and gave us the country we live in today. Everywhere you looked, from the House of Commons to the school common room, from the recording studio to the television screen, from the railways to the rear-view mirror, from the inner space of the tortured mind to the outer space of the moon, the country was (as Bob Dylan put it that year) 'busy being born'. Change wasn't just in the air – it *was* the air, the air everyone breathed all day long.

'We all dressed up,' the melodramatically cynical John Lennon once said of the 1960s, but 'nothing happened'.[1] The photographer David Bailey wasn't even sure about the numbers. The sixties, he claimed, were 'great for 2000 people living in London, a very elitist thing, a naïve kind of attitude before the accountants took over'.[2] Picking up and running with this revisionist baton, the historian Dominic Sandbrook has argued that though during the sixties a 'small group of affluent, self-confident young people ... welcomed change, millions of others clung firmly to what they knew and loved'.[3] You could say pretty much the same thing about the Russian Revolution, of course. Yet who would claim that the communist Russia of 1926 was the same place as the Tsarist autocracy of 1916? So too with Britain in the sixties. Of course not everyone was a psychedelic painter or pop-star poet. Nor were many people actively involved in the counterculture (that balmy cocktail of New Left Marxism, Eastern mysticism, Left Bank existentialism and whatever drugs you could lay your hands on) that burgeoned in 1965. But for good or ill, those who were involved were the advance guard of a new sensibility, and the reverberations of what they made happen that year were heard and felt by everyone in the country. We all of us live lives that are shaped and structured by the changes that took place that year. You can hymn or hate those changes, but you can't deny that they took place. There is Britain before 1965 and Britain after 1965, and they are not the same thing.

Culturally, the year was a time of innovatory tumult. This was the year that the great British public finally got to grips with the modernist project of the preceding hundred years, the year when everyone from comedians to pop singers, from TV writers to film directors, began to admit to the constructed nature of their imaginary worlds and got self-conscious with their artistry. What Bertolt Brecht had called the 'Fourth Wall' – the imaginary barrier that separated audiences from actors in the theatre – came tumbling down. The star of a mainstream movie melodrama turned to the camera to address the viewer directly. The nightmare visions of surrealism were rendered suburban and domestic. Writers of putatively action-packed espionage novels repeatedly tried to show that their imaginary thrills and spills not only bore no relation to the workings of the real world, but actually existed in order to disguise what was really going on. On the musical front, the Rolling Stones' '(I Can't Get No) Satisfaction' sexed up the top 20, Dusty Springfield popularised black music in the BBC's hitherto middle-of-the-road Saturday night variety slot, Bob Dylan abandoned protest for pop as he travelled the UK on a controversial tour, Robert Moog invented the future of rock with his electronic synthesiser, and the Beatles came of age as songwriters with the LSD-inspired *Rubber Soul*.

But LSD was everywhere in 1965. It's biggest advocate was the radical psychiatrist R. D. Laing who that year set up an experimental community in London's East End, in which patients and therapists lived together with the aim of exploring the landscapes of schizophrenia. The writer John Fowles was on similar terrain in *The Magus*, a novel of existential abreaction that dumped a stiff-upper-lipped Englishman straight out of central casting for Victorian Britain into a paranoid, erotic nightmare. (Novels might otherwise be thought conspicuous by their comparative absence from this book. The reason is twofold. First, not much of the fiction published here in 1965 has really stood the test of time.[*]

---

[*] The jury is still out on Norman Mailer's *An American Dream*, but even had that book been a guaranteed, copper-bottomed masterpiece it wouldn't have featured here because it's, well, an American dream.

Second – perhaps as a corollary, perhaps as a symptom – this is the year that Britain's once largely literary culture made way for one in which cinema and television and song became the dominant media for the telling of stories. Young people in the sixties weren't great readers – though they might seem so by comparison with their counterparts today – largely because the baby boomers were the first generation to have been raised in what Robert Hughes once called the 'amniotic glare'[4] of television.)

But do the sixties genuinely exist? Can we really demarcate one decade from another, one year from another? Or is history, like time itself, a continuum in which change never happens because change is all that ever happens? Perhaps, but it doesn't feel like that to us. It doesn't feel like that because whether or not time exists, we ourselves exist only as temporal beings. And even though time itself is a human construct, it is precisely because of its constructed nature that it matters so much to us. Years, decades, quarter-centuries, half-centuries – such are the periodic structures that we use to make sense of our lives. And how else to make sense of Britain today than to see the sixties as the pivotal decade in the twentieth century – the decade you have to understand in order to have an inkling of where we are today.

Why 1965? Simply because it was the pivotal year in that pivotal decade. For all the envy you might feel at having missed out on 1967's Summer of Love, for all the trouble-tastic talk of May 1968, the events of those years can't begin to compete with 1965 for the variety of *concrete* changes they brought to the way the average life was lived in Britain. Moreover, 1965 is the hinge year in the now commonly accepted historical bracket of the so-called 'long sixties'. It falls precisely midway through the eighteen-year period that begins in 1956 with the Suez Crisis and the opening of John Osborne's *Look Back in Anger*, and ends in 1973 with the Yom Kippur War and the massive hike in the price of oil and David Bowie's *Aladdin Sane*. Add in the fact that 1965 was the year that the first baby boomers came of age and became eligible to vote (the age being twenty-one back then) and it is plain that this is the year around which the cultural revolution of the sixties turned.

Given the accession of all those baby boomers to the electoral arena it should hardly come as a surprise that there was political change in 1965, too. This was the year that the aristocrat-dominated Conservative Party chose the grammar school educated son of a Kentish carpenter, Edward Heath, to be its first non-blue-blooded leader. At the very same moment, Harold Wilson's Labour government set about dismantling the heavily demarcated, tripartite structure of post-war education, replacing it with the non-selective comprehensive system. The death penalty was finally abolished that year, too, and when Roy Jenkins was appointed Home Secretary in December 1965 he immediately let it be known that he would be refusing to sign birching orders for prisoners – the first step, he said, in his plan to civilise what he considered a brutish culture. Over the next two years he would become the chief architect of the 'permissive' society we still inhabit, with liberalising legislation on homosexuality, divorce, abortion, race and censorship.

There was something a little permissive about the job market, too. In 1965, the percentage of people unemployed stood at around 1.5 per cent. In other words, if you wanted a job, you had one. And if you didn't want the job you had, you chucked it in, walked round the corner, and got another. It is mighty easy, in such easeful circumstances, to acquiesce to – or even take part in – a cultural revolution. Still and all, there is no denying that the post-war consensus that any government's first duty was to use public spending to ensure full employment was beginning to fray. The baby boomers who had benefited most from that settlement, who had lived only under governments bent on slaying what William Beveridge had called pre-war Britain's five evils – want, disease, ignorance, squalor and idleness – were too short-sighted to keep the system going.

Short-sighted and tight-fisted. In his song 'Sunny Afternoon', the Kinks' leading light Ray Davies (a first-year baby boomer, born in 1944) was to be heard bemoaning the fact that 'the taxman's taken all my dough', thus abandoning him to life in a 'stately home'. Almost simultaneously, one of the sixties' greatest poets of sybaritic hedonism, the Beatles' guitarist George Harrison (born a year before the baby boom, in 1943), got in on the act with the lyrically risible 'Taxman', an attack on the then top tax rate of nineteen shillings and sixpence (97.5p) in the pound.* It is not, as Burke said, given to men to be able to tax and to please at the same time, of course. Nonetheless, the generation who had voted for the establishment of the welfare state might have expected a little more loyalty from the generation who had supped of it from birth.

This is not the place to argue the merits or defects of Keynesian economics (though it is only fair to point out that the author believes that no other economic policy was ever so beneficial to so many for so long). But it needs to be made clear that twenty years into the social democratic experiment, the national mood was changing. Memories of the 1930s and the slump that had done so much to engender the country's move to macroeconomic management were fading. The old, who remembered those years of dread and despair, were dying off. The young – the post-war baby boomers who had known nothing but the Keynesian comfort blanket, and who were beginning to realise that their numbers meant they called an awful lot of shots – were blasé almost to the point of unconsciousness about the golden age in which they had been brought up.

* Anyone who thinks the Beatles the ur-emblems of countercultural insurrection would do well to remember that when they took themselves off to India, to learn about the delights of transcendental meditation, Ringo insisted on bringing a suitcase full of baked beans with him. Sagely enough, in the opinion of John Lennon, who thought the food on offer at the ashram of the Maharishi Mahesh Yogi 'lousy'.

All of which means that when Margaret Thatcher claimed that the Britain of the 1980s was 'reaping what was sown in the sixties' she wasn't wrong. What she didn't grasp was that it was she who was doing the reaping. The neo-liberal revolution Thatcher launched in the eighties (and that six years since the global financial crash that blew it clean out of the water somehow continues to sail blithely on) was born out of precisely those 'fashionable theories and permissive claptrap [of the sixties which] set the scene for a society in which old values of discipline and restraint were denigrated'.[5] Baffled though Mrs Thatcher would have been by the thought, there isn't any great gulf between the sixties' long-haired, dope-smoking rocker who wants you to 'Get off my back, man', and the eighties-and-onwards' no-nonsense bankster or business body who wants the state to keep well clear of the workings of the market.* The Thatcher revolution wasn't a response to the sixties revolution. Like the songs and movies, the shows and series, the plays and paintings and poems to which we now turn, it was part of it.

---

* To be sure, there was more to the counterculture than its infantile wish for absolute freedom. Unlike the neo-liberals who trailed in their wake, the hippies were genuine conservatives disgusted at what they saw as the empty-headed materialism (in both the consumerist and secularist senses of the word) of an increasingly irreligious culture. At heart, the hippies were missionaries without a church. Far from being the beginning of something, then the counterculture was the end of something – a world view that had emphasised not the here and now of consumer capitalism but an afterlife that was yours to work for.

1

GOODBYE TO ALL THAT

In which our stage is set

'If it is agreed that those who seek to rebuild what Mr Churchill likes to call "traditional" Britain have no hope of fulfilling that end, it follows that there must be a new Britain in a new civilization.'

Harold Laski[1]

'History has many cunning passages, contrived corridors'

T. S. Eliot, 'Gerontion'

He had loathed the modern world. He had loathed modern culture. Most of all, he had loathed modern painting. Though Evelyn Waugh had thought him 'always in the wrong'[2] he had thought Waugh right to have one of his characters argue that 'modern art is all bosh'.[3] True, when Graham Sutherland was commissioned to paint his portrait he called the resultant picture 'a remarkable example of modern art'.[4] In private though, he was rather less given to irony. The picture, he said, made him look like a 'down-and-out drunk who has been picked out of the gutter in the Strand'.[5] As soon as he decently could, he had his wife burn it. An amateur watercolourist himself, he once asked the President of the Royal Academy, Sir Alfred Munnings, whether he detested Picasso – and if so, then 'would you join with me in kicking his something, something, something?' 'Yes, sir,' Munnings told a laughing RA audience he had gleefully replied. 'I would.'[6]

But Munnings had died at the end of the fifties, and now, five years later and almost two weeks since what turned out to be his final stroke, Winston Churchill's own 'great heart was still'.[7] It was 24 January 1965, and for the next six days, before his funeral at St Paul's Cathedral, Victorian Britain, imperial Britain – the Britain that had made Churchill and that he had spent the bulk of his ninety years trying to remake – lived again. Within hours of his death Buckingham Palace announced that Churchill was to be given a state funeral – the first non-royal to be granted such an honour since the burial of William Gladstone in 1898. On that occasion Queen Victoria had only reluctantly acceded to Parliament's request. This time round, there was no such dithering. Indeed, the gun carriage that transported Churchill's coffin to the funeral service in St Paul's was the same one that had been used to take Victoria to her own final send-off.

For the Queen thought as highly of Churchill as most of her subjects did. Churchill had once said of Queen Elizabeth II that 'All the film people in the world, if they had scoured the globe, could not have found anyone so suited to the part.'[8] It was a compliment the Queen was happy to return. She was certain that the British couldn't have found a man more fitted to leading them through the war against Hitler. Like Sir Edward Bridges, the wartime cabinet secretary, she believed that only Churchill had 'had the power to make the nation believe that it could win'.[9] And so, not content with kick-starting the organisation of the funeral for a commoner, she let it be known that she would be in attendance at the ceremony.

Before that, though, there was the lying-in-state. During the course of Churchill's final days, the streets around his home at Hyde Park Gate hadn't been short of well-wishers and lookers-on, all busy mumbling silent prayers and wondering whether their country, and even their world, would ever make sense again. At any one time no fewer than 250 people had maintained that cold, wet watch on their wartime leader. But their numbers were as nothing when set against the crowds that would turn up to say their last farewells to 'good old Winnie'. For the three days preceding the funeral, on 30 January, Churchill's catafalque was placed in Westminster Hall, during which time more than 300,000 people filed past to pay their last respects. And on the day of the funeral itself, with Big Ben silenced, hundreds of thousands more turned out to watch the gun carriage that took Churchill's coffin through the streets of central London to St Paul's. Many further millions around the globe watched the proceedings on television. A great national production number though Churchill's funeral was, it was also, like the moon landing that would follow it four years later, one of the world historical events of the 1960s.

For what was being commemorated wasn't merely the death of one man. Just this once, people were right to talk about the end of an era. Or eras. As Clement Attlee, who had replaced Churchill as Prime Minister after the war, once said, there was about him 'a layer of seventeenth century, a layer of eighteenth century, a layer of nineteenth century and possibly even a layer of twentieth century. You were never sure which layer would be uppermost.'[10] Never sure, perhaps, but in general it was a good bet to put your money on Churchill's nineteenth-century layer coming out on top. He was nothing if not a child of Britain's imperial age. Like Macaulay, from whose books of Whig history he learned so much, he was happy to count himself a member of 'the greatest and most highly civilised people that ever the world saw'.[11] Macaulay gave Churchill the faith to believe in his own knee-jerk notion that

Britain was the moral and political leader of the world. Right to the end he never doubted that he had been born into the country whose duty it was to civilise anyone unlucky enough to have been born elsewhere.

Certainly he had been born into the Whig interpretation of history. He was a descendant of John Churchill, the most successful general of his age, and the man appointed by Queen Anne as the first Duke of Marlborough. A couple of years later, after Churchill's victory against French and Bavarian troops at the Battle of Blenheim, the Queen and a grateful nation gifted the duke the wherewithal (£300,000 of wherewithal*) to build Blenheim Palace. Designed by Sir John Vanbrugh, this top-heavy slice of English baroque was finished in the early 1720s. And it was there, a century and half later, on 30 November 1874, that Winston Churchill came into this world.

His military sensibility was spotted early. Churchill's father, Randolph, a Whiggishly wet Tory (and very briefly Chancellor of the Exchequer who foresaw, if not invented, the idea of the twentieth-century welfare state), never thought much of young Winston's intellect. Indeed, he never thought much of – or about – Winston at all. But he liked the way his son played with his toy soldiers. He seemed to be having more than just fun with them. He seemed to be thinking about how best they could be used in the field. If the Church wouldn't be quite right for him, much less the law – let alone politics – then perhaps he could make something of himself in the forces. After 'Army Class' at Harrow Winston enrolled at the Royal Military College at Sandhurst in September 1893. (It took more than one go: he failed the entrance exam not once but twice.)

Short of leg and pigeon of chest (Churchill was known to disparage himself as a pygmy), his greatest joy at Sandhurst lay in riding. So much so that against his father's wishes that he join an

---

* Around £33 million today.

infantry regiment – the 60th Rifles – he determined to sign up with the cavalry. Fortunately for Churchill, his mother, Jennie, was a friend of Colonel John Brabazon of the 4th Queen's Own Hussars, and on 20 February 1895 (not uncoincidentally less than a month after Randolph Churchill's death) Winston was enrolled into their number. Even now, with his father gone, he was determined to prove himself a hero in action in the hope of winning for himself the approval and acclaim he felt he had been denied.

At the same time, he wasn't certain that a military career would be enough. He wanted, he told his mother, not just to be there in the thick of the action but to be back home telling people about it, too. He wanted, in short, to be a reporter. Once again, Jennie pulled some strings, and soon enough Winston found himself in Cuba writing war reports for the *Daily Graphic*: 'When first in the dim light of early morning I saw the shores of Cuba rise and define themselves from dark-blue horizons,' Churchill wrote, in one of his early pieces, 'I felt as if I sailed with Long John Silver and first gazed on Treasure Island. Here was a place where real things were going on. Here was a scene of vital action. Here was a place where anything might happen. Here was a place where something would certainly happen. Here I might leave my bones.'[12] Here, too, he might start building a reputation as a master of the English language.

Subsequently, Churchill would see service in India (on the North-West Frontier), in the Sudan, and in the second Boer War. There is no doubting his bravery – he seems to have been thrilled at the thought that death could be so near at hand, and thrilled yet more by the faith it granted him in his invincibility – but nor is there any denying that what really made his name were the Ripping Yarns-style stories (by now he was writing for the *Morning Post*, too) and books he spun out of his adventures. And yet believe in this stuff though he did, Churchill was sage enough to see that the jingoistic jig was up. 'It did seem such a pity that it all had to be make-believe', he recorded in the first volume of his memoirs. 'If it had only been 100 years earlier what splendid times we should have had!'[13]

But there are different kinds of splendour, and by 1899 Churchill had made enough money from book sales to be able to contemplate the political career his father had thought beyond him. He didn't win the by-election he fought in Oldham that year – a special correspondent for *The Times* called Churchill out for taking 'too much pain with his orations' and not appreciating that the good people of Oldham 'prefer solid argument to smart epigrams'[14] – though little more than a year later he was elected the town's MP in the general election of 1900.

Still, a version of *The Times*' reporter's criticism would dog Churchill for the next four decades. Even his admirers thought that his high-flying rhetoric encouraged him to treat events in the real world as if they were just acts in a drama that was forever descending into dullness unless he was on hand to liven things up. Witness his decision, in April 1915, four years into his stint as First Lord of the Admiralty, to launch an assault on the Gallipoli peninsula in what is now Turkey. Yes, had the mission been a success it would have opened up a sea route to Russia (still an ally at that time). But all the evidence shows that Churchill had conceived of the assault for rather less rational reasons. Bored with the endless, dirge-like slog that was the Western Front, he wanted a big, show-stopping number to jolt this hitherto dull war into a second act full of derring-do. It didn't work out like that. Gallipoli was a disaster for the Allies. They lost more than 70,000 men there before their eventual withdrawal. The only show that was stopped was Churchill's. He was forced to resign from the Admiralty (and perhaps to seek a kind of atonement in active service on the dreaded Western Front). From now on he would be mistrusted not just for his phrase-turning but for treating the theatre of war as no more than a theatre.

Even as late as the mid-thirties, when Churchill was telling the world that Adolf Hitler was up to no good, the powers that be were still turning a deaf ear to him. They thought Churchill was worried by Hitler simply because he (Hitler) was another stentorian stage-strutter. They thought Churchill's love of warmongering led him to exaggerate the threats of others. But they were wrong – and Churchill was right when he said that Hitler was more than just another blustering chancer. Their mistake only heightened Churchill's lustre when he was invited back to the top table after everyone realised that Hitler really was up to no good.

At first he found himself back in charge of the Admiralty, where within months he had engineered something that looked very much like a second Gallipoli – a botched expedition to Norway that ended in retreat. The man who had once rued the notion 'that the age of wars between civilized nations had come to an end for ever' had miscalculated.[15] Stuck in his imperial fantasies, he hadn't stopped to wonder about the threat his battlecruisers could face from the air. This time around, though, it wasn't Churchill who took the blame, but the Prime Minister, Neville Chamberlain. When he resigned, after a way too narrow win on a no-confidence motion ('Go! Go! Go!' howled the opposition), a coalition government was formed to take Britain through the war. Churchill was a shoo-in for the leader.*

Cometh the hour, cometh the man. Except that in Churchill's case things worked the other way around. The man had always been there – he'd just been waiting for the hour in which to prove it. He had always known that it was one day going to fall to him

---

* In fact, Chamberlain's Foreign Secretary, Lord Halifax, was the shoo-in. But he felt himself unable to lead the government – not only because he would have had to do so from the House of Lords but because the man who was running the Admiralty was so obviously the man for the job. Halifax may, too, have feared that Hitler had already won the war – and that he didn't want to be the PM who admitted the fact.

to lead his country through a great crisis. Hitler and his 'Narsis'* were that crisis, and Churchill admitted to 'a profound sense of relief' that he could at last 'walk ... with destiny' in the fight against him.[16]

On 13 May 1940, his first Monday in office, Churchill addressed the House of Commons. 'I have nothing to offer', he told them, 'but blood, toil, tears and sweat.' In fact, as the speech couldn't help but make clear, he had something else to offer: his speeches themselves. For all Waugh's talk of Churchill's 'sham Augustan prose', for all the carping that his rhetoric was all idiom and no style – 'like a court dress of rather tarnished grandeur from a theatrical costumier's'[17] – Churchill spoke for the nation. Six days after that first prime ministerial address, on Trinity Sunday, he told the country about the successes Hitler's forces were enjoying in France, and about how there would soon have to be a fight 'for all that Britain is, and all that Britain means'.

Nearly all that Britain was was listening. Throughout the war an average of seven in ten people tuned in to hear Churchill's war broadcasts. Their effect on national morale cannot be exaggerated. Even today, three quarters of a century on, you can't read or listen to them without feeling your eyes moisten. Roy Jenkins wasn't wrong when he said that Churchill at the microphone or podium was 'inclined to go over several tops'.[18] But as great actors know – and Churchill was one of their number; had he not been, nobody would have believed in him – there are times when going over the top is the only way to get under the skin. Some stories are so ridiculous they have to be told hammily. Churchill's story about Britain being able to resist the Nazis was one of them. Until the Americans joined the war, his rhetoric was all the country had to fight with.

With Hitler vanquished, Churchill and the Tories were thrown out of government. The solidarity he had invoked and embodied

---

* Churchill's hilarious habitual mispronunciation of the word was surely deliberate.

in wartime was thought unsuited to the peace. His values seemed out of date. Not that he was forgotten. His memory went on being cherished long after the country decided he had nothing more to offer them. And although over the years it would become a commonplace cat-among-the-pigeons contrarianism to suggest that Britain's victory in the war against Hitler had been largely illusory and almost entirely delusory, the revisionists never won many converts. When, a few days after Churchill's death, the historian John Grigg suggested that for Britain 'the next few days should act as a tonic rather than a sedative' there was no doubt that he was going out on a limb.[19]

Funerals are by definition celebrations of past glories, but wasn't there something hysterical about the way the British said their goodbyes to Churchill? Were they really just farewelling one of their country's more romantic visionaries, or were they, in fact, bidding adieu to romantic visions about the country itself? Were the British so moved by the end of what *Private Eye* had taken to calling 'the greatest dying Englishman' because they saw reflected in it the end of the Britain he had done so much to bolster and burnish? The Queen might have been of the opinion that 'the survival of this country and the sister nations of the Commonwealth in the face of the greatest danger that has ever threatened them will be a perpetual memorial to his leadership'[20] but there were those who believed land and leader yet more intimately entwined. As Charles de Gaulle was heard to say when he was advised of Churchill's death, 'Now Britain is no longer a great power.'[21]

De Gaulle was just the man to know. Two years earlier the French President had rebuffed Churchill's second successor as leader of the Conservative Party, Harold Macmillan, when he had made a belated entreaty to join the European Economic Community (EEC). (Macmillan, it should be pointed out, had worried that Churchill, an arch Atlanticist, would himself come out against the proposal.) De Gaulle vetoed the application because he feared that allowing the laggardly Brits into the EEC (who, had they signed up to the club when it was first mooted, amid the ash and ruin of the immediate post-war years, could likely have run the show from the get-go) would result in 'a colossal Atlantic community dependent on America'.[22] And yet, while de Gaulle and so many other European and world leaders were lined up to pay their respects at Churchill's funeral, neither the American President, Lyndon B. Johnson, nor any member of his administration could be bothered to make the journey across the Atlantic. 'Sometimes,' the French poet and statesman Alphonse de Lamartine remarked, 'when one person is missing, the whole world seems depopulated.'[23] For all those crowds, for all that hustle and bustle, Churchill's funeral was a tiny bit depopulated. A page in history had not, it seemed, been turned for the Americans.

Hitherto, Churchill had walked hand in hand with history. Indeed, a decade or so earlier, in a post-war collection of tribute essays, A. L. Rowse had suggested that 'Winston Churchill sums up the whole first half of our century.'[24] The survivor of an ambush at the Khyber Pass, he had lived on into the age of Hiroshima and the Campaign for Nuclear Disarmament.* Name any major event in his country's recent past and Churchill had been there, from the Siege of Malakand to the general strike, from the Boer War to the Blitz. He was, said, Isaiah Berlin, 'a gigantic historical figure . . . a legendary hero who belongs to myth as much as to reality, the largest human being of our times'.[25] The *Daily Express* was even more rampant in its adoration. 'History', Lord Beaverbrook's paper mournfully informed its readers, 'was with us while he lived.'[26]

---

* A campaign that Churchill, surprisingly enough, had some secret sympathy for. Not that his reasons were remotely conventional ones. He disapproved of nuclear weapons because they put an end to the need for more traditional forms of combat. He thought such combat brought out the best in men, paving the way for social progress. Like the Futurists – another group of modernist painters whose work he would have despised – he thought of war as social hygiene, a cleanser of the body politic.

So did Lyndon Johnson's no-show at Churchill's funeral mean that history was now against us? Or were such thoughts part of what the then Labour housing minister Richard Crossman called mere 'self-condolence on the end of our imperial destiny – with Churchill as its symbol'?[27] Certainly history was all we seemed to have when Churchill walked among us. Livewire though he had so often been in defending past visions, he was a deadweight when it came to forward thinking. Churchill wasn't wrong when he said that 'a nation that forgets its past has no future', but he could never see that a nation that forgets that its past isn't its present hasn't much of a future either. As President Eisenhower more than once complained of Churchill during the fifties, he doesn't 'think in terms of today, but rather only those of the war years'.[28]

For Churchill had no grasp of the social and political forces that had reshaped the world during his lifetime. He had fought the war not to build a new world but to save the British Empire he had been born into. Even if that had been possible – and since that Empire was long dead before the war the possibility did not meaningfully exist – his countrymen wouldn't have allowed it. Churchill might have wanted time to stand still, but they did not. Though they supported him unquestioningly throughout the war, everyone but Churchill could see that they wouldn't support him once it was over. Half a century or so before, Churchill had told the then Prime Minister, Lloyd George, 'You're not going to get your new world. The old world is a good enough place for me, and there's life in the old dog yet. It's going to sit up and wag its tail.'[29] But the new world had come anyway, and even though post-war shortages and rationing ensured that Churchill was voted back into 10 Downing Street in 1951, the price of his return had been his party's acceptance of the Keynesian post-war settlement of a welfare state and economic policies geared to full employment. 'I have', Churchill told his eldest daughter Diana a few years before his death, 'achieved a great deal to achieve nothing in the end.'[30]

Not that his achievements were over quite yet. In life Churchill had liberated his people from the threat of tyranny. In death he would liberate them some more – liberate them from what the novelist John Fowles was simultaneously calling 'the grotesquely elongated shadow . . . of that monstrous dwarf Queen Victoria'.[31] Cultures do not change overnight, of course. Nonetheless, John Grigg's suggestion that Churchill's death 'relieves us of a psychological burden'[32] was surely right. Churchill's passing licensed a whole vision of the past to pass too.

The funeral ceremony over, Churchill's coffin was drummed down to the Thames at Tower Pier. A nineteen-gun salute was fired as it was placed on the *Havengore* launch and taken upriver to the pier outside the Royal Festival Hall. From there a hearse transported the coffin on to Waterloo station, where the Queen's Royal Irish Hussars took over, carrying it to Platform 11 and putting it on a Battle of Britain-class locomotive called *Winston Churchill*. En route to the Oxfordshire of Churchill's birth, the train passed through station after station thronged with mourners (who had bought platform tickets for the privilege of watching it flash by). Churchill was finally laid to rest at a small private ceremony in the parish churchyard of Bladon, the place where he had worshipped as a boy and where his parents were also buried, in a plot within sight of the family home at Blenheim Palace.

Churchill's coffin had been made from oak trees that grew on the Blenheim estate, but the ropes that lowered it into the hard January earth had come from further afield. They had been made a hundred or so miles away, in Somerset – in the hamlet of East Coker, near Yeovil. An unremarkable fact and an unremarkable place – or anyway it would be were it not for the fact that twenty-five years earlier, during the months leading up to the Battle of Britain, a poem entitled 'East Coker' had been published in the Easter issue of a small-circulation magazine called the *New English Weekly*. It turned out to be a popular read, so popular, in fact, that the magazine reprinted it twice more in May and June of that year, before Faber & Faber published it in stand-alone pamphlet form that September, selling a handsome 12,000 copies or so. Good going for a characteristically difficult, eight-page verse from the pen of T. S. Eliot. Indeed, Eliot confessed himself to being worried somewhat by the poem's popularity, suggesting – only half jokingly – to a fellow editor at Faber that such success surely meant it 'couldn't be very good'.[33]

Certainly 'East Coker' was a tougher read than its sales figures suggest. No poem that requires for its understanding an insight into the philosophy of Heraclitus and the thought of St John of the Cross might be fancied destined for bestseller status. Yet 'East Coker's popularity is fairly easily accounted for. Before it did anything else – and it did an awful lot – Eliot's poem embodied and expressed the need for cultural continuity at a time when the British felt under threat of cultural extinction. Even as the poem was published, the British army, forced back by Hitler's troops, was in retreat from France. Soon enough, it was widely feared, those same Nazi troops would be crossing the Channel and invading England. The Englishman's world might be about to be changed out of all recognition – but here was Eliot telling his readers an older England survived and would always survive. Amen to that, you can almost hear Churchill saying. Because while Churchill would have had no time for Eliot's intricacies and enigmas, he would have applauded his searching commitment to deeper continuities than a secular age allows. Like the Eliot of 'Little Gidding' (the final instalment of what Eliot came to call his *Four Quartets*; 'East Coker' was the second), Churchill was forever adamant that 'History is now and England.'

Not that the inspiration behind 'East Coker' was purely cultural. Eliot had personal reasons for writing about the place, too. A little more than two centuries before Eliot's birth, in St Louis, Missouri, in 1888, his ancestor Andrew Elyot had left East Coker for the

New World. Eliot himself made the same journey in reverse, so far in reverse in fact that in the run-up to his fortieth birthday he became a British citizen and entered the Anglican Church. Eliot's visit to East Coker was not a chance one, then, and he was sufficiently moved by the place to arrange for his funeral ashes to be buried there in St Michael's Church. And on 8 January 1965, five days after Eliot's death and just two days before the stroke that would finally fell Winston Churchill, that is where they were taken:

> Here, whence his forbears sprang, a man is laid
> As dust, in quiet earth, whose written word
> Helped many thousands broken and dismayed
> Among the ruins of triumphant wrong.

That is the then Poet Laureate John Masefield's tribute to Eliot, though anything less Eliot-like it is hard to imagine.[34] At eighty-six, Masefield had been born a mere ten years before Eliot, but in aesthetic styles and ambitions the two men might have been generations apart.

For Eliot was the great modernist innovator of English poetry, a writer whose most characteristic verse even as encyclopaedic a critic as Cyril Connolly could describe as 'almost unintelligible'.[35] Eliot wouldn't have disagreed, nor have been aggrieved at the suggestion that a great many of his most famous poems were pretty much incomprehensible. 'I wasn't even bothering,' he said of his early masterpiece *The Waste Land*, 'whether I understood what I was saying ... it was a question of not being able to – of having more to say than one knew how to say, and something one wanted to put into words and rhythm which one didn't have the command of words and rhythm to put in a way immediately apprehensible.'[36]

Indeed, when the poem was published in the UK, in October

1922 in the inaugural issue of Eliot's magazine *The Criterion*, it came accompanied by several pages of notes that purported to explicate, or at least ground by means of reference, its more enigmatic passages. (Twelve years later, the artist Marcel Duchamp's *The Green Box* would provide much the same kind of interpretative flapdoodle for his inscrutable painting on two glass panels, *The Bride Stripped Bare by Her Bachelors, Even* [1915–23] – another work that conceived of contemporary sex as mechanised, alienated and resolutely profane.) Such mock hermeneutics were necessary, Eliot argued, because 'Poets in our civilisation, as it exists at present, must be difficult ... the poet must become more and more comprehensive, more allusive, more indirect, to force, to dislocate if necessary, language into his meaning.'[37] Like all the modernists, that is, Eliot believed that the language of art had to change when there is change within the culture it both reflects and embodies – and in a culture as fractured as that of Europe after the Great War that meant greatly changed art.

Almost a century on, we can, perhaps, more easily grasp the stuttering, shuttling, cut-up cubism of Eliot's technique than its first readers did. *The Waste Land*'s riven, multi-voiced structure is plainly an attempt at rendering the chaotic cacophony of modern city life – though that was far from plain at the time. Like Stravinsky's *Le Sacre du printemps*, a work Eliot pronounced 'very remarkable', *The Waste Land* worked to 'transform the rhythm of the steppes into the scream of the motor horn, the rattle of machinery, the grind of wheels, the beating of iron and steel, the roar of the underground railway, and the other barbaric cries of modern life; and to transform these despairing noises into music'.[38] But that music, Eliot acknowledged, 'was too strange and new to please very many people'.[39] So too *The Waste Land*. What the bulk of its first readers saw wasn't an evocation of chaos but chaos itself – pure, unadulterated and almost minatory in its ambiguities. Reading *The Waste Land* is like watching an early television slip in and out of tuning:

fractured, staccato moments of visual and verbal sense amid the hiss and crackle of the void.

As to what the poem might mean – well, the idea that it might mean anything, at least in the sense of *meaning* to mean something, is as meaningless as asking what a TV itself means. Certainly Eliot wasn't the man to offer any help. Asked by an undergraduate at an Oxford Poetry Club seminar what he had meant by the line 'Lady, three white leopards sat under a juniper tree' (from the 1930 poem 'Ash Wednesday'), Eliot told him that he had meant 'Lady, three white leopards sat under a juniper tree'.[40] And a decade or so after *The Waste Land* he took issue with what he called 'some of the more approving critics [who] said that [the poem] had expressed the "disillusionment of a generation", which is nonsense. I may have expressed for them their own illusion of being disillusioned, but that did not form part of my intention.'[41] No, indeed, because intention didn't enter into it: 'I wonder what an *intention* means! One wants to get something off one's chest. One doesn't quite know what it is that one wants to get off the chest until one's got it off. But I couldn't apply the word *intention* positively to any of my poems.'[42]

Which meant, of course, that no one else could have the definitive last word on them either. As a critic and poet Eliot was adamant, at least in his younger days, that no interpretation of a work of art was any more valid than any other. Indeed, he often claimed to prefer reading verse in languages he couldn't really converse in, the better to *hear* its poetic soundscape. Even more daringly, he was of the opinion that nothing a writer or painter has to say about his or her work is of any more import than what any individual reader or viewer makes of it.

Subsequently though, Eliot's philosophy – but not, paradoxically, his verse – became a lot more traditional in outlook and aspiration. 'He was a great conservative containing a great radical,' obituarised John Updike, who rightly saw that Eliot's potency sprang from his 'participation in this century's despair'.[43] In later years, indeed, the despair was all he had – and Eliot seemed to partake of it with greed. As early as 1928, only six years on from the publication of *The Waste Land*, he could describe his 'general point of view . . . as classicist in literature, royalist in politics, and Anglo-catholic in religion'.[44] At the same time he substituted for the high formalist abstractions of his early criticism the kind of historicist contextualisation the modern movement might have been invented to subvert.

Because for all that he was one of the holy figures of modernism (so iconic he once filled a football stadium for a lecture; so iconic he was mobbed by students shouting 'Viva Eliot!' while picking up an honorary degree in Rome in 1958), Eliot had little time for the modern world – a world that he loathed for its lack of a coherent morality. Unlike the average modernist, Eliot saw modernism not as a critique of modernity but as its caterwauling offspring. Modernism was part and parcel of modernity and as such a horrible combination of romanticism, liberalism and secularism. As Lionel Trilling has suggested, one of the key themes of *The Waste Land* is the idea that in 'modern life vulgarity has triumphed over the ancient pieties'.[45]

As the years went by it became ever more clear that Eliot, who took to calling Richard III the last legitimate English king (and wearing a white flower on the anniversary of the Battle of Bosworth Field), would have liked history to end around the time that Shakespeare was writing *Hamlet*. Groucho Marx, whom Eliot befriended in the last years of his (Eliot's) life, famously didn't want to belong to any club that would have him as a member. Eliot was rather more exclusive. He didn't want to belong to a club that would allow anyone else to join. As Lawrence Alloway put it, Eliot 'never doubted the essentially aristocratic nature of culture'.[46] Just so. You don't have to go along with John Carey's line that modernism was an elitist masquerade designed to put the lower orders in their place (by reminding them that there were certain areas of aesthetic life that were off-limits to their limited sensibilities) to acknowledge that Eliot had no time for the idea of liberal democracy.[47] Nor need you concede Peter Ackroyd's suggestion that having 'helped to create the idea of a modern movement with his own "difficult poetry"', Eliot then 'assisted at its burial',[48] to see that the man who during the twenties worked references from his beloved music hall into the elsewhere fearsomely learned *The Waste Land* might not be quite the same man as the one who in November 1958 wrote to *The Times* to say that he worried that the recent advent of independent television would be a threat to the standards of the BBC.

No less than Churchill's death, the passing of the high priest of high culture would licence a revolution. In the months following, the modernism Eliot had helped invent was imported into the pop culture he had loathed. And that pop culture becaue part of the high culture he loved. Indeed, only a week after Eliot's death, the *Observer* – by some measure the newspaper with the highest brow in Britain – had appointed its first 'critic of pop culture'. On January 10, when George Melly's first column appeared, it may have surprised, even shocked an audience used to the mandarin tones of Philip Toynbee and Cyril Connolly and Kenneth Tynan and Eliot himself telling them what was what in the world of culture on a Sunday morning. By the end of the year, though, it would be no more – and certainly no less – than what was expected.

History isn't, of course it isn't, the biography of great men. That doesn't mean, though, that the deaths of the likes of Winston Churchill and T. S. Eliot, the choice and master spirits of their age, don't reverberate through national life. The heavens might not themselves have blazed forth the death of these princes, but consciously or not their countrymen registered the fact that two guardians of the past were gone.

The poet who died on 4 January 1965 detested the cultural

world he had helped bring into being. And the statesman who died three weeks later had fought for the freedom of his country only to find himself more and more disapproving of what that freedom had led to and was being used for. Eliot and Churchill were men out of time. Now, though, they were out of it altogether – and the nation that had for so long been dominated by their backward-looking fantasies turned its attentions to the future.

Right on cue, the future arrived. A couple of weeks after Churchill's funeral, the American spaceship *Ranger 8* landed on the moon. The next day the front pages of the papers were covered with pictures of the moon's 'frothy surface'. To be sure, there was for most people no more to these monochrome relief studies than met the eye. Nonetheless, the mission itself, with its promise of extraterrestrial adventure and excitement, couldn't help but foment a feeling of change being in the air. Over the next twelve months Britain would finally say goodbye to its fusty, crusty days-of-empire reveries and turn that feeling into fact.

2

FAR OUT, MAN!

In which Britain gets surreal

'We have no intention of changing men's habits, but we have hopes of proving to them how fragile their thoughts are, and what unstable foundations, over what cellars they have erected their unsteady houses.'

Surrealist declaration, 27 January 1925

On 9 January 1965, peak-time television viewers were treated to the sight of John Lennon running and jumping and cycling through the English countryside to the accompaniment of the 'Winter' movement of Vivaldi's *The Four Seasons*. To the accompaniment, too, of a clipped yet doleful monotone, reciting nonsense about 'burly ive' and 'Big daley' from Lennon's new poem 'Deaf Ted, Danoota, (and me)'.[1] We have come a long way from 'She loves you, yeah, yeah, yeah'.

Not that Lennon was (as yet) a fully signed-up modernist. He was not writing T. S. Eliot-style free verse. The iambic tetrameters and pentameters and tight rhyme schemes that Lennon the songwriter forever cleaved to made his work at least rhythmically immediately comprehensible. But nor would any of the poems in his 1965 collection and *A Spaniard in the Works* have qualified for the monthly prize later set up by Auberon Waugh in the pages of the *Literary Review*. Rhyme and scan though they might have done, Lennon's poems never fulfilled what one suspects was Waugh's most vital requirement – that of making sense.

Indeed, for the MP Charles Curran, the publication of Lennon's gibberish was cause for national panic. After reading out three verses of 'Deaf Ted, Danoota, (and me)' to the House of Commons in order to draw attention to what he called Lennon's 'state of pathetic near-literacy',[2] the Conservative MP for Uxbridge wondered whether anyone would now dare deny his long-held claim that educational standards in Britain were slipping. Alas for Curran, his harangue did nothing to stop Lennon's collection of verse going on to be one of 1965's bestsellers. Fifty years on, his books have rarely been out of print.

Back when Lennon's poetry was first being heard and read, parochial English critics made much of the impact that the likes of Lewis Carroll and Edward Lear had had on his style – influences he was only too happy to acknowledge. Yet while there can be no arguing about the debts 'Deaf Ted, Danoota, (and me)' owes to, say, Lear's 'The Jabberwocky', nor is there any denying that something more continental, something rather more self-consciously modernist was at work on it, too. Lennon was introducing the mainstream Britons who made up the Beatles' audience to the anarchic aesthetic of surrealism.

Of all the twentieth century's art isms, surrealism was the one most bent on liberation. No art before or since has been so deliberately anti-authoritarian, as the titles of the movement's two journals – *The Surrealist Revolution* and *Surrealism in the Service of Revolution* – rather suggest. 'Surrealism', wrote the movement's ringmaster André Breton in its official manifesto, 'is a means of total liberation . . . and of everything resembling it. We are determined to create a revolution.' The surrealists believed that the hollow values of High European bourgeois liberalism had paved the way for the horrors of the First World War. Idealists rather than materialists, they were out to provoke such paroxysms of thought and feeling that their viewers and readers would begin to question the very fundamentals of their existence – politics, religion, money, sex, death. Anti-scientistic, anti-technological and (foreshadowing that very sixties sentiment) flirtatiously Marxist, the surrealists hoped to bring about a new spirituality that could take on the forces of capitalism's shallow empiricism. (Most of the surrealists had been raised Catholic, and kick as they did against the idea of faith, they never really abandoned it.*) Though the news of the Stalinist terror led to their abandonment of communism, the surrealists never gave up on the idea that art's essential function was the criticism of bourgeois life. John Lennon thought rock and roll existed to do the same thing.

What did Lennon's fans, who heretofore had heard in his songs lines no more surreal than the (Ringo Starr-inspired) 'It's been a hard day's night', make of his impenetrable burble? Who can say, though one thing is certain: Lennon's newly enigmatic style did nothing to put them off his work. Though from now on his lyrical (and musical) output would become increasingly shaped by the Dadaist and surrealist aesthetics he had learned about at art school a decade or so earlier, the fans who liked nothing more than a love plaint sung to a catchy tune wouldn't be put off the Beatles' records.

For the first time, that is, a mass audience was showing itself willing to countenance and contemplate art that disavowed the very British realist cum rationalist aesthetic in favour of a kind of chaotic designer-nonsense. Hitherto, surrealism – indeed, modernist art

---

* As had been the actor Patrick McGoohan who in 1965 was conceiving his paranoiac-critical surrealist television drama, *The Prisoner*.

generally – had always been a minority taste. The minority in question was the bourgeoisie. Modernism, as Lionel Trilling once put it, was a kind of middle-class revolt against the existence of the middle class.[3] Now, though, half a century on from the artistic revolution inaugurated by the likes of Breton and Eliot, British mass culture was coming to embrace avant-garde ambiguity, experimentation and non sequitur. Modernism, which from its earliest days had defined itself as existing in opposition to popular culture, was being co-opted by entertainment aimed at a mass audience. Nothing would ever be the same again.

As preparation for the writing of his second book Lennon had worked his way through large (if partial) chunks of the English canon – something he had signally failed to do as a schoolboy a decade earlier. His researches took him as near to the present day as Joyce's *Finnegans Wake*, at nearly 700 pages long surely the most challenging novel that came out of British literary modernism. Not, it should be said, that the notoriously indolent Lennon had worked his way through the book wholesale. 'It was great,' he said at the time, 'and I dug it and felt as though [Joyce] was an old friend. But I couldn't make it right through the book.'[4] Wherever he did get to, though, it was far enough for the message to have sunk in. Joyce's fingerprints are all over the work that his young wannabe apprentice published in 1965. What is 'The Singularge Experience of Miss Anne Duffield', with its detective hero Shamrock Wolmbs, but an exercise in Joycean wordplay? Wouldn't the inventor of 'Sir Tristram, violer d'amores', that hero who 'wielderfight his penisolate war', have enjoyed the exploits of 'Harrassed Wilsod' and 'Sir Alice Doubtless-Whom' in the recent 'General Erection'? How could an Irish linguistic revolutionary have resisted a book by a Liverpudlian that wanted to throw *A Spaniard in the Works*?

For the book's cover photograph, Lennon was dressed in the hat and cape of a Spanish matador, for all the world as if posing for one of those late Picasso portraits of oh so mortal flesh. Except that not even Picasso had ever thought to place (or paint) a two-headed spanner in his subject's hands. Just such a tool was to be seen in Lennon's gloved fist, though, at once a visual nod to the wordplay in the title of his collection and an absurdist clue to the surrealist clashes that were to be found within its covers.* It was all a far cry from the smiley, jump-up-and-down imagery to be seen on the four LP sleeves the Beatles had thus far put their name to. And indeed, *A Spaniard in the Works* was a far more accurate pointer to the direction the band would subsequently take than the *Help!* album that would go on sale a couple of months after the publication of Lennon's book. That album, recorded in mid-February, just a few weeks after Lennon's televised poetry recital, was very much a standard-issue rock and roll release – a handful of stompers and a handful of ballads written and produced at speed for a market that was plainly nowhere near reaching saturation point.

On the other hand, the movie *Help!* that accompanied the album had an awful lot in common with Lennon's verse. To be sure, the picture was built around scenes of the Fabs singing and dancing, and could be sold to the kids as an opportunity to see and not just hear their idols in action. But Richard Lester's film is, too, one of the central surrealist texts of the sixties – and being a film aimed squarely at a mass audience it did as much to popularise an otherwise esoteric revolutionary aesthetic as Lennon's verse. With its sudden, random changes of location, its *Alice in Wonderland*-style shrinking stars, its wacky interpolations and juxtapositions (at one

* Not to be outdone, Bob Dylan, to whose own newly modernist songwriting we shall return, was simultaneously claiming to collect 'monkey wrenches, all sizes and shapes' – and was photographed holding a pair of pliers for the gatefold sleeve of his next but one album, *Blonde on Blonde* (1966). See Dylan's interview with Nora Ephron and Susan Edmiston in *Positively Tie Dream*, August 1965. Reprinted in Jonathan Cott (ed), *Bob Dylan: The Essential Interviews* (Wenner, 2006), p.51.

point a gas-pipe pierces the navel of the subject of an Elizabethan portrait), *Help!* was a Magritte or a Max Ernst image come to life – a dislocated dreamscape in which to ask for explanations would be as meaningless as to expect them to be forthcoming. Even the Beatles' performances, if one can so dignify their stilted, startled, reaction-free style of acting, contrive to be part of the movie's surrealist air. Precisely by dint of their failure to respond to the magical mysteries Lester's picture throws at them, the Fabs seem to embody the surrealist demand that we surrender to the irrational.

By contrast, the only surreal thing about the album *Help!* was the fact that its stand-out ballad, the otherwise defiantly middle-of-the-road song 'Yesterday', by Paul McCartney, had begun life with the working title 'Scrambled Eggs' – the kind of flaccid, deliquescent substance that loomed large in the iconography of that other Spaniard in *Help!*'s works, Salvador Dalí. Indeed, had Dalí, many of whose paintings featured bodies so liquefied and distended they have to be held up by crutches, ever got round to reading Lennon's book he could have been forgiven for wondering where the idea of a budgie so fat he has to 'wear a crutch' might have originated.

Yet the example of Lennon's increasingly madcap dreamscapes was not lost on McCartney. Soon enough he was engaged in his own crash-course in twentieth-century art and music – a course that, characteristically, took him far deeper into avant-garde aesthetics than a little light nonsense verse. By the end of the year the erstwhile soppy romantic – not for nothing did Lennon complain that McCartney wrote too many songs for old women – was composing automaton mantras that would pave the way for the Summer of Love. It was during that summer that the Queen is reputed to have remarked that 'the Beatles are getting awfully strange these days'. There was something to the insight, but Her Majesty was a couple of years behind the times. It was in 1965 that the mop tops went modernist.

They weren't the only ones. Modernism was everywhere in Britain in 1965. Nowhere was this more apparent than in *Not Only . . . But Also*, the television show in which Lennon had acted out 'Deaf Ted, Danoota, (and me)'. Conceived by the BBC's Light Entertainment department as a component in their Saturday night prime-time schedules, *Not Only . . .* had originally been going to be called 'The Dudley Moore Show'. As such, it had been designed as a showcase for Moore's talents as a jazz-influenced pianist and charmingly handsome, light comedian-style host who would each week welcome a different guest into the studio. Brilliant a musician and entertainer as Moore was, though, he was more than a little nervous about what would in effect be his debut as a solo performer away from the revue-style *Beyond the Fringe* collective in which he had made his name. Feeling the need for a little hand-holding, he asked one of his *Fringe* co-stars, the comedian Peter Cook, to be the guest on 'The Dudley Moore Show' trial run. Cook, who was then mainly working for the independent television channels and was desperate to make a name for himself on the BBC, instantly agreed. He had just one proviso: that he would not have to write or perform sketches that could in any way be construed as political.

This was a real about-turn. When, a few years earlier, Cook had made his name, it had been as a swingeing satirist forever looking to trade blows with anyone he regarded as a member of the establishment. Nobody, not even the Prime Minister, was safe from mockery when Cook was around. Indeed, in 1961, when the then PM Harold Macmillan showed up for a performance of *Beyond the Fringe* at the Fortune Theatre, Cook actually pointed at him from the stage midway through proceedings and commenced to ad-lib in the fruity slur that passed for his impersonation of Supermac: 'When I've a spare evening, there's nothing I like better than to wander over to a theatre and sit there listening to a group of sappy, urgent, vibrant young satirists, with a stupid great grin spread all over my silly face.' Even now, half a century and more of insurrectionary mickey-taking on, there is something unsettling about this verbal assault on a prime minister. No surprises, then, that back in those more deferential days, the West End audience was dumbstruck at the audacity of Cook's outrage. Cook himself, though, was nothing daunted by the panicked silence in the theatre. Comedians crave laughter, yet rather than back off from his attack, Cook only redoubled his sneering insults, rejoicing, like the Dadaists of interwar Europe before him, in his capacity to shock. Still, by 1965 Cook was doing nothing more satirical than advertise Watneys Red Barrel beer on television. Never happy with the 'spokesman of a generation'-style labels that journalists were forever trying to pin on him, he had, he said, washed his hands of politically inspired comedy.

There were several reasons for this volte-face. Cook was still chafing at the BBC's recent rejection of his proposal for a television show that took a satirical look at the week's news – and chafing all the more at the fact that the Beeb had subsequently offered the MC's role in an eerily similar-sounding show to David Frost, one of Cook's acolytes from his university days, and a man he ever after referred to as 'the Bubonic plagiarist'. (Almost a quarter of a century on from what Cook saw as Frost's hijacking of his idea, Frost rang his hero to invite him to a dinner party he was giving for Prince Andrew and his then bride-to-be Sarah Ferguson. 'Hang on a minute', Cook said, 'I'll have to check my diary' – wherein he claimed to have discovered that he was 'watching television that night'. His only regret, Cook was fond of reminding people throughout his life, was having saved Frost from drowning.)

But it wasn't just the fact that his mocking take on the deference culture had been adopted by all and sundry that was putting Cook off any further adventures in satire. Having been educated to embody that culture (he had read Modern Languages at Cambridge

with a view to entering the Foreign Office), Cook was at heart a
thoroughly establishment figure. For all his undoubted anger at the
status quo, he never entertained fantasies of radical social change.
When, a couple of years earlier, he and his friend Nicholas Luard
had set up a club facetiously called the 'Establishment' in London's
Soho, it was because they wanted a comedy venue 'where we could
be more outrageous than we could be on stage'.[5] But even as the
Establishment was opening its doors to the public Cook was dis-
missing the notion that it might have any concrete effect on the
body politic. As he self-mockingly told a television reporter, the
club had been modelled on the cabarets of Weimar Berlin that had
done 'so much to stop the rise of Hitler and prevent the outbreak
of the Second World War'. Humour, as André Breton's friend
Jacques Vaché once observed, is 'a feeling – I almost said a sense –
and that too – of the theatrical uselessness [...] of everything. *When
you know*.'[6] Cook, it seems fair to say, knew.

Along with such scepticism went an instinctive small-c con-
servatism. John Bird has remembered how, during a summer
vacation at Cook's parents' house near Bognor Regis, the two college chums had taken a walk through a nearby – and thanks to
gale-force winds all but deserted – golf course. At one point, Bird
stumbled in a rabbit hole and fell to the ground, cursing mildly as
he did so. 'Shhhh,' said an astonishingly earnest Cook, a moment
as supremely surreal as it is slavish to ceremony.[7] But as the *Spitting
Image* creator Roger Law, who knew Cook in the early sixties, has
said of his friend's political leanings: 'I really thought things could
be changed a bit – a lot of people made that mistake in my generation. But I don't think Peter was fooled for a minute.'[8] Hence
Kathleen Tynan's dismissal of Cook as a pessimist who 'thinks the
human race cannot be improved and that there's no point trying.
He believes that everyone, without exception in the whole history
of the world, has been exclusively motivated by greed, lust or power
mania.'[9] Hence, too, Jonathan Miller's dismissal of Cook as just a

standard-issue 'home-counties Tory [...] the most upstanding, traditional upholder of everything English and everything establishment'.[10] Indeed, Cook had once told Miller that he worried that their wartime sketch in *Beyond the Fringe*, in which Cook's commanding officer ordered Miller's flight lieutenant to fly off to Dresden and not come back because 'we need a futile gesture at this stage of the war', might be too cynical for those members of the audience who had lived through the real thing. Seen in that light, Cook's off-the-cuff assault on Macmillan might have been as shocked as it was shocking – an admonitory heckle at the fact of a Conservative prime minister wasting his valuable time watching some silly undergraduate revue.

What really counted, though, in Cook's dismissal of satire was the fact of its inescapable topicality. Topicality, Cook had come to think, meant ephemerality. Worried though he was by the success of Frost and *That Was The Week That Was*, he was also wise to the fact that, no matter how hilarious it started out seeming, comic material that traded on the events of the day would look a lot less funny a few months – or even weeks – down the line. Successful mainstream television entertainment, on the other hand, might well be repeated – thus earning its creators another royalty cheque. So Cook was delighted when the audience research department at the BBC reported this kind of reaction to *Not Only . . . But Also*: 'different . . . and especially appreciated in some quarters because it did not rely for its humour on politics, crime or rude satire'. His gamble about spokesmen for a generation soon passing their sell-by date had paid off. Within a few short months of its first transmissions on BBC2, *Not Only . . . But Also* was repeated on BBC1 during the prime-time summer schedules.

Even today, fifty years on, there is something slightly surprising about this success. T. S. Eliot's mentor Ezra Pound once defined literature as news that stays news. The daringly modern comedy material Peter Cook and Dudley Moore wrote in 1965 is still

daringly modern. Parts of the show can still baffle and intrigue.*
Not because they rely on dated references – *Not Only . . . But Also*
still has a startlingly up-to-the-minute feel – but because of their
almost wilful meaninglessness.

How to explain a show which opened with the sight of a smiling, tailcoated and dickie-bowed Cook and Moore striding along
the deck of a warship moored by Tower Bridge, sitting at a piano
and . . . suddenly being raised into the air, baby grand and all, and
lowered into and beneath the water? How to account for the fact
that once down under the surface of the Thames our two intrepid
hosts continue tickling the ivories – and we continue hearing the
tune they're picking out, wobbly and gurgled though those watery
acoustics make it? How to explain that as the two of them spout –
the word is apt – garbled nonsense at one another, Peter proceeds
to comb his hair while Dudley pours him a cup of tea? And that
then, tempted by the sight of a scantily clad mermaid, our two
heroes swim out of shot and . . . walk, still tailcoated and bow-tied,
on to the stage of the BBC theatre?

No one could claim that this set piece affords the funniest
couple of minutes that *Not Only . . . But Also* served up. Nonetheless, it served as a matchless manifesto for the kind of dislocating
nonsense the next few Saturday nights were to offer television
viewers. Here you were, watching the prime-time slot, and it was
as if the atonal, rhythm-free piano of Hugo Ball and the tuneless,

---

* Alas, parts are all we have. You can't actually see the show any more, at least in full. The
BBC, in its infinite wisdom, saw fit to record over the tapes of the bulk of the first series –
even though Cook offered to buy the tapes off them. So it is only the first half of the first
series of *Not Only . . . But Also* that we still have access to – provided, that is, you have
access to a DVD player that can play Region 1 (i.e. American) discs. The BBC itself has
not released anything but snippets of the show. Nor would any of this exist without the
foresight of the show's producer, Joe McGrath, who broke BBC rules and had several of
the shows filmed by a 35mm camera as they went out live. The American disc is called
The Best of What's Left of Not Only . . .

automaton chanting of Emmy Hennings that Zurich's Café Odeon had played host to four decades and more before, had been brought into your front room. It's a measure of how weirdly unsettling the show was (and remains) that matters only seemed to be made weirder still when our two erstwhile underwater pianists proceeded to ask us to 'give a big hand for Miss Cilla Black'. But then, as the godfather of Dada and surrealism Alfred Jarry once said, 'laughter is born out of the discovery of contradictions.'[11]

Above all, the original Dadaists prized spontaneity – not a quality one associates with pre-recorded television shows. Still, Moore and Cook (especially Cook, who would go on to become one of the most daringly off-the-cuff television performers, a man chat-show hosts both worshipped for his breathless fecundity and worried over for taking them they knew not where) did their best to make the show feel as if it were being made up on the hoof.

Cook loved to make Moore laugh, for instance, and regularly withheld from rehearsal scripts lines of dialogue he was going to use for the show proper, the better to surprise his partner in mid-performance. The most celebrated of these moments occurs in a sketch written for what were to become the show's two most beloved characters, Pete 'n' Dud, in which Dud tells Pete that in bed the previous night Jane Russell touched him on the cheek, and Cook – in what is plainly for Moore an out-of-the-blue moment – asks 'Which cheek was that, Dud?' So funny was this sequence, which was filmed for the one-off trial run of what became *Not Only ... But Also*, that although it distressed the BBC's head of light entertainment, Tom Sloan, it also ensured Cook was signed up for the whole series. ('If this is light entertainment', Sloan was heard to say, 'I'm in the wrong business.' At which point BBC2's controller, Michael Peacock, turned to him and said, 'I think, Tom, you're in the wrong business.')[12]

If Cook's off-the-cuff comic instincts were of a piece with the surrealist love of automatic writing, so too were Moore's jazz piano-playing interludes. To the unpractised ear, Moore's dissonant vamping and broken rhythms could (and still can) sound almost random in their leaps and lurches in and out of key and tempo. During one show, Moore duetted with the singer Marian Montgomery on Bernice Petkere's 'Close Your Eyes',* and as well as vamping luxuriantly at the piano he suddenly started skatting at the microphone, an extraordinary stream of high-pitched baby gurgles, squeals and screeches pouring out of him, all in perfect time with the drum and double-bass accompaniment that made up the rest of the Dudley Moore Trio.

Beneath that modernist fooling around with form, of course, was the perfectly precise musical training and technique that had helped win Moore his Oxford scholarship. Similarly, beneath Cook's love of the abstruse and the illogical and the downright crazy, beat the heart of a mightily old-fashioned entertainer. You don't have to watch Cook in action for too long before you realise that he fancied himself as a matinee idol. Tall, slim, elegant and ravishingly handsome, he might, had he been a better actor, have got away with it.

Like many a surrealist before him, Cook was born into middle-class privilege (in 1937), the son of a Foreign Office diplomat, Alec Cook, who had married a solicitor's daughter, Margaret Mayo. If that biographical sketch sounds bald, then never forget that Cook himself grew up knowing little more about his parents than those few facts. Like his father before him – or, rather, *not* like his father before him, who never met *his* father – Cook was sent away to school (Radley) at an early age. Meanwhile Alec, and sometimes Margaret with him, decamped to various points in Africa on government business. Cook never got over what he saw as this abandonment. Though there are photographs of him as a teenager, home for the holidays or in the long vac before going up to Cambridge, photographs in

---

* With which Doris Day and André Previn had had such randomising fun on their great album of 1962, *Duet*.

which he is plainly a loving brother to his younger sisters Sarah and Elizabeth, his adult life was marked out by an inability to ever really talk to anybody one on one. When his mother died, in 1984, just a few months before his own very early death at the age of fifty-seven, Cook took to telling everyone he was now an orphan.

As a child, Cook's two big loves were football (then an emphatically working-class game and frowned upon at the rugby-playing Radley), from which passion came the affection that marks out his portrayals of even the most dim-witted oik; and Lewis Carroll, whose nonsensical fantasies helped raise aloft his own flights of comic madness. Who – indeed, what – are the leaping nuns of the Order of Saint Beryl, who breakfast on 'hard-boiled fish' and spend their days bouncing and pirouetting on trampolines 'Leaping here, leaping there, leaping, leaping everywhere'? Who, if not evacuees from a chapter of *Alice Through the Looking Glass* that Carroll never quite got round to writing? What is Sir Arthur Streeb-Greebling doing training ravens to fly underwater – confessedly without much success – if not auditioning for a part in Carroll's fantasy world?

Lewis Carroll was a surrealist before the fact. The dramatist N. F. Simpson was a surrealist long after the original art movement had lost its interwar impetus. His first play, the one-act comedy *A Resounding Tinkle*, opened at the Royal Court Theatre in 1958 to a resounding roar of critical approval, if not resounding sales at the box office. (An earlier, two-act version had come third in the *Observer*'s competition for new writers the year previous.) It tells the story of Bro and Middie Paradocks, a suburban couple with a pet elephant that they are considering exchanging for a pet snake. The trouble is, a snake might be too short – and though they could easily have it lengthened, won't that make it narrower? Then the phone rings. A friend is worried about her eagle – might its eyesight be on the wane? Whatever, here comes the play's much mentioned 'Uncle Ted' – who turns out to be a rather lovely young lady ... You get the picture. *A Resounding Tinkle* was as close to the Comte de Lautréamont's surrealist ideal of 'a chance encounter of an umbrella and a sewing machine on an operating table' as even René Magritte could have painted. It was also a key influence on Peter Cook.

For what really ensured *A Resounding Tinkle*'s resounding victory over Loamshire* aesthetics was an amateur production put on by one of the Cambridge drama societies in January 1959. The director of this show was John Bird (still, thanks to Rory Bremner, a regular star of our TV screens). An aficionado of surrealism, Bird had already mounted a production of an Ionesco play – and was determined to demonstrate that Simpson was in the same league. For the role of Middie Paradock he settled on the young Eleanor Bron. As to who should get the role of Middie's husband, Bro, Bird was in no doubt: Bron's fellow Modern Languages undergraduate, Peter Cook.

Bird had seen Cook on stage at various Footlights smokers in which his 'Mr Boylett Speaks' interludes (to call them sketches would be to grant them a form they singularly, and calculatedly, lacked) had stolen the show. Wearing an old macintosh and a knocked-about trilby, Boylett had shambled on to the stage, sat himself down on a bench, and proceeded to drone through a series of seemingly random, determinedly turgid monologues on the working routines of ants or the length of the human intestine or his plans for world domination. It didn't and doesn't sound like much, yet within hours of Boylett's debut, the whole of Cambridge was imitating him. (Even today, more than half a century on, many of us unwittingly slip into Boylett's strangulated, nasal tones for the purposes of acting out the boring character of a story.) It was this vision of a man slavishly devoted to tedium that Bird wanted for the centrepiece of his production of Simpson's play – a production that would turn out so successful that the Royal Court actually took it

* The word is Kenneth Tynan's – minted to describe any play set largely in drawing rooms and featuring young people carrying tennis rackets.

to London for a performance, perhaps to see where they had gone wrong with their original showing.*

John Bird, it should be said, has poured scorn on the idea that Cook's comedy was in any way inspired by his appearance in the surreal high jinks of *A Resounding Tinkle*. After all, argues Bird, the Dadaist material Cook had been putting on at Cambridge had originated long before he had read and appeared in Simpson's play. And there are those for whom the idea of Cook ever having read anything is laughably ludicrous. According to his *Beyond the Fringe* compadre Alan Bennett, Cook thought books at best a waste of time – and at worst an active con.[13] Certainly he was never an assiduous student, though he was near perfectly assiduous in steering clear of all reading material save that provided by the racing pages. And with free-form talents as high soaring as his, why would he have any need of learning or training? As John Lahr has pointed out, Cook's comic skills were 'almost fully formed [by the time he was] a teenager. He had already worked out his major comic manoeuvre: to combine the suburban with the surreal.'[14]

Fair enough, though even at the most basic level it is plain that Cook's penchant for assonantly repetitive character names (Sir Arthur Streeb-Greebling, Herman Hermitz) owes something to the Kirby Groomkirby of *A Resounding Tinkle*. Moreover, there are reasons for believing Cook to have been better schooled in twentieth-century aesthetics than he was happy to let on. As with so many of the cleverest students, he liked to give the impression of never having done any work. As with so many middle-class boys who love football, he could feel obliged to keep quiet about matters cultural. Yet if there's a clearer exposition of the ideas underlying impressionism than the sketch in which Pete and Dud discuss Debussy, I'd like to read it.[15]

---

* Intriguingly, the Royal Court that same year of 1959 hired Dudley Moore to write the music for Simpson's follow-up to *A Resounding Tinkle*, *One Way Pendulum*.

For Cook was far more learned and erudite than he liked to let on. While his Cambridge studies, such as they were, introduced him to the work of absurdist writers such as Franz Kafka, André Gide and Jean-Paul Sartre, he was already well in the know about surrealism. In 1956, the year before he went up to Pembroke (and the year everyone else was going to see *Look Back in Anger*), Cook summered in Paris – where he became every inch the gap-year culture vulture. One night he saw Edith Piaf, the next Abel Gance's six and a half hour epic, *Napoleon*. One night he caught Brecht's *Threepenny Opera*, the next Jacques Mauclair's second production of Ionesco's *Les Chaises*. (The first production, five years earlier, had been a disaster.) *Les Chaises* is a play about an old couple anticipating the arrival of hundreds of important guests – who turn out to be imaginary. Not so much *Waiting for Godot* as waiting for god knows what, it ends with the couple jumping into the sea – precisely the kind of peremptory, purpose-free ending so many of the sketches in *Not Only ... But Also* built towards.

History has not vouchsafed us the details of Cook's Parisian gallery-going exploits, but this 1990 interview with Ludovic Kennedy suggests he used his time in the key modernist city to bone up on his isms. What, asked Ludo, had Paris been like in the twenties?

Cook (as Sir Arthur Streeb Greebling): ...a bit like in the 1960s actually, only in black and white and without any subtitles. I was very poor, had a pathetically weedy little moustache and I was absolutely homeless. But I was young and I desperately wanted to paint.
Ludo: You knocked at the first door you came to.
Cook: Yes, and I painted it. There was no answer, but the door swung open and there in the centre of the room was this most peculiar melting bed draped over an ironing board. I'd stumbled into the garret of Salvador Dalí.[16]

Later on, Sir Arthur tells Ludo about meeting Piaf, as well as his exploits with the rest of the surrealists, including the 'frightful' Magritte and his 'stupid little waxed moustache on his bottom'. Moustaches, bottoms – might Cook be thinking of Marcel Duchamp's Dada-inaugurating *L.H.O.O.Q.* (1919)? This last is a reproduction of the *Mona Lisa* with a waxed moustache and goatee pencilled in, and the letters of whose title, pronounced phonetically in French, state that 'Elle a chaud au cul' – she has a hot ass. Could it be that behind Sir Arthur's own stupid moustache, Cook was actually something of an aesthete? Certainly only someone au fait with art historical debates could have written the famous 'At the Art Gallery' sketch from *Not Only . . . But Also*. With its gags about 'Da vinci cartoons' and cultural relativism (Pete and Dud don't get Leonardo's joke, but as Dud argues, '*The Mousetrap* did terribly in Pakistan'), not to mention its puns on the name Pissarro, the sketch bespeaks a writer at home with the Western canon. Like the Parisian cubists of half a century earlier, Cook was always fond of seeing what happened when high culture met mass culture.*

In the end it was this cultural clash cum fusion that mattered most about *Not Only . . . But Also*. Like Philip Larkin, who said that assembling a volume of verse always put him in mind of being a circus barker ('make 'em laugh, make 'em cry, bring on the dancing girls'), Cook and Moore loved the showbiz side of variety. But their unconscious inclinations were still to produce comedy that

---

* For the same reason, the narrator of the 'Deaf Ted, Danoota, (and me)' film incants Lennon's sliver of nonsense in a version of the staccato, stentorian screech Laurence Olivier had used for his *Richard III* a decade earlier. The joke was turned back on itself a few weeks after the show's broadcast, when Peter Sellers – who had practically insisted he be a guest on *Not Only . . . But Also* – went into the recording studio to lay down his own version of Lennon's 'A Hard Day's Night'. For this version of the song, though, the Beatles' producer George Martin – who had made his name back in the fifties working on Sellers's records – eschewed jangling electric guitars and pounding drums in favour of pipes and lutes, the better to form the backdrop to Sellers's eerily accurate impersonation of Olivier's Richard acting out Lennon's anguished lyric.

asked questions rather than just evaded them. Just as John Lennon's poetry-performing appearance on the show foreshadowed the more self-consciously arty music for which the Beatles would soon abandon pop, so Cook and Moore's laugh-a-second sketches introduced mainstream audiences to concepts and characters far off the mainstream purview.

All of which means that *Not Only . . . But Also* had far more practical effect than Cook's more openly political work. Inspirationally angry though satire could be, its barefaced ideological impetus meant it always ended up preaching to the converted. Far more subversive, Cook had discovered (or stumbled upon), was to challenge the status quo with the kind of nonsensical, distorted visions the Parisian painters and writers of half a century previous had pioneered. Not that their work had ever gained much more than a minority audience. As Bro Paradock puts it in *A Resounding Tinkle*, 'it takes a trained mind to relish a non sequitur'. And it took Peter Cook's mind to realise that the ideal form for the short-circuiting narrative switchbacks that surrealist storytelling depends on was the comic sketch. That is why Buñuel and Dalí's *Un Chien Andalou* (1928) is far superior to their *L'Age d'Or* (1930); while the latter clocks in at over an hour long, the former lasts little more than twenty minutes. Beyond that kind of time frame, even the most inventive nonsense can grow tiresome. And it is why though one can listen to the coiling nonsense of the Beatles' 'I Am the Walrus' over and over again, nobody has ever got more than a few pages in to, say, André Breton's autobiographical account of his relations with a madwoman, *Nadja*.

In the surrealist manifesto of 1924, Breton defined the movement's aesthetic as 'Psychic automatism in its pure state, by which one proposes to express – verbally, by means of the written word, or in any other manner – the actual functioning of thought. Dictated by thought, in the absence of any control exercised by reason, exempt from any aesthetic or moral concern.'[17] He might have been describing *Repulsion*, Roman Polanski's hit horror movie which told, the poster declaimed, of 'the nightmare world of a Virgin's dreams' and which lived up to its title by shocking and sickening audiences on its release, in the summer of 1965. Unlike most fifty-year-old horror, though, *Repulsion* is still shocking today. Next to it, the *Frankenstein* and *Dracula* cycles that Hammer studios had been working through since the late fifties don't even look tame. They look utterly insignificant.

The movie tells of a few days in the life of Carole Ledoux (Catherine Deneuve), a manicurist at a ritzy London beauty parlour who shares a flat with her sister Hélène (Yvonne Furneaux). Also around for much of the time, and much to Carole's distress, is Hélène's yobbish middle-class lover, Michael (Ian Hendry). Not that Carole thinks much of her own putative boyfriend, Colin (John Fraser), either. Whenever he comes near her she pushes him away, and when he does manage to snatch a struggling kiss she spends the next five minutes at the sink rinsing herself off. Soon enough she has battered him to death, and not long after that she despatches her landlord to a similarly bloody fate. For some reason (and despite the repeated track-in shots to a close-up of what we assume is Hélène as a child at her family home, Polanski is very careful to never give us a reason), Hélène can't stand to be near men. Does she just hate them? Does she hate them because she hates the idea of sex? Does she hate herself for *not* hating the idea of sex, and therefore hate men for making her want it? Answers come there none.

And yet, on the other hand, answers come there several. *Repulsion* cunningly allows of all these and other readings. Like Polanski himself, who has admitted that 'for as far back as I can remember, the line between fantasy and reality has been hopelessly blurred',[18] Hélène lives in a world that bears only fleeting and passing resemblance to the one we all believe we inhabit. Unsurprisingly, she doesn't have a clue as to why she is as she is. (There was going to be a third murder in the picture: Michael's cuckolded wife was going to show up at the flat demanding to know where he was, and then chance on Colin's corpse in the bath before being bumped off herself. Because such a murder was utterly explicable by everyday human motivation, though, Polanski ditched it.)

The genius of Polanski's expressionistically surreal direction, which takes us as far into a disturbed consciousness as any movie has ever done, is to ensure that we don't know what Carole's about, either. Malignant or otherwise, she is as motiveless as the Iago of Coleridge's essay on *Othello*. If the function of most horror pictures is to close its viewers off from the world, to make them fearful of what goes on outside their own head, *Repulsion* works in precisely the opposite way, taking us deep inside the mind of a woman who turns, as the movie goes on, into a killer, without once having us think about condemning her. As Polanski remarked at the time, '*Repulsion* ... will shock some people, jolt them ... it is the study of a girl's disintegration ... I'm concerned with *showing* something; exposing a little bit of human behaviour that society likes to keep hidden, because then everyone can pretend it doesn't exist. But it does exist, and by lifting the curtain on the forbidden subject, I think one liberates it from this secrecy and shame.'[19] That could be Breton speaking, and though it would be over-egging things to suggest that the movie had anything to do with the parliamentary decision, a few weeks after its release, to abolish the death penalty, still, Polanski's picture was part of the mood of those liberating times. René Magritte once said that he conceived of his art 'as material signs of the freedom of thought'.[20] So too Polanski, who was adamant that 'I owe my apprenticeship to surrealism. For ten years, and even when I made my first film, I viewed things solely by its light. There was something of the "angry young man" about me as I opposed a society that really exasperated me. In the twilight days of Stalinism, to have a passion for surrealism was to be drawn to forbidden fruit.'[21]

The cinema, as André Bazin made his name arguing, is almost reflexively realist. Yet the context of Polanski's film renders every image literally *surreal*. Everything about *Repulsion* is suggestive of a world *beneath* the surface of the quotidian and banal that even the most gruesome horror movies necessarily inhabit. 'My mood then endowed the moulding of a door with a mysterious existence': once more the words are Magritte's, but they might have been Polanski's, who can make objects as mundane as a toothbrush glass – or even the folds and rivulets on the sheets of an unmade bed – seem pregnant with dread. By gluing a row of nails to its sole, Man Ray's *Gift* (1921) made a humble iron both functionless and fearful. Polanski doesn't even need the nails for the scene in which we watch Carole press her clothes with an iron that isn't plugged in.[*]

Salvador Dalí used to say that he painted by means of what he called a 'paranoid-critical method', a method that revolved around the idea of looking at something and seeing something else. Something similar is going on in *Repulsion*, where an empty bathroom plughole can look like an invitation to Hades, where some ageing potatoes look like monsters from another world, where the walls of Carole's apartment can suddenly and violently sunder themselves or become as flaccid as the heads of so many Dalí canvases.[†] Indeed, the rotting, fly-strewn rabbit she leaves out on a plate in her living room is almost precisely the same shape as the cold,

---

[*] The ironing board was also, of course, central to the iconography of the kitchen-sink drama. Whole swathes of the dialogic tedium that is John Osborne's *Look Back in Anger* take place over and across one.

[†] Even the most devout Polanski worshipper might, however, question whether the twin-pronged gashes Carole is forever espying in walls and pavements aren't a tad over-determined. As to the determinedly frigid Carole's line about 'I must get this crack mended', it is almost worthy of Benny Hill. On the other hand, as Magritte said, 'The cracks we see in our houses and on our faces seemed to me more eloquent in the sky.'

slimy, effeminately eyelashed blob that serves as a portrait of the artist in Dalí's most famous painting, *The Persistence of Memory* (1931).

But the most astonishing aspect of Polanski's surrealism is that it is conceived in the grainy monochrome imagery the British cinema had long relied on to evoke notions of the naturalistic. Black and white photography meant grit and grime and northern industrialism, it meant the trials and torments of tough working-class lives lived in small houses and smaller kitchens. Indeed, movies like *Room at the Top* (1959) and *Saturday Night and Sunday Morning* (1960) – as well, of course, as *Look Back in Anger* (1959) – had been labelled 'kitchen-sink dramas'. What with all that rotting food, all that incessant hand-cleaning, not to mention all that blood that must be washed away from the cut-throat razor Carole uses to cut her landlord's throat, the kitchen sink looms large in *Repulsion*, too. But this isn't kitchen-sink drama. It's kitchen-sink dread. At one point a radio bulletin informs us that the government's Health Secretary has found eels swimming out of the plughole in his sink. Like Magritte before him, Polanski had concluded that disturbing visions are all the more disturbing when set in the context of the matter-of-fact here and now rather than amid the paraphernalia of the fantastical and gothic.

As with interiors, so with exteriors. The streets of Chelsea and West Kensington which form the backdrop to the bulk of *Repulsion* (the scenes inside the apartment were filmed on set at Twickenham) had been the landscape of a thousand British pictures – *Genevieve*, *The League of Gentlemen*, *Spring in Park Lane*, etc. – before it. In those movies, though, it had figured as a topography of the utmost stability – the topography of the comfortably well-off Britain that had come through the inclusively social democratic consensus years almost untouched. Even the late-in-the day Beats and proto hippies who were increasingly taking this area of west London over as the sixties wore on, conceived of the place as a spaced-out urban paradise. Indeed, just as Polanski and his cinematographer Gil Taylor were transforming those arenas of the new consumerism Thurloe

Place and the Old Brompton Road into bulging, buckling, emblems of the modern mind, that nominally alternative songwriter Donovan was singing about what he called 'Sunny South Kensington', as if the place were some heavenly garden laid on by the dope god for the tired of partying. Donovan's song told of 'the girl with the silk Chinese blouse on/ You know she ain't no freak'. But the Catherine Deneuve of Polanksi's picture emphatically is a freak. Certain of her murderous activities in sunny South Kensington might have troubled even Breton – who had once suggested that the essential surrealist act would 'consist of dashing down the street, pistol in hand, and firing blindly, as fast as you can pull the trigger, into the crowd'.

Not that they trouble anyone over much whilst watching the picture. The expressionistic rigour of Polanski's surrealism ensures that we are, if not ever quite 'with' Carole, then never defiantly 'against' her. By means of his constantly roving camera and his ingeniously constructed set (which in best *Alice in Wonderland* style can be loudly sundered in front of our eyes, and which features rooms and corridors that bubble and grow – or sag and shrink – before us), Polanski serves up the cinema's most convincing impression of madness ever. One feels, watching *Repulsion*, that one knows what it might be like to be unhinged from reality. When the British Board of Film Censors' then head, Sir John Trevelyan, gave *Repulsion* the once-over for classification, he did so in the company of Dr Steven Blake, a psychiatrist who had long advised him on films of a sexual or violent nature. Lucky for the worried Polanski, Trevelyan demanded no cuts, but it was Dr Blake who really bowled the director over. How, Blake wanted to know, did he come to know so much about what it was to be a paranoid schizophrenic?[*]

Not that knowing anything about paranoia or schizophrenia

---

[*] Intriguingly, Jonathan Miller – himself a doctor – who had caught parts of Peter Cook's various performances at Cambridge, asked his new partner the very same question when they began working together on *Beyond the Fringe*.

helps you get a grip on *Repulsion*. Polanski's film owes many debts to Hitchcock's *Psycho* (1960), but by eschewing any *Psycho*-style explicatory denouement it avoids descending into what Orson Welles liked to call 'dollar-book Freud'. The all-understanding psychiatrist, whose presence in Hitchcock's movie allowed everyone to leave the cinema certain of his or her own sanity, is conspicuous by his absence here. *Repulsion* leaves you as destabilised, as uncertain of your grasp on the empirical, as the great surrealists of the past would have wished. 'Reason', Francis Picabia once said, 'shows us things in a light which conceals what they really are. And, in the last resort, what are they?'[22] There is, though, no rational light shed in *Repulsion*. In its place, the movie offers what Dalí called the surrealist's ability to 'systematise confusion and contribute to the total discrediting of the world of reality'.[23]

There is, on the other hand, no denying that the movie stacks the deck against its marker of stiff-collared repression. John Fraser's Colin is as thoroughgoing a dullard as any in British cinema, an 'anyone for tennis' type of chap who would be quite at home courting one of the over-enunciated starlets who a decade earlier had poured like warm treacle out of the Rank Charm School and on to location shoots in the streets of west London. One of the points of *Repulsion* (as of so many Polanski movies) is the comeuppance of this type of soft-spoken, safe-as-houses knight in whining amour. And so, disturbing as Carole's murder of Colin is, with its repeated close-ups of blood spraying on to the furniture of her flat, there can't be many people in the audience lamenting his loss. Polanski's instinctive siding with victims, Deneuve's fragile beauty (made all the more fragile by the wide-angle lenses Polanski insisted on shooting her through,* the

---

* Much to Gil Taylor's distress. As all photographers know, a short telephoto is the lens most suited to flattering portrait subjects. 'I hate doing this to a beautiful woman,' Polanski records Taylor as saying during the shoot. See *Roman* by Roman Polanski (Heinemann, 1984), p.188.

monstrous ribaldry of Colin's charm-free pub pals John (James Villiers) and Reggie (Hugh Futcher): all conspire to ensure that we won't come on like hanging judges no matter what Carole does.

This is doubly unusual, not only because the conventions of the horror movie were and are resolutely anti-feminist, but because surrealism itself was never even remotely an arena for women's rights. Driven as they may have been by the idea of sexual liberation, the original surrealists conceived of it only in male terms. As inheritors of nineteenth-century romanticism's fascination with the Belle Dame sans Merci, the surrealists saw woman as at best a distant goddess, at worst as a Medusan castrator. Think of Hans Bellmer's *Doll* (1935), a collection of tinted, monochrome images of a jointed wooden dummy arranged in various, violently provocative poses, and that, eight decades on, retains its power to shock.

Polanski aside, though, the other key members of the second wave of surrealism were no more liberated in their sexuality than its original progenitors. Pop music, like so much surrealism, had its roots in the medieval notion of courtly love, though there was nothing courtly about even the sweetest Beatles number. Read on the page, a line like 'She loves you, yeah, yeah, yeah' looks blandly repetitive – but can anyone *just* read it? Can anyone pass their eyes over those six simple words and not hear the chaotic, carnal howl with which the Beatles booted up the sixties? To be sure, Beatles' titles like 'Love Me Do' or 'I Want to Hold Your Hand' are as metonymically distanced as anything by Rodgers and Hart or the Gershwin brothers, but the open-hearted, open-throated manner in which the songs are sung leave no doubt as to their base agenda. The monotonous etiquette of 'Please Please Me' is belied by the record's shrill urgency. You'll go down in my estimation, Lennon warns the song's antagonist, if you won't go down in my bed.

In his printed work he was more suggestive still. Here he is in the titular story from *A Spaniard in the Works*: 'They were married in the fallout, with the Lairds blessing of course, he also gave them a "wee gifty" as he put it, which was a useful addition to their bottom lawyer.'[24] One doesn't have to be Shamrock Womlbs to work out what's going on there, nor to see that Shamrock's fellow characters, 'Jack the nipple' and a woman who having got off the bus 'as uterus at Nats Café and took up her position', are the result of something more neurotically suggestive than simple wordplay.

But for your full-blown sixties surrealist misogyny you needed Peter Cook. In one studio skit with Moore he all but reinvented Bellmer's infamous work, making what he at least seemed to think was sport with an inflatable doll. After kicking it and wrestling with it, he jumped on its stomach, thereby turning inside out what Cook calls its 'plastic twat' and effectively giving the doll a sex-change. Difficult as it was and is for audiences to sit through such yobbish violence, it was more difficult still for Moore to endure. 'I shudder at times,' he once said, thinking back on the sessions. 'My head obviously drops a few times during the filming. I think his hatred for women was fairly apparent there.'[25] And so it was. Thankfully, Britain in 1965 also played host to a surge of feminist painters and poets and novelists ready to fight back.

3

YOU'RE GOING TO LOSE
THAT GIRL

In which painters, writers and filmmakers lay the
ground for Britain's feminist revolution

*'Women are never stronger than when they arm themselves
with their weaknesses.'*

Marquise du Deffand

As the cab worked its way up Madison Avenue it dawned on
Bridget Riley that she'd arrived in America long before her
transatlantic flight had touched down at JFK an hour or so ago.
The nearer she got to the Museum of Modern Art, the more
apparent it was that New York couldn't get enough of her. Everywhere she looked she could see reproductions of her paintings.
Not just on the invitation to The Responsive Eye, the MOMA
show at which her work was to make its American debut. Not just
on the cover of the show's catalogue, which curator William Seitz
had chosen to illustrate with a detail from her 1963 painting *Fall*.
Not just on the posters for the Richard Feigen Gallery, which was
simultaneously hosting a solo Riley show and had elected to

advertise the fact with a similar, neurotically wavy detail from *Current* (1964).

Astonishing as this high–cultural ubiquity was for an all–but–unheard–of 33-year-old English painter, it was more astonishing still that Manhattan itself seemed to be filled with her imagery. Look out at one side of the street and her paintings were being used as the backdrop to store window displays. Look out at the other and there were rolls of pricey wallpaper on sale, printed with patterns she had so carefully worked up on canvas only a few months before. And then there were the women – decked out in chequerboard A-line frocks here, toting aggressively striped black and white hand-bags there. Inside the Museum of Modern Art it was harder still to pick out her work. 'About half the people there were wearing clothes based on my paintings,' she said.[1] Later on she would find out that you could even kit yourself out in Bridget Riley under-wear – underwear mightily easily displayed when worn under the miniskirts that Mary Quant launched from her boutique Bazaar in London's Kings Road in the spring of 1965.

It was all very unsettling – which given the nature of the work Riley was showing in New York seems only fair. No paintings since the hermetic cubism of Picasso and Braque had done more to subvert the onlooker's relationship to the apprehensible world. Certainly the paintings she brought to America in 1965 assaulted the retina and destabilised the psyche. Unbriefed gallery-goers fan-cying they were turning up for just another show of blurry British bucolic were in for a shock with the cut and thrust of Riley's visu-als. Like Sherlock Holmes, she is forever reminding the Watsons in the gallery that looking does not guarantee seeing, and that seeing does not guarantee belief.

But then, not everyone was a believer. The feminist critic and theorist Rosalind Kraus, at the time a dedicated follower of Clement Greenberg's proscriptions for flattened out, post-painterly abstraction, found Riley's work no better than 'timidly pleasant'.[2]

And the ease with which her imagery was hijacked by the fashion industry led others to wonder whether her paintings offered anything more than the kind of visual workout you get on a visit to the optician. Returning to England after three weeks in America, Riley confessed to 'feelings of violation and disillusionment'.[3] It would, she said, 'take at least twenty years before anyone looks at my paintings seriously again'.[4]

In the event, it took about twenty minutes. Op art, the half-parody, half-pastiche of a name for the sub-movement into which Riley's work was casually dump-binned in 1965, was over almost as soon as it was begun. Half a century on from her conquest of America (a conquest made all the more emphatic by the fact that for the twenty years since the end of the war American painters had pretty much single-handedly held sway over Western visual culture), Riley goes on developing as an artist of vigorous, unimpeachable intelligence. The images that made her name, meanwhile, remain emblazoned on the popular consciousness like so much radioactive razzle-dazzle. Icons of high sixties' nostalgia her wavy, stripy, dotty monochromes might be, but there is no denying that these emblems of what became psychedelic London have retained their power to upend expectations.

No matter how familiar Riley's work looks in reproduction, to see it in the flesh is to be reminded that no eye is capable of fully grasping everything in front of it. The tension people feel in front of a Riley, the air of unease her canvases instil, is quite intentional. 'I want', she said shortly after the success of *The Responsive Eye*, 'the disturbance [prompted by my paintings] to arise naturally, in visual terms out of the inherent energies and characteristics of the elements which I use. I also want it to have a quality of inevitability. There should, that is to say, be something akin to a sense of recognition within the works, so that the spectator experiences at one and the same time something known and something unknown.'[5] To stand in front of Riley's work is to feel, as one's grip on what one takes for reality slackens and slips away, oneself standing on aesthetic quicksand.

Glance at a painting like *Burn* (1964) and you might take it for a rigorously organised grid of black triangles on a white ground. Look some more though, and the grid starts to decompose in front of your eyes. Those black triangles aren't geometrically uniform, for instance, though nor are their differences random. Each one is a minute adjustment of its predecessor on the grid, their lines and points pivoting leftward or rightward as they move toward the centre of the canvas. And then, just as you become aware of such individuating subtleties, the whole image begins to buckle and swell, undulating to and fro before your eyes. The triangles move in and out of focus. Then the white ground disappears. It's not a ground at all, you realise, but another arrangement of (seemingly inverted) triangles. Then the triangles disappear and you're look-ing at a 3D relief map of a network of pyramids, one plane in the sun, one in shadow. Then the whole image starts moving, rotating first clockwise then back again. Locked in yet labile, Riley's work was both pre-modern in its commitment to structure and form, and preternaturally modern and impressionistic in its conviction that what counted above all was perception. As Riley has suggested, her imagery is 'hard to understand because the elements I used seemed so far removed from the experience they produced'.[6]

It's not that there's more to Riley's work than meets the eye. It's that no eye – no human eye, at any rate – is able to cope simulta-neously with everything it meets in images like *Burn*. You can't take it in at a glance, but nor will the painting allow you to rest your gaze for too long in one place. Hence it's impossible to convince yourself that your eyes are merely being fooled and that the paint-ing really is no more than a bunch of triangles. Riley's illusions are too powerful for rational thought to countermand them. That is why moving on from one of her pictures always feels like a wrench. Exquisitely exhausting, they never let you feel you've penetrated their mystery. Just as you think you've navigated through to the heart of the tunnel cum maze that are the *Blaze* paintings (1962), you realise that you're not only back where you began but that you've learned nothing on your travels across and around the canvas. As one trapdoor closes, another one opens.

Unusually for abstract work that rewards repeated looking, Riley's effects aren't achieved by brushwork. Not for her the scumbled facture and *passage* of a Cézanne, the signature slashes and whiplash arabesques of a Pollock, the ruggedly emotive impasto of a de Kooning. Riley's pictures were and are as smooth and licked as ice cream, and once they have been plotted and planned, their rhymes and rhythms worked out, she leaves it to her assistants to actually put paint on board. Such tactile anonymity was of a piece with much post-painterly abstraction of the late fifties and sixties. Yet Riley's work stands out from the Greenbergian colour-field crowd by refusing its blasé languor, its splashy, easy-on-the-eye sybaritics. Friendly though she became with Barnett Newman (whose lawyer she hired to try to stop any more of her ideas being stolen by those fashion designers and store owners), Riley's aggressive, stand-to-attention images had nothing to do with the numinous tranquillity of his 'zip' paintings.

Nor, though, did Riley's work have any links with that of the pop artists then holding sway over the New York art scene. There is nothing less gluttonous and Warholian, nothing less representational and Lichtensteinian than the puritan monochromes that Riley brought to New York in 1965. So much so that among British painters she was surely the least likely candidate for taking the United States by storm. The contemporaneous American success of Riley's fellow Brits Gerald Laing and Peter Phillips is at least partly explicable by the fact that they were working within the dominant American idioms of the day. Laing's enormous portrait of *Brigitte Bardot* (1962), for instance, with its dotty, blown-up haziness is Warhol meets Lichtenstein – though the target signage painted on Bardot's face links the work with that of Jasper Johns, too. Phillips had clearly studied Johns as well, but though his iconography – Marilyn, Lana – was decidedly American, the porcelain politesse of his brushwork was absolutely English. As with the Beatles and rock and roll, these painters were effectively export- ing stolen goods back to the culture they had been filched from. Not so Riley. Her bone-dry abstractions spoke to an austerity unimaginable amid the luxuriant plenty of post-war America.

And yet Riley's work was popular with audiences who normally steered clear of non-representational art. 'Op is very much a pro- letarian art,' she once said. 'As long as you have a pair of eyes, you can see it. It will do as much for you as the art historian or the big critic.'[7] And so, just as John Lennon and Peter Cook had introduced the mass audience to Dada and surrealism, so Riley's paintings brought abstraction – long modernism's villain-in-chief for the 'I don't know much about art but I know what I like' crowd – within the purview of mainstream culture. Whether or not her images evoked for the masses what Riley hoped they might – the sensation of 'the freshness of a walk across the cliffs in the early morning, the blackness of the sea in deep shadow or the shiver of tiny grasses blown by the wind'[8] – they certainly found their way into the con- sciousness of the age. Loathe though she did the frocks and handbags patterned on her paintings, the dayglo dynamism of hippie psychedelia is inconceivable without her example. So too the mind-bending shows that rock bands began to have fun with in 1965. All those lights and lasers, all those whirling, amorphous, multicoloured projections, all those tabs of acid: to enter Kensing- ton's Countdown Club and see, say, Pink Floyd on stage was to walk into a kind of life-sized Riley. Soon enough, people were tripping out in front of Riley's canvases proper.

Riley was shocked. Why should anyone want to get bombed in front of work as painstaking and refined and demanding of close and sober attention as hers? Three decades on from the spaced-out, psychotropic sixties she remembered 'being told, as though it were some sort of compliment, that it was the greatest kick to go down and smoke in front of my painting *Fall*'.[9] 'Even the word perception', Riley griped, 'suddenly became, thanks to the popularity of Aldous Huxley's *The Doors of Perception*, linked with the drug culture of the sixties.'[10] And so it did, though it ought to be pointed out that one of the first people to make the link was the guy who had helped make her a big name in America. In his introduction to the catalogue for The Responsive Eye, William Seitz argued not only for the hallucinatory effects of the 'pure energy' on display in Riley's work, but also that such effects were magnified 'under the influence of the drugs mescaline and LSD'.[11]

Riley herself has always maintained that her early sixties images 'were never simply about how fascinating it might be to take black and white and put them together into those optically dynamic configurations'. Rather, 'they were an attempt to say something about stabilities and instabilities, certainties and uncertainties.'[12] Fair enough – though a painter whose art is forever reminding its viewers that they are not always in charge of their senses was likely always going to be inviting to people whose main aim in life was taking leave of their own. What was Syd Barrett, an art-school boy turned rock star acid-head, doing painting the floorboards of his Earls Court flat in Riley-style alternate-coloured stripes if not transforming his home into something resembling an op art image?

For Riley's talk of instability and uncertainty would hardly have been alien to Barrett and the other zoned-out relativists of the late sixties hippie crowd. What were these dopers and snorters seeking if not a religious-style release from the rational and the somatic? What did they want if not a refuge from the uncertainty and instability they saw all around them – a refuge they believed was to be found in the utopia of the id. In a sense, the drug culture was just a chemically inspired rewrite of modernist formalism. What counted wasn't meaning but sensation. Clive Bell thought the function of art was to remove you from your necessarily partisan take on the world and allow you to see things from a position of Kantian disinterest. Dropping a tab of acid achieved the same end without your having to leave the sofa (let alone labour through the third critique) – though as Riley's distress at junkies having smoked in front of *Fall* (1963) reminds us, a belt and braces approach to Bloomsbury-style transcendence was clearly an optional extra.

Not that the counterculture's penchant for psychedelia was all that goaded Riley. Worse, far worse, than being taken for the in-house painter of the drug culture was being taken for any kind of representative of womanhood. A photograph by Lord Snowdon, who posed her in her studio glancing sideways at the camera, her ostentatiously bare feet in the foreground of the image, helped her become famous; but it helped, too, she later thought, to suggest feminine levity. 'Women artists didn't know how to present themselves in photographs then,' she has said. 'I didn't know enough to say no when he asked me to take off my shoes.' But while she didn't want 'to turn [her]self into a travesty of femininity' and didn't believe that her 'femininity should be an issue' she was also determined not 'to make a fetish of it not being an issue'.[13] Small wonder that Riley has maintained that feminism is not for her. While not denying that society made it hard for women artists, she has always been adamant that 'few male artists have avoided analogous physical and sociological problems.'[14] As for women's liberation, it seemed to her 'a naïve concept' at least 'when applied to artists . . . It raises issues which in this context are quite absurd . . . artists who happen to be women need this particular form of hysteria like they need a hole in the head.'[15]

Maybe so, yet Riley's work, and the fame it brought, would be one of the motors behind the rise of feminism in the sixties. The mere fact of her success in what was still predominantly a male world cannot have helped being an inspiration to young women. Moreover, her paintings seemed almost macho in their aesthetic: all those hard edges, all those finely calibrated measurements, all those logical progressions, all that harsh black and white paint. Whether they were intended to or not, Riley's images broke down sexual as well as aesthetic barriers.

Artists at work, Riley once said, are neither male nor female but hermaphrodites – and she goes so far as to include in the category 'Renoir, who is supposed to have said that he painted his paintings with his prick'.[16] Renoir was talking figuratively, of course, though perhaps not figuratively enough for Shigeko Kubota who in July 1965 was to be found squatting above canvases she had laid out on the floor, a paintbrush affixed to her underwear, at work on what she called her *Vagina Painting*. As an agitprop response to Yves Klein's body paintings of the late fifties and early sixties, there was something to Kubota's concept. Not even the most fiendishly disinterested aesthete had ever quite managed to justify those pictures in which a dandyishly dinner-jacketed Klein had hurled the contents of a tin of his favourite blue paint at a succession of naked lovelies and then barked orders at them to drag and roll and rub their bodies across his picture surface. In front of an audience. (And captured on film: you can watch them to this day on YouTube.) Whatever else it was – and there *are* painterly delights to be had from Klein's so-called body pictures – this was a bump and grind show for the highbrow crowd.

But the suggestion that Kubota had bigger fish to fry, the idea that her *Vagina Painting* wasn't just an attack on Klein but on the putatively macho abstractions of Jackson Pollock, was way off beam. The tabloids might have mockingly called the Pollock they caught dancing and gyrating around his canvases Jack the Dripper, but nobody who has actually looked at his work could hold on to the notion that it was the product of aggression or even bravado. Graceful in their curving and looping lines and skeins, misty and airy in their overall conception of space, these paintings are less laddish than ladylike. And for all the randomness of his whirling dervish technique, Pollock turned out to have had far more control of his effects than

Kubota – whose work counts only for its performative effects. As ideological happenings, Kubota's work has some small claim on cultural history. As painting proper, it was ineffectual to the point of obsolescence.

Bridget Riley's influence was everywhere in 1965, though – and not only in art galleries but on movie and television screens, too. We shall deal with *The Avengers* in a later chapter, but *The Knack . . . and How to Get It*, Richard Lester's second film of 1965,* was an abstract, Rileyesque romp through the London her eye-popping paintings were prompting to swing.

Ann Jellicoe's original, pretty much abstract play, which premiered in 1961 – just as Riley was beginning to explore her hard-edged style – begins with a scene-setting instruction that might be a description of a Riley canvas: 'A room. The distribution of the paint is determined by the way the light falls . . . The paint is darkest where the shadows are darkest and light where they are most light.'[17] Later on, one of Jellicoe's characters, a habitual paintbrush wielder called Tom, points out that 'That white horse you see in the park could be a zebra synchronized with the railings',[18] precisely the kind of counsel for cautiousness over visual certitude that Riley's own stripey images insist on.

Lester's film makes even more sport with such optical doubt – so much so that at times even Rita Tushingham's plain old chequered tweed cap can seem like a graph paper sketch for one of Riley's more rigorously patterned canvases. The house in which much of what one only hesitantly calls the film's action takes place (and in which the entirety of the original play was set) looks from the outside like a standard-issue suburban London terrace. From the inside, though, it's an optical wonderland of Möbius strip-style staircases that, like Riley's more maze-like paintings, go nowhere. It's a critical commonplace that Lester's use of freeze-frame images, jump-cut editing

---

* Though *The Knack* was actually released before *Help!*

and alienating intertitles, not to mention his ignoring every rule of classical storytelling, were stolen from Truffaut and Godard and the other French moviemakers who had surfed the so-called New Wave of the late fifties and early sixties. Doubtless this perceived sense of *homage* did the film no harm at Cannes, where it won the Palme d'Or. Still, *The Knack*'s destabilising visuals owed as much and more to Riley's optical assault courses as they did to Godard's wilful editing and Truffaut's worship of spontaneity. And while in Jellicoe's play Tom smears a window with Windolene because 'It's as good as net curtains only better,'[19] Lester's whole movie has a gauzy, halated feel that speaks to the furl and pitch of the grey paintings Riley had showed in New York. Even the movie's repeated and rapid zooms in and out are cinematic equivalents for the jittery cut and thrust that undermines the flatness of Riley's imagery.

They are also, of course, jokily jerky metaphors for the movie's thrusting, priapic theme. For unlike Riley, Lester's real interest is in the changing sexual dynamic of sixties Britain. Stripped to its bare bones, the play and movie (which, incidentally, Jellicoe hated) tell the story of three house-sharers, Tolen, Tom and Colin (Ray Brooks, Donal Donnelly and Michael Crawford) who are, respectively, highly successful, reasonably successful and not at all successful at seducing women. Enter Nancy (Tushingham), a north-country lass who has lost her way to the YWCA. Her sexual innocence pulls the rug from under this Freudian triumvirate (ego, super-ego, id) – though not before Tolen has tried to have his wicked way with her. Tried and failed, a failure hammered home when Nancy chooses to go off with the meek and mild Colin (and the genteel Victorian bedstead we have earlier watched them push through the London streets).*

---

* Irresistible, given Richard Lester's work with the Beatles – in 1964 he had directed them in *A Hard Day's Night*, and having finished work on *The Knack* would direct them in *Help!* – to suggest that John Lennon and Yoko Ono's peacenik bed-ins of the later sixties owed something to Colin and Nancy's example . . .

Tolen, on the other hand, is as pumped up and macho as a Nazi fervent. Certainly there is something of the storm trooper about his all-black clothes, his shiny black boots (repeated close-ups of which Lester treats us to as they kick-start his even shinier black motorbike), his obsession with power and ritual humiliation. 'Girls', he tells his housemates, 'don't get raped unless they want it.' Were it not for the fact that his argument has been so dramatically disproven, he might be the fascist that Sylvia Plath was contemporaneously (and yet posthumously) declaring that every woman adores.[20]

That sentiment was to be found in 'Daddy', likely the most famous poem in Plath's *Ariel*, a book that had taken the quiet world of poetry by storm a few weeks before *The Knack* was released. In Britain alone it had sold 8,000 copies in hardback and fully 20,000 in paperback by the time of the May '68 riots. The book has never been out of print since. Good going for a slim collection of violently free verse documenting the breakdown and near dissolution of a personality in catatonic freefall. Reassuring and cosy *Ariel* is not – and 'Daddy' and sundry other poems in the book have served as a clarion call to legions of critics and fans who have claimed Plath as a feminist heroine and martyr.

It helped, let us not deny it, that Plath had committed suicide a couple of years before the book saw the light of day. Plath's friend and editor Al Alvarez once suggested that the poems in *Ariel* read as if they were written after her death, which is only a way of saying that separating Plath's life from Plath's poetry would be a thankless critical task. No one is suggesting that her suicide was a stunt (although Alvarez is surely not deranged for believing that the evidence found at the flat where she died suggests she was making a cry for help rather than a final sign-off[22]), but nor is there any denying that she suffered for her art. Humphrey Bogart said that dying young was the best career-move James Dean ever made. It didn't do Sylvia Plath's reputation any harm either. Suicide didn't increase the value of her poetry, but it gave it a currency it might not otherwise have earned.

Plath's suicide apart, it is the idea of *Ariel* as a document of near man-eating shrewishness that has kept it in the public eye. Published around the same time as Betty Friedan's *Feminine Mystique*, *Ariel* is one of the longest-standing riders of the second-wave of feminism. While it was largely in America that an organised and coherent women's movement was burgeoning, in the Britain of 1965 what Frederic Jameson once called the political unconscious was dreaming a feminist culture into being. *Ariel* was one of its essential texts. As its continuing sales figures suggest, the book has been bought and read by far more people than the average poetry collection. Philip Larkin, who called Plath 'a kind of Hammer Films poet',[23] thought her too extreme a character to identify with.[24] Yet mothers and housewives whose only interest in verse was teaching their children nursery rhymes found themselves reading it, and recognising in the gothic bleat of its carefully crazed urgency something of their own constricted lives.

Larkin, whose own life was far from average, was on to something about Plath's weirdness though. As a role model for those who had seen through the feminine mystique, this suicidal neurotic who in 'Daddy' openly acknowledged her unresolved Electra complex was hardly ideal. In fact, Plath's father had died two decades and more earlier, when she was just eight, of diabetes (undiagnosed until far too late in the day) and, subsequently, gangrene. Biography is always a hazardous art, but there is something to be said for the idea that the furiously competitive Plath devoted the rest of her life to trying to get her father back.

Her drive to success was fearsome. A straight-As student in school, she won prizes for her writing and was publishing poems and short stories in prestigious magazines when still a teenager. And while studying at Smith College she won not one but *two* prizes: having sent poems into a competition under different names, she ended up taking both first and second place. For the rest of her life she would be obsessed by her position in the cultural pecking order, a position that felt more rather than less precarious because of her marriage to a man whose place in it always seemed fixed.

Not that she was incapable of subsuming her ambitions. As the 23-year-old Plath wrote in her journal in 1956, she was on the lookout for 'some sort of blazing love that I can live with', and that she was 'inclined to babies and bed and brilliant friends and a magnificent stimulating home where geniuses drink gin in the kitchen after a delectable dinner . . . this is what I was meant to make for a man, and to give him this colossal reservoir of faith and love for him to swim in daily, and to give him children, lots of them in great pain and pride.'[26] And if that is not quite the voice of radical feminism speaking, much less is Plath's admission that if her hopes of marrying another poet came true, she'd want him to be more successful than her. Certainly for all the time and effort she put into her own verse during her years with Ted Hughes, she spent as much if not more on keeping his work in the public eye. Early on in their marriage she promised him that there would never be fewer than twenty of his poems circulating magazine editors' offices. She was as good as her word, and within a year of their wedding, in June 1956, Hughes's debut collection, *The Hawk in the Rain*, was published.

The literary support mechanism that constituted a good part of the marriage was, it should be said, mutual. Hughes never stopped telling Plath that she had it in her to be one of the best poets of the age. Soon enough she was publishing verse in the *Spectator*, *Harper's*, the *Times Literary Supplement* and the *Observer* (where Alvarez was poetry editor). After the fruits of this early work were gathered up for a collection called *The Colossus* (1960), the *New Yorker* paid her a first refusal retainer on all subsequent work for the then handsome annual fee of $100. Shortly after marrying Hughes she noted that with his help she was certain she could produce a book that would 'hit the critics violently'.[27] Four short years later she had done just that.

From the start, though, Plath's relationship with Hughes had been marked out by its own violence. In 'Daddy', which was written almost seven years to the day after her first meeting with Hughes at a party in Cambridge, Plath talks of a vampire having drunk her blood for just that length of time. Still the fact remains that Plath had fangs of her own and enjoyed using them. At that meeting, Plath, who at 5 feet 9 inches herself was not short, found herself bowled over by what she calls 'that big, dark, hunky boy, the only one there huge enough for me'. Their eyes kept meeting through the crowd, and eventually they got talking. And then, suddenly, 'he kissed me bang smash on the mouth and ripped my hair band off . . . and my favourite silver earrings: hah, I shall keep, he barked. And when he kissed my neck I bit him long and hard on the cheek, and when we came out of the room, blood was running down his face.'[28] Plath, who had a scar on her own cheek from one of her earlier attempts at suicide, had no hopes that she would get it together with Hughes (who was living and working in London). Still, she confided to her journal, it would have been good to 'try just this once, my force against his'.[29]

This account, Hughes always claimed, was overblown, and it is likely that Plath, who before talking to Hughes had been hitting the whisky bottle hard, went a little over the top in her reporting of it. But, report it she did, for all the world like some teenager recalling her first night out. Which means that even if everything she said wasn't verifiably true, it was nonetheless a record of how she imagined a relationship with Hughes might pan out. And anyway, we have it on the authority of his friend Lucas Myers that Hughes was indeed bitten on the face that night.

Thanks to his height and burly build and craggy features, as well as to the blood and bone imagery of much of his verse, Hughes is commonly conceived of as a man (and a poet) who was rather more physical than he was cerebral. Still, if his friends are to be trusted, he was a moderate chap, rarely to be seen drunk, and who, Myers says, 'never allowed himself to lose control of himself in any way'.[30] Nor does Myers believe his friend was a violent man – at least, 'he never did anything violent that I saw. He never even made a violent gesture.' And though Myers acknowledges that 'there was violence in his poetry' he argues that this wasn't autobiographical but observational – 'it expressed the violence of the universe.'[31] We do not have to take this as gospel, of course, though you will seek in vain for anything in the Hughes's oeuvre as autobiographically violent as Plath's 'Burning the Letters'.

The poem tells of how, in July 1962, during the final, protracted breakdown of the marriage, Plath broke into Hughes's study in the north Devon rectory they had moved into the year previous, rifled through his papers – the bulk of them letters, though there may have been some unfinished verse among them, too – before hauling them off to the garden and burning the lot. Her mother, who was visiting from America, looked on appalled. As well she might, since a writer can suffer no act of violence worse than the destruction of work in progress. And how much viler the violence is if its perpetrator is another writer. Plath, though, was a vandal of old. Eighteen months earlier, when the couple were still living in London, Hughes had found himself a job with the BBC's Schools Broadcasting Department. Alas, on the strength of one telephone conversation with the department's head, Moira Doolan, Plath decided that the tone of the woman's voice meant she was Hughes's lover – at which point she tore to shreds not only all the work on his desk but also his Complete Shakespeare.[32] Hughes said that he never held these acts against Plath, but that doesn't mean we should refrain from calling them what they were.[33]

Plath's poetry, though, was nourished on paranoid fury. As her college friend Nancy Hunter Steiner said, Plath liked to engineer crises in her life because of the creative stimulus they gave her.[34] And Hughes was surely right when he said that Plath's pre-*Ariel* work –

her novel *The Bell Jar* and the poems collected in *The Colossus* – 'were like impurities thrown off from the various stages of the inner transformation, by products of the internal work.'[35] What he couldn't quite bring himself to say was that her work only really came together when their marriage broke down. Formally satisfying as her earlier verse could be, too much of it smelled of the lamp. Plath's bust-up with Hughes was a boon to her poetry, not merely because it gave her a subject, but because it granted the violence-infused outpourings it engendered (written at what Hughes once described as dictation speed), an energy her previous work had signally lacked.

The strikingly violent line in 'Daddy' about the telephone being cut off at the root is justly famous, but it had its own roots in a striking act of violence. One day at their house in Devon, Plath answered the phone to be asked by a man whether 'Ted Hughes' was there. Except that she didn't believe it really was a man on the other end of the line. She suspected Hughes (rightly enough) of carrying on an affair with Assia Wevill (who with her husband had sublet the Hughes' London apartment a few months earlier). Wevill had, for a woman, a deep voice. Ergo, concluded Plath, the deep voice asking not for 'Ted' or 'Mr Hughes' must belong to her. And so, having handed the receiver over to Hughes, she yanked the phone line out of the socket at the wall.

For Plath's supporters, though, such destruction is as nothing when set beside the demolition job Hughes did on the original *Ariel* manuscript. For the fact is that not all of the poems Plath had written on the collapse of her marriage made it into the edition of the book that was published in 1965. Indeed, the book that came out in Britain that year differed in several ways from the 'Ariel' that Hughes had found among Plath's things. That manuscript was made up of forty-one poems collected into a black ring-binder, together with various drafts for both its title page (at one point Plath was going to call the book 'The Rival', at another 'Daddy and other poems') and contents page. (As ordered on the last version of the contents page, the book would have kicked off with the word 'Love' and come to a finish with the word 'Spring', a movement that suggests the book's mood was not meant to be wholly tenebrous.)

The *Ariel* that Hughes put together for Faber & Faber, though, contained only forty poems – and not all of them had been listed on Plath's contents page. Indeed, fully twelve of the poems in that ring-binder – 'The Rabbit Catcher'; 'Thalidomide'; 'Barren Woman'; 'A Secret'; 'The Jailer'; 'The Detective'; 'Magi'; 'The Other'; 'Stopped Dead'; 'The Courage of Shutting-Up'; 'Purdah'; and 'Amnesiac' – were missing from the published collection. In their place were a dozen or so poems written after the completion of what Plath considered *her* 'Ariel' and which she had put aside in consideration for a future third collection of her verse.

The reasoning behind Hughes's restructuring was simple enough. He believed that the 'Ariel' Plath had envisaged publishing would allow readers too much insight into the breakdown of their relationship. Because quite as much as these poems are evidence of a personality in free-fall, they are also a fever chart of rage and grief at the failure of a marriage. So it was that the book that eventually saw the light of day 'omitted', as Hughes put it, 'some of the more personally aggressive poems from 1962, and might have omitted one or two more if she had not already published them herself in magazines'.[37]

It is possible, of course, that had Plath lived she would herself have restructured the book. As the drafts prove, she was constantly tinkering with *Ariel*'s order and contents. More than that, her marriage to Hughes was not categorically over. Neither side had filed for divorce and both were hopeful that things might one day be patched up. Had that come to pass, Plath may well have excised some of the more heedless and hurtful poems herself. We'll never know.

But as far as Plath's admirers were concerned, Hughes's editing of the manuscript had been an outrageous intrusion, an arrogant rewriting of poetic history designed to safeguard his own reputation.

Never mind that he was himself still in a state of shocked self-recrimination at the terrible way his marriage had ended.* Never mind that
he was now the single father of two young children (who had been
asleep in the room above the kitchen when their mother had killed
herself), and wanted to protect what was left of their childhood.†
Never mind that the later poems he had worked into the book had
themselves been folded into the manuscript by Plath herself – as if,
had she lived, she might have one day worked them into the running
order. Never mind that 'within six years of that first publication all
her late poems were published in collections – all that she'd put in
her own *Ariel*, and those she'd kept out.'[38] Never mind that Hughes,
who had copyright control over everything from Plath's notebooks
to the letters she had written to family and friends, had no need to
publish any of her verse – whether 'more personally aggressive'
towards him or not. Never mind that he was in fact legally entitled
to pulp the lot. Never mind all that: it was plain to his critics that
Hughes the impugned adulterer had been in conflict with Hughes
the widower executor. Bluntly, he had edited *Ariel* not with an ear
for Plath's poetry but with merely an eye for his own reputation.

Well, maybe, though readers less ideologically swayed will not
regret the lack of the boorish 'Wintering' from *Ariel*, nor the omission of the agitprop angst that is 'The Rabbit Catcher'. Even if you
believe that poem to offer an accurate depiction of how being
married to Hughes had come to seem to Plath, there is no denying its over-determined metaphors would sit mighty uneasily with
the rigorously controlled anguish of the verse that made it into the

---

* Assia Wevill, the woman he had run away with, would herself commit suicide (by the
same head in the oven technique Plath had used) a few years later.
† Indeed, as late as 1992, when the children were into their thirties, Hughes took public
exception to Jacqueline Rose's book *The Haunting of Sylvia Plath* (Virago, 1991) because
it read Plath's 'The Rabbit Catcher' as a fantasy of bisexuality, 'presenting her', said
Hughes, 'in a role that I vividly felt to be humiliating to Sylvia Plath's children'. See the
Times Literary Supplement, 24 April 1992, for Hughes's letter on the subject.

book as originally published. Whatever else Hughes did when editing the 'Ariel' manuscript, then, there can be no doubt that his cuts helped in the success of a book that did so much to promulgate sixties feminism.

How much of an active feminist was Plath herself? Not much of one, unless you believe, with one of her biographers, Linda Wagner-Martin, that any female poet who reads other female poets is a feminist, or that any female poet who thinks she is talented and that her work is worthy of attention is a feminist.[39] And even if such could be proven whimsy the fact would remain that the young Plath had signed up pretty much wholesale to the apple-pie and gingham-frock vision of the Eisenhower America she had come of age in. Certainly at Cambridge, where she came to read English as a Fulbright scholar in 1955, she was dismissive of what she called the college's 'spinster bluestockings' and adamant that she wanted to have 'millions of babies'.[40]

Reading the descriptions of Hughes in Plath's letters home to her mother we might be reading the script of a Doris Day and Rock Hudson picture. Hughes, Plath writes, is a 'rugged, kind, magnificent man, who has no scrap of false vanity', he is 'the strongest man in the world'[41] and is 'twice as tall as all the little stumpy people' and 'a large, hulking, healthy Adam . . . a singer, story-teller, lion and world-wanderer, a vagabond who will never stop'.[42] She was sure that the boys at the Cambridge secondary school where he began teaching shortly after their marriage 'must really admire him; he is such a strong, fascinating person, compared to the other sissy teachers they get.'[43] As Janet Malcolm has said, in her *Journals* Plath goes on and on seeing Hughes as an 'overgrown Adonis/Aryan superman'.[44]

All of which raises another question. How badly is Plath's verse vitiated by its recourse to Nazi imagery? Adorno famously said that there could be no poetry after Auschwitz, yet in 'Lady Lazarus' Plath recalls the aftermath of a failed suicide attempt when her pallor put her in mind of the lampshades the Nazis fashoned from Jews' skin. And even if you're just about tempted to allow that simile, in 'Daddy' she imagines a train taking her off to Dachau, to Auschwitz, to Belsen.[45]

It's not just that using the Holocaust as a metaphor for private pain – what Plath calls elsewhere in the poem her 'weird luck' – is in bad taste. It's that such Grand Guignol hamming does nothing to illuminate the rage she wants to share. No one doubts Plath's psychic torments, if only because no sane person would ever compare their sufferings to those of the innocent victims of the death camps.* But nor is there any denying that Plath's poetic gift was rendered merely rhetorical by such hysteria, such histrionics. It's bad enough that history is being dragged used to aggrandise Plath's sufferings; far worse that the aggrandisement only denigrates the sufferings of history's victims. Adolescence might just about excuse the entertainment of such fantasies, but childish things must eventually be put away, and poetic licence can always be revoked.

The problem is that it isn't for her poetry that Plath is really revered. What matters about her most to her legions of admirers is not her poetry but her suffering. Just as rage was 'Plath's muse',[46] so it became the guiding light for her fans. Irving Howe once argued that the extremity of Plath's derangement debarred her from ever illuminating the human condition, but it was just this kind of claim the radical feminists trailing on Plath's tails wanted to take issue with. Plath only looked deranged, they argued, if you were yourself a deranged patriarch. If you were a woman living under patriarchy, Plath's sufferings made perfect sense. Hence the urgency with which they spoke to the emerging feminist sensibility of 1965.

In 'The Jailer', one of the poems Hughes held back from the first edition of *Ariel*, Plath wrote of having been drugged and raped and

---

* Though it is only right to point out that it was not the Jews who were famous for burning books.

described herself as the mechanism of her assailant's wet dreams. She might have been writing a diary entry for Miranda, the kidnapped heroine of John Fowles's first novel *The Collector*, a movie version of which was released in 1965. The book and the film tell a simple yet deeply disturbing story, centring on one Frederick Clegg, a sociopathic young town hall clerk and amateur lepidopterist, and Miranda, the girl he has been trailing obsessively for months. Alas for Miranda, when Clegg wins a fortune on the pools, he buys a big house in the country, converts the cellar into something just about habitable, and takes her prisoner there.

Sketched out like that, Fowles's novel might be the template for any number of recent Scandinavian psychological shockers. Just so, for *The Collector* is never less than a highly competent thriller. But it is rather more than that, too. For Fowles, *The Collector* was an allegory of capitalism in which a habitually despised but now wealthy member of the working class (Fowles calls them 'the Many' and 'Them'[47]) takes revenge on the culture he has been brought up to defer to by kidnapping one of the 'Few' (or 'Us', as Fowles unabashedly puts it) in the forlorn hope that once the barriers are down she might come to love him. 'I tried to show', Fowles once said, 'that [Clegg's] evil was largely, perhaps wholly, the result of a bad education, a mean environment.'[48] Fair enough, though there's no way around the fact that Fowles, for all his redoubtable skills as a narrator, never once makes us feel like taking Clegg's side. True, the picture he paints of Miranda makes her seem priggish and pretentious, but priggishness and pretentiousness are not crimes, and even if they were they would hardly compare to Clegg's crimes of kidnap and (eventually) manslaughter. Certainly few readers could ever share Miranda's belief, confided to her diary, that 'He's the one in prison.' (William Wyler's film of the book tries to complicate things by casting as Clegg not some loathsome brute but the beautifully epicene Terence Stamp. Alas, neither Wyler's over-emphatic direction nor

Stamp's underpowered performance roughen the surface of what has become, in the move from novel to film, mere well-oiled melodrama.)

Fowles's comments aside, his story makes rather more sense when seen as a parable of the horrors of marriage. Clegg has no interest in Miranda as a human being. She is someone he has worshipped from afar, but she remains no more than an image to him, an image that, like one of his butterflies, exists not to move through space and time, but to be pinned down and pored over. Like Charles Smithson, the hero of Fowles's third novel, *The French Lieutenant's Woman* (1969), Clegg hasn't learned that 'the desire to hold and the desire to enjoy are mutually destructive.'[49] As Miranda notes in her diary, 'He doesn't care what I say or how I feel . . . my feelings are meaningless to him – it's the fact that he's got me.'[50] Unlike Clegg's butterflies, though, Miranda can talk back. Alas, once she does so and Clegg gets to know something about her, he quickly falls out of love with what reveals itself to be not some angelic ideal but a flesh and blood human being with needs and desires of its own. Only towards the end of the story, when Miranda has fallen badly ill (and can no longer talk back), does Clegg again feel what passes for his version of warmth toward her. That's because he isn't interested in Miranda as Miranda, only in his fantasy of what she might be.

The Freudian term for this kind of thing is obsessional neurosis, though there is another, more poetic (and yet far more commonplace) name for it: romantic love. Certainly you couldn't get a cigarette paper between Clegg's early idealised objectifications of the perfect, though wholly unknown, Miranda and the denial of otherness – two become one – that is the essential prerequisite for the fantasy of romantic love. But if Fowles was a writer of romances – and he was – the striking fact about the structure of *The Collector* is its reversal of the form's basic terms: instead of releasing the heroine from captivity in order that she become his lover ('Rapunzel,

Rapunzel, let down your hair'), Fowles's (anti-) hero is the captor and his house the prison of the woman he would have as his wife.[51] His hope is that by holding her prisoner he can mould her into the woman of his dreams and thereby make her love him, or at least need him.

But it was *The Magus*, Fowles's second published novel, which he finally completed in March 1965 after twelve years of writing and rewriting, that cemented his reputation as one of the second wave of feminism's most vital male cheerleaders. The book was an immediate bestseller – and unlike many bestsellers one that went on to be fondly remembered. Indeed, when Fowles published a revised second edition of *The Magus*, twelve years after its first appearance (during which time it had never been out of print), the book became a bestseller all over again. Whatever its faults – and despite its near gratuitous readability *The Magus* is shot through with them – the book plainly spoke to Fowles's 'Many' rather than just his 'Few'.

There is no mystery about why this should have been so. For all its self-conscious artistry, its modernist meddling with form, its philosophical trickery and general air of booga-wooga mysticism, the book pulls like a train. It might occupy more than 600 pages of closely set type, but nobody ever takes long to get through them. And, boy, does it stay with you. Thirty years after I first read the novel, its fictional island of Phraxos (modelled on the Spetses Fowles had spent time teaching on during the fifties) remains one of the fantasy landscapes of my mind. I can no more wait to get back there, than I can stop myself envying anyone about to read *The Magus* for the first time.

Like Frederick Clegg before him, Nicholas Urfe, the narrator of *The Magus*, is a self-confessed projector of fantasies. 'Like a medieval king,' he writes of his dream of Greece in the novel, 'I had fallen in love with the picture long before I saw the reality.'[52] If landscapes were the only object of his reconstructive reveries no harm would be done, but Nicholas has a tendency to treat women in a similarly dreamy way. He either idealises them as unapproachable angels, or demonises them as all too approachable whores. A man of what he himself calls 'congenital promiscuity',[53] he is at heart a puritan.

Not that he is anything like self-aware enough to know it. His parents, he tells us on the first page of the book, were both victims and practitioners of a narrow-minded, Victorian value system that crippled them for life. The rest of the novel is essentially a long, dramatised upbraiding of such casual generational contempt, a *bildungsroman* whose essential lesson for Nicholas is that far from being the liberated mid-twentieth century existentialist he takes himself to be, he is in fact a stiff-upper-lipped Englishman straight from the central casting couch of Freudian repression. He likes sex, but he despises any woman who feels similarly. His punishment is to find himself dumped into a surreal continental nightmare wherein a succession of prick-teasing apparitions make him realise he has only been affecting to despise the hangover from nineteenth-century boarding school morality he has grown up under.

It should be clear from that that one of *The Magus*'s most profound effects for the sixties lay in its introducing into the culture what we might call a post-Lawrentian vision of sexuality. Not for Fowles's characters those epiphanic glimpses of the eternal that Lawrence's men and women are forever experiencing during lovemaking. We are firmly grounded on planet earth here. It isn't that Fowles's descriptions of the sexual act (far more explicit in the revised edition, of course, but suggestive enough in 1965) are anything other than the higher baloney. It's that they're *meant* to be baloney. Unlike Lawrence's, Fowles's – or, more properly, Nicholas's – evocations of carnality are the merest romantic afflatus. Like Frederick Clegg (who is counselled by Miranda that 'sex is just an activity, like anything else. It's not dirty, it's just two people playing with each other's bodies. Like dancing'[54]), Nicholas is taught that romance and sex have very little to do with one another. Out of such insights would come the summer of love.*

The Magus has been criticised for its ambiguous ending,† for leaving us in two minds as to whether Nicholas has grown through his sufferings and whether he is now in a position to embark on a mature relationship with his girlfriend of old, Alison. Yet this is to miss the point of a novel which has argued throughout that the only thing that truly counts is individual choice, individual decision. Unlike a classical, three-act story (which it in so many ways resembles), *The Magus* never arrives at that moment when its hero grasps just what has been going on and knows just what to do about it. By the end of the novel he is as certain as any hero can be that he is in charge of his own destiny. He just hasn't got a clue what that means. It's up to him to decide.

And, by the same token, it's up to us. One's responsibility, as a properly sentient being in the Fowlesian universe, is to exercise one's judgement on such moral questions and decide for oneself whether Nicholas has been improved by the torments he has had to endure. (Fowles, incidentally, was in no doubt that Nicholas was a better man for his misadventures on Phraxos. It is he, after all, who is the narrator of his tale – and he makes no bones about painting himself as an arrant swine.)

* *The Magus*'s influence wasn't just on the body politic. Patrick McGoohan's *The Prisoner*, which thanks to its continued (indeed, almost continual) showing on television and its forever being re-released on video and DVD has become one of the ur-sixties texts, would have been inconceivable without Fowles's example. It's not just the show's basic storyline – a man finding out who he really is within the confines of an artily hostile environment. It's McGoohan's reliance on a drugged-out sensibility, a sensibility that finds as much pleasure in distrusting as in trusting empirical evidence, that has its origins in Fowles. Even those people who eschewed the delights of dope and LSD that the sixties offered could get a semblance of the experience by reading *The Magus* or watching McGoohan's endlessly repetitive, hypnotically spiralling, hallucinatory Rorschach blot of a spy thriller.
† Four years later *The French Lieutenant's Woman* would wholly refuse the idea of closure, with Fowles's highly self-conscious narrator nudging us to choose first this denouement then that in a succession of chapters offering wholly different endings.

Fowles was a lifelong socialist, but by a quaint irony it has perhaps been *The Magus*'s emphasis on the individual's responsibility to him or her self that has ensured the novel has lasted. For all its status as a harbinger of the druggy, psyched-out culture of the late sixties, the novel's unrelenting grip on us speaks as much if not more to the neo-liberal revolution that took place in the seventies and eighties. Even without Fowles's self-confessed belief in the aristos and the hoi polloi, the us and the them, the elect and the ill-bred, there is no missing the fact that *The Magus*, like so much of sixties culture, served to presage the rampant individualism the Thatcher governments were going to invoke and inspire. As Penelope Mortimer argued in a damning yet deeply insightful review of the novel's first edition, Nicholas Urfe was really just 'a middle-class Alfie'.*[55]

By the same token, Diana Scott, the titular lead of John Schlesinger's *Darling*, was a kind of female Alfie – a post-feminist before the fact. Diana was played by Julie Christie, who once described the character as the very embodiment 'of a woman who would actually go out and pursue her own goal'.[56] And score a few own-goals while she's about it, one can't help adding, since the picture that Schlesinger and his writer, Frederic Raphael, paint of Diana as she jaunts about Europe is as damning as any composition the pre-Magus-moralised Nicholas Urfe could have conjured up.

Because *Darling* is as confused a movie as any in history. For all its emphasis on the vacuous ethics of the advertising and modelling world in which Diana earns her living, Raphael's clever

---

* Bill Naughton's *Alfie* was filmed in 1966, with perhaps the sixties' most crucial forerunner of the Thatcher era, Michael Caine, in the lead role. Two years later, Caine also took the lead in Guy Green's woefully misguided film version of Fowles's novel – a film that prompted Woody Allen to suggest that if he could have his life over again he'd do everything the same 'except see *The Magus*'. Fowles, incidentally, thought Caine 'a natural bastard, so I suppose he's a sort of natural casting', adding in his journal that he found such 'ultra-hard young princes of limelight … very ugly'. (John Fowles, *The Journals: Volume 1* [Jonathan Cape, 2003], p.630.)

clever, punning, cryptic crossword-solving, literally unspeakable dialogue comes across as all the more hollow for thinking itself morally cutting. And while Schlesinger saw himself as engaged in a criticism of the burgeoning permissive society and 'the emotional coldness ... [and] loneliness that Diana's kind of life must lead to',[57] his movie turns out to be highly reliant on that permissiveness for its repeated shots of Christie's bikini-clad or lingerie-clad (and at one point naked) body. Despite the film's glamour and glitz, it is best seen as a late inheritor of the kitchen-sink tradition on which we have already touched. Schlesinger had in fact directed one of the entries in that mini-genre, 1962's *A Kind of Loving*, though it is Jack Clayton's version of John Braine's *Room at the Top* (1959) that *Darling*'s vision of a young (wo)man on the make most closely resembles. The crucial difference between Diana Scott and Braine's Joe Lampton, of course, is that he wreaks havoc on the lives of all around him while she ends up harming no one but herself.

In that sense, *Darling* was less a foretaste of the feminism 1965 was about to unleash than a pre-emptive attack on it by suggesting that such liberation will bring only whorish misery. (Two years later Schlesinger and Raphael told the same story all over again in a very swinging yet very sorry version of Hardy's *Far From the Madding Crowd* with Christie risibly miscast as Bathsheba and Terence Stamp even more laughably playing Sergeant Troy.) Far better, *Darling* counsels its audience, to find happiness through living an average life.

And yet the film has no real vision of normality to offer. Inspired by the moral quagmire Federico Fellini had attempted to cross in *La Dolce Vita* (1959), *Darling* has a cast of characters that is really no more than a gaggle of gargoyles. The film offers up not one decent, humane person for us to identify with, let alone for us to observe Diane's heartless shenanigans through. Even its, for the time near obligatory, abortion scene, is painted not as a moment of agonised doubt (as it is in Margaret Drabble's *The Millstone*, published the month after *Darling* was released), nor as a moment of moral self-recrimination (as it was in *Saturday Night and Sunday Morning*), but as just another lifestyle choice.

Yet in its vision of a young woman who knows not what she wants as long as she's having a good time, Schlesinger and Raphael's story pointed with eerie acuity to the hollowed-out materialism and spurious, self-congratulatory consciousness-raising that was to grow out of the sixties revolution. Perhaps without quite knowing it, the movie suggested that sixties feminism was less a movement of existential liberation than one predicated upon and determined entirely by the capitalist economy.

Which doesn't mean that women's lives and roles weren't changing in 1965. On 12 August, for instance, just a few weeks before *Darling* opened, the barrister Elizabeth Lane became the first woman to be appointed to the High Court bench.* At the same time, she was made DBE (comparable with the knighthoods customarily conferred on male High Court judges). Doubtless because of her sex she was assigned to the Probate, Divorce and Admiralty Division (subsequently renamed the Family Division), where she more than once demonstrated a kindlier than usual approach to the problems of families in the throes of separation or divorce. Herself the mother of a mentally disabled son who had died aged only fourteen, Lane was famous for understanding the needs of children at those times when families were under strain. 'It often seemed to me', she said in retirement, 'that children were happier with two parents who quarrelled than when deprived of one of them, although obviously quarrelling or violence might reach such a pitch that it was better for the children if their parents did part.'[58]

And increasing numbers of parents were separating through and beyond 1965. Marriage and its requisite 2.4 children were no longer

---

* It would be nine long years before another female judge was appointed to the High Court – again to the family division – in the shape of Mrs Rose Heilbron.

seen as the prerequisites for a normal and fulfilled life. Ambitions outside the four walls of the family home were licensed for women in a way they hadn't been since the war (and had been then only because so many of the men were away). After the two immediate post-war decades of doing little but child-rearing and running the family home, women were more and more to be found earning a living in factories and offices across the land. Hence one of the reasons for the increase in divorce rates (which all but doubled between 1965 and 1970, and doubled again by 1975[59]): women were earning their own money and becoming less dependent on their husbands. And since they were less dependent on their husbands, the divorce courts need have less fear that such newly single women would be a burden on the state. Men – or at least some of them – were perhaps understandably resentful of this change in lifestyle. Surveyed just as Diana Scott was blazing a trail across the nation's cinema screens, more than 30 per cent of them admitted to disliking the idea of their wives going out to work. One in fifteen went so far as to say that a woman's place was in the home.[60]

But thanks to the cultural revolution of 1965 there was an increasing belief among young women that the shape of their lives need not have been marked out for them by the template of their own childhood. Questioning the rules for how the labours of married life might be parcelled out was one of the key themes of so much film and fiction that year. Its first theoretical fruit was borne a few short months later, when Juliet Mitchell's 'Women: the Longest Revolution' appeared in the pages of the *New Left Review*. Bestselling books by Germaine Greer (*The Female Eunuch*) and Kate Millet (*Sexual Politics*) would follow shortly on its heels. Within a couple of decades women's studies – in which the work of Sylvia Plath figured heavily – would become not only a staple course at universities but a component course for pretty much any humanities student. Poetry, Auden famously said, 'makes nothing happen'. Except that sometimes it does.

4

THE FREEDOM TRAP

In which the car guns the motor of the Thatcher revolution

'The car has become an article of dress without which we feel uncertain, unclad and incomplete in the urban compound.'[1]

Marshall McLuhan

We'd all like one. We'd all love one of those strap-to-your-back jet-pack gizmos with which James Bond flees the French foe at the start of 1965's 007 blockbuster, *Thunderball*, before stowing it in the boot of his Aston Martin and quipping to the inevitable waiting girl that 'no well-dressed man should be without one'. Back then, of course, we'd have loved a jet pack for the fun of it – the orgiastic thrill of solo flights above the everyday. Nowadays, though, Bond's airborne gadget appeals as much more of a workaday tool. How much better to cut through the rush-hour traffic – or even the non-rush-hour traffic – than by floating glee-fully above it?

To be sure, a jet pack mightn't be the safest way of getting around, but let's not kid ourselves that driving a car is all that safe either. As J. G. Ballard, the writer of *Crash*, once argued,* 'Most of us, when we drive our cars, willingly accept a degree of risk for ourselves, our wives and children which we could regard as criminally negligent in any other field – the wiring of electrical appliances, say, or the design of a bridge or apartment block, the competence of a surgeon or midwife. Yet the rough equivalent of speeding on unchecked tyres along a fast dual carriageway at the end of a tiring day at the office is lying in a hot bath with a blazing three-bar electric fire balanced on the edge below a half-open window rattling in a rising gale.'[2]

For the fact is that in ethical terms very few of us are up to the task of driving. We can pass the practical skills test all right, but we're never asked until far too late in the day whether we understand or are even aware of the moral dilemmas intrinsic to making a tonne and more of metal race at speeds that render intelligent decision-making an impossibility. It was surely not random choice that led Nicholas Mosley to make a troubled Oxford philosopher the central consciousness of *Accident*, his 1965 novel about the moral fall-out from a car crash. For Mosley's forty-something don Stephen, life is enough of an ethical quagmire without questions as to what getting behind the wheel does to the human soul obtruding on it.†

That is why, long before it starts firing bullets from its front indicator lights and shooting high-pressure jets of water from its rear lights, even before its driver slashes the tyres of anyone daring to try

---

* In the pages of the magazine *Drive* – a commission as mind-boggling as, say, Jeremy Clarkson being asked to write a history of environmentalism.

† Mosley wasn't on to anything new. Half a century earlier, in 1913 – little more than a decade after the commencement of mass automobile manufacture – an Austrian Olympic gold cyclist turned motoring journalist called Adolf Schmal was to be found confessing that he knew 'kind, well-bred, and considerate people who, as soon as they feel the steering wheel in their hands and the gas pedal under their foot are seized by an automotive frenzy'. Quoted in Dietmar Fack, *Automobil, Verkehr un Erziehung: Motorisierung und Sozialisation zwischen Beschleunigung und Anpassung, 1885–1945* (Leske & Budrichnn, 2000), p.149.

to go faster than him, and even before he ejects an oriental heavy through its roof panel, James Bond's unashamedly desirable Aston Martin DB5* looks like a weapon. From its fearsome, sharkish grille, through its vampirically toothsome bumper guards to its gunmetal skin, this is a tank with sex appeal. Who needs a Walther PPK when a car itself is a licence to kill?

All of which helps explain the fact that far more people die on the roads than do in train and even plane crashes. Indeed, only a couple of years ago it was calculated that the number of people killed on the roads every day is equivalent to those killed in a dozen jumbo jet crashes. Small wonder that the twentieth century was witness to some 30 million road-related deaths. To help put that figure in perspective, consider that it represents around half the number of people who died in the Second World War. Alternatively, think of it as accounting for the deaths of about twice as many of the people who perished in the First World War. There is no way of pretending that these aren't astonishing figures. As the economist E. J. Mishan argued back in the sixties, 'The sacrifice of a life or two by primitive communities in the belief that it ensured a good harvest seem humane in comparison with the implicit decision to kill some tens of thousands yearly that the pleasures of private motoring be upheld.'[3]

Mishan's book was published in 1967, two years after the most perilous year on the roads in our history. Because with just shy of 8,000 people killed and almost 400,000 injured during its twelve-month span, 1965 was the worst year for road casualties in Britain. Car accidents had been building to such numbers for some time.[4] Over the course of the previous fifteen years, road casualty numbers had all but doubled. It is true that the number of vehicles in use

---

* In April 2011 the newly married Prince William was allowed to drive his father's Aston Martin DB5 convertible from Buckingham Palace to St James's Palace. The jury is still out on whether this humanised Wills, by making him prey to the same fantasies and desires as our own, or made him and his father seem more out of touch with the needs of real people than they are not so fondly imagined to be.

during that period had virtually trebled – so that proportionally speaking road accidents and injuries were on the slide. Still, there was no getting away from the suggestion that the future looked a whole lot worse. Figures produced for the Department of Transport in 1965 suggested that by the turn of the century fully half a million people could be expected to meet their death on the road every year.

And so, three days before Christmas, the then Transport Minister, Tom Fraser, imposed an experimental speed limit of 70 miles an hour on all Britain's hitherto unrestricted roads.* Meanwhile, Dr Murray Mackay, of the Road Accident Research Unit at the University of Birmingham, began an intensive and systematic study of road accidents and their causes.[5] His core conclusion was that the old saw about accidents will happen was wrong. There was, of course, an element of bad luck in a small number of road accidents; but the majority of them were caused by driver error – usually, he said, a very basic error.

According to Mackay, accident-prone drivers shared several key personality traits, chief among them aggression, self-obsession and rebelliousness. Immature, incautious and off-balance, they are people incapable of thinking things through; hence their propensity for risk-taking.† A few years later these findings were backed up by Dr Terence Willett of Reading University. About a third of people involved in driving offences, he found, were people 'with anti-social tendencies generally. They didn't seem to have any particular regard for their families or their employers or anyone else. Their interests were self-interests ... Most of our studies suggest that an individual's attitude to society generally are reflected in their

---

* Germany, as so often, was ahead of the game. In 1965 it introduced variable speed limits on the A8 route between Munich and Salzburg; it would be another thirty years before Britain did the same, on certain sections of the M25.

† Troubled and troubling, such people's career patterns tended to be erratic, too, though such waywardness was a lot easier to spot in an age of full employment. These days, pretty much anyone's CV can look shy of narrative structure.

driving behaviour.'[6] The problem is, of course, that taking risks on the road isn't just dangerous for the risk-taker. It puts non-risk-taking people at risk too. As Nick says to that 'rotten driver' Jordan Baker in *The Great Gatsby*, the problem with driving carelessly is that one day you might meet someone coming from the other direction who is driving carelessly too. The old joke about the most dangerous bit of a car being the nut behind the steering wheel turns out to be mighty close to the truth.

Not that accidents were all down to the driver. As the title of Ralph Nader's 1965 bestseller, *Unsafe at Any Speed*, pointed out, cars as they were then manufactured really were accidents waiting to happen.[7] The book, which argued that motor manufacturers were almost completely indifferent to the safety of their cars, can lay claim to being one of the most influential ever published.* Thanks to Nader's efforts, car safety technologies have improved enormously in the fifty years since his book's publication. Cars withstand impact from the front and side so much more effectively than they did when Sean Connery's James Bond was throwing them round corners. They also brake without locking or skidding so much more efficiently than they did back then. (Though to be fair, Nader always said that British car brakes, as well as British tyres, were way ahead of their American counterparts. He was astonished, though, that seat belts weren't compulsory in British cars, and baffled by the fact that we had yet to do anything about tackling exhaust emissions.[8])

No less importantly, car interiors have been rendered so much safer for the driver and passengers. The spiked shaft that supported the pre-collapsible steering wheel, for instance, ran the infamous nut behind it a close second in the danger stakes. And then there

---

* So influential that General Motors hired private detectives to follow Nader in the hope of getting some dirt on him. Not only did they find nothing discreditable, but they were themselves discredited when the investigation came to light and the company had to apologise before a Senate subcommittee.

was the console. When Nader was writing, car fascias weren't at all like the padded, curvaceous bulks of today. Back then they were all sharp edges and hard wood – just perfect for cutting and crushing you in the event of a smash. And let's not forget about the windscreen that the force of a crash could send you flying through. In Nader's day windscreens were made of glass, and a smash would have them shattering into shards that could blind and maim. Or kill. Even if the screen managed to remain in one piece, the force of a crash tended to make the windscreen tilt to the horizontal – thereby making it a perfect guillotine.*

Not that talk of the dangers of cars and government statutes on the speed they could be driven at put people off driving any. Car passenger mileage was booming. The number of cars on the road almost doubled between the end of the fifties and the end of the sixties, from 9 million to 16 million vehicles. (Over the half century that led up to the turn of the millennium, the number of cars and vans in Britain increased tenfold to some 24 million vehicles. Ten years later there were 31.25 million vehicles on Britain's roads – one for every two people in the country.†

And woe betide the poor pedestrian who got in the driver's way. That at least was the suggestion of the Master of the Worshipful Company of Carmen, Colonel John Pye. Traffic should be allowed to go faster, he said, including through towns and cities. 'A look should be taken at the widths of pavements,' he wrote, 'and, where possible, steps be taken to cut them down to widen the road space

---

* All these developments, motoring provocateurs like to argue, have only made driving more dangerous. Improvements in car safety, the argument runs, only encourage drivers to be more reckless – safe in the knowledge that they will escape any accident largely unscathed. There is something to such ruthless logic, of course, though there is rather more to the argument that the roads would be far, far safer places if anyone who believes in such facetious sophistry were disqualified from driving.

† This may turn out to have been a peak. In April 2010 the *Daily Telegraph* reported that the number of cars on the roads had dropped – to 31,035,791 – for the first time since the Second World War.

[. . .] there should be more control of pedestrians.'[9] Astonishingly, nobody objected.

Nobody objected because more and more people wanted to get off their bikes and into a car of their own. During the first half of the sixties, the mileage covered by Britain's bicyclists went down by 40 per cent, from an average of 125 miles per person per year in 1961 to 75 miles per person just four years later. (Since not everyone cycled, individual mileages – or non-mileages – were, of course, rather higher than those figures suggest.)[10]

So it was that by the mid-sixties motorways were springing up all over Britain. These were the first major road-building projects since before the Second World War, and they transformed the country far more radically than we are apt to realise, let alone admit. It is no exaggeration to say that motorways made for the biggest changes to the landscape and soundscape of our countryside since the canal- and mill-building programmes of the Industrial Revolution. Hence the claim in the *British Medical Journal* in September 1965 'that the hearing of the population as a whole has begun to be affected by the rise in ambient noise in cities through the growth of mechanisation in transport'.[11] Forget concerns about safety or pollution or the environment and contemplate for a moment the peace and the silence we abandoned for what Margaret Thatcher once called the 'great car economy'.

Abandon it we did, though. In the spring of 1965 almost 700,000 people visited the London Motor Show at Earls Court, a few short weeks after the British Motor Corporation had announced that the millionth Mini had rolled off its Longbridge assembly line. (Mini production peaked that year, in fact, with 345,245 of the cars hitting the forecourts – almost 30,000 a month.) Popular with the increasingly mobile housewife about town,* the car was also a big hit

---

* A fact that outraged its designer, the unashamedly homosexual Alec Issigonis. 'What could be worse', he was heard to mutter, 'than a suburban housewife with money?'

with the rich and (in)famous. Back in January, the racing driver Timo Mäkinen had won the Monte Carlo Rally in a Mini Cooper S, and everyone from the disgraced former Secretary of State for War, John Profumo, to the two good-time girls who had brought a peremptory end to his career a couple of years earlier, Christine Keeler and Mandy Rice-Davies, were to be seen at the wheel of their Minis. By the end of the year, when Paul McCartney acquired a Mini Cooper S with Radford styling (just for dotting around town in, you understand: for longer journeys Macca still favoured his 007-style Aston Martin) all the Beatles save Ringo Starr were proud owners of a Mini. Ringo owned two of them.

Soon enough, such transports of delight began to find their way into the Fabs' songs. In early autumn, after motoring down from London to John Lennon's house in Weybridge, McCartney sang for his writing partner a tune and lyric he was working on whose hook line was 'You can buy me diamond rings'. Lennon vetoed this sentiment (he called it 'crap' to be precise), arguing correctly enough that diamond rings had already featured in a couple of Beatles numbers. His suggested replacement line was the rather less romantic 'Baby, you can drive my car'. That sentiment would turn out to be the opening words of 'Drive My Car', the opening song on what would turn out to be the Beatles' finest album yet, *Rubber Soul*. Celebratory songs about cars and their drivers and their love affairs had been a staple of rock and roll since its inception a decade earlier, of course. 'Drive My Car', though, turned out to be a rather dark little comic tale about spurned love and materialist aspiration. (Eighteen months later, when the Beatles recorded one of their greatest songs, 'A Day in the Life', Lennon proved himself yet more in tune with the zeitgeist when he took for his subject the apocalyptic fallout from a lethal car smash.)

Meanwhile, the official cross-party line on the effects of car pollution began to wobble. In June, Lord Lindgren, the Parliamentary Secretary to the Ministry of Transport in the upper house, admitted that 'recent investigations in London have shown that some danger is likely to arise' from the inhalation of car exhaust fumes.[12] Six months later, in the Commons, the Minister of Transport, Tom Fraser, said that he couldn't disagree with those findings.[13] Over the next few months, the Royal Society of Health heard from Dr L. E. Reed, of the government's Warren Spring Laboratory, who advised that action must be taken against car pollution, as well as from the Ministry of Transport's deputy chief mechanical engineer, H. D. Fawell, who said regulations for the control of exhaust emissions might have to be put in place. No such rules came into being (although the ever-playful Alec Issigonis was said to be toying with the idea of building a Mini that would puff along by means of a steam engine). Cheese-paring economics can be the only explanation for this emission omission, because the fact is that Britain's car-makers were already having to implement such technological alterations for cars that were to be exported to America.

That's right: fifty years ago, just as the British government was kicking discussion of the downsides of the car revolution into the long grass, those gas-guzzlers across the Atlantic were already beginning to worry about the threats from CO_2 emissions. As early as 1965, the Environmental Pollution Panel of the President's Science Advisory Committee was arguing that by the end of the twentieth century the extra carbon dioxide that results from the burning of oil and petrol 'may be sufficient to produce measurable and perhaps marked changes in climate, and will almost certainly cause significant changes in the temperature and other properties of the stratosphere'. Needless to say, 'the climactic changes that may be produced by the increased carbon dioxide content could be deleterious from the point of view of human beings.'[14] They argued, too, that mass car usage was having an impact on global warming. Given the effects of CO_2 on temperature, they said, it was not impossible that come the century's end the average temperature near the earth's surface may well have increased by a few degrees.

Inactive as Britain's leaders were, though, there were those among us who were out to question – and in some cases actively subvert – the ever-growing car culture. As early as 1958 the town planner Colin Buchanan's *Mixed Blessing: The Motor in Britain* had ruminated on how the country might look if car usage continued to increase.* Five years on, Buchanan followed that government report with another that became so talked about it was published in the more reader-friendly form of a Penguin Special – *Traffic in Towns*. One of the arguments of the book, which became a bestseller, was that it was becoming impossible 'to spend any time on the study of the future of traffic in towns without at once being appalled by the magnitude of the emergency that is coming upon us. We are nourishing at immense cost a monster of great potential destructiveness, and yet we love him dearly. To refuse to accept the challenge it presents would be an act of defeatism.'[15] Once again, alas, the challenge was refused – at least in Buchanan's own country.

Yet the popularity of *Traffic in Towns* – which, for all its boosterish faith in technological progress, suggested government control may be needed to limit the number of cars on the road – led, in 1965, to the translation of its predecessor into French and German, and it was across Europe that a 'down with the motorcar' movement really began to burgeon that year. In Helsinki an anti-car group issued its members with hammers, the better to damage the paintwork of any vehicle breaking rules and regulations. In Amsterdam a group calling themselves the 'Provos' fought to ban all cars from

---

* The French political activist Guy Debord was having mighty similar thoughts: 'It is not a matter of opposing the automobile as an evil in itself,' he wrote in his 'Situationist Theses on Traffic'. 'It is its extreme concentration in the cities that has led to the negation of its function. Urbanism should certainly not ignore the automobile, but even less should it accept it as its central theme. It should reckon on gradually phasing it out. In any case, we can envision the banning of auto traffic from the central areas of certain new complexes, as well as from a few old cities.' Guy Debord, 'Situationist Theses on Traffic', *Internationale Situationiste* 3, November 1959.

the city centre, at the same time introducing a fleet of all-white bicycles intended for the free use of anyone in the city. (Forty-five years later, the Mayor of London Boris Johnson would announce a similar scheme, this time sponsored by an international bank and with an annual subscription fee to boot.) In France, meanwhile, the art historian Michel Ragon published a memoir of the national capital, *Paris, hier, aujourd'hui, demain*, in which he bemoaned the increasing American influence on French life not least because over there they had 'destroyed so much for freeways and parking that they will soon realise that there are no longer any cities!'.[16]

Harold Wilson's government, however, which had won the election on the back of a campaign promising that it would harness the 'white heat of the technological revolution', contrived to read Buchanan's book through spectacles even Pangloss might have pronounced too roseate. Only build more roads, they said, and all would be for the best. Indeed, even as *Traffic in Towns* was climbing the bestseller lists around the world, the newly formed Greater London Council (which opened for business on 1 April 1965, under Labour control) was announcing plans for the building of what it called a 'motorway box' around central London – a ring-road that would speed and distribute traffic into and around the city while avoiding the centre where at all possible. A year later, the government's 'Cars for Cities' report was to be found arguing for the construction of aerial urban roads designed exclusively for Mini-sized cars and complete with Mini-sized parking spaces.

Reactions to the idea of urban motorways were mixed – and occasionally downright confused. In March 1965, for instance, when the eastern end of the M4* was opened for business and traffic from the west began speeding into London, the Chiswick Motorway Liaison Committee began campaigning against what one reporter called 'the

---

* One of the engineers on this final section of the motorway had been Sandy Darling, father of the future Transport Secretary (and Chancellor of the Exchequer), Alistair.

monster roads nosing into Britain's cities'.[17] And yet just a couple of years later, when the Tories gained control of the GLC in 1967 they did so on the back of a campaign for speeding up motorway construction. 'Some people', the Tory leader Edward Heath had told the Society of Motor Manufacturers and Traders the previous year, 'would like to push us into a frame of mind in which it is considered anti-social to own a car, selfish to drive one, and positively sinful to take it into a built-up area.'[18] By 1968 the Conservatives would publish a pamphlet entitled 'The Plight of the Motorist'.

Not everyone saw the plight, though. By the time the first section of the London box had been opened – the elevated section of the Westway that starts near Paddington station – popular opposition to urban motoring was growing. Pictures of the Westway, which showed cars zooming into and out of the city mere feet from the upper-storey bedroom windows of local residents, did nothing to sell the plan to an increasingly sceptical public. Londoners, most of whom didn't own cars, were distinctly unimpressed by the idea of public money being spent on roads that would help well-heeled suburbanites on their journeys to and from their homes in the shires and their work in the city. Moreover, the clearance of housing stock necessary for the box's construction would make London even shorter of homes than it already was.

One of the reasons for this shortage was the increasing trend for the new middle classes to move into areas of London which had for several generations been looked askance at by professionals. Because even though throughout the sixties some 50,000 people a year abandoned the city for the suburbs,* those young people who did come to London subsequent to the Rent Act of March

---

* Paradoxically, people said they were fleeing the city because they felt the increasing numbers of cars was making life unbearable there, while at the same time saying that they could only contemplate moving to the countryside because of the greater mobility their car afforded them. See Brian Ladd, *Autophobia: Love and Hate in the Automotive Age* (University of Chicago Press, 2008), pp.98 and 160.

1965* had no intention of living in the bedsits and small flats that so many large Victorian and Georgian houses had been split up into over the past few years. Instead, they took to buying up such properties wholesale and then set about reconverting them back into single homes.

Among the areas first taken over by what the locals called the 'knockers-through' were the squares and crescents of the Barnsbury area of Islington. (At the time, prior to what we now refer to as gentrification, almost two-thirds – 62 per cent – of the area's residents were living in shared accommodation. Across London, the average was 30 per cent.)[19] Rightly admiring and protective of what they saw as the area's distinctive architectural beauty, the knockers-through set up the Barnsbury Association – and early in 1965 succeeded in establishing the village as Britain's first Conservation Area. (Alas, they weren't so lucky with the Packington estate, not half a mile east of Barnsbury. This collection of rat-infested early and mid-Victorian terraces was just as ripe for gentrification, but Islington Council bought the houses up in 1965 and, aided by some strong-arm work from the Permanent Secretary at the Department of Housing, Dame Evelyn Sharp, demolished them in short order.[20])

One of the Association's first aims was the establishment of a roads management scheme designed to 'revive [Barnsbury's] "village" character – and identity as a living unit'. 'Through traffic', said the Association's David Wager, a local resident who worked as a town planner, 'must be excluded, and necessarily provided for, by creating proper urban through routes around the boundaries of the area.'[21] The result was a network of blocked-off turns, one-way streets and 'back doubles' (to use the taxi driver's vernacular) that could mystify even the most knowledgeable local. It was also rather more by way

* Which, by freezing rents on the bulk of unfurnished properties while increasing security of tenure, had the effect of encouraging many of London's still Dickensianly greedy landlords to look for other ways of turning a shilling.

of peace and quiet than Barnsbury's new residents had been used to. That said, traffic noise wasn't done away with but merely reallocated. For all their solidarity with the evictees from the Packington estate, all the Barnsbury Association's new roads scheme really succeeded in doing was siphoning traffic out of its own streets and on to those in the surrounding, and still predominantly working-class, area.

Elsewhere around the country, though, peace and quiet were getting harder and harder to find. Even on the 267-mile-long* Pennine Way, Britain's first officially sanctioned long-distance walking route, which was opened in full in April 1965, walkers were rarely far enough away from a car to be assured of enjoying the contemplative silence they were seeking. Traffic in Manchester, which Pennine Wayers passed by within a few miles of setting off on their walk, was burgeoning – as it was in cities across the land. Indeed, a few years later the people of Birmingham were told that the cars on the city's Gravelly Hill Interchange could be heard by Pennine Way walkers as far away as 60 miles to the north.

Gravelly Hill is more commonly referred to as Spaghetti Junction, the monicker it was given in June 1965 when a reporter for the *Birmingham Evening Mail* described the plans he had seen for the motorway interchange as 'a cross between a plate of spaghetti and an unsuccessful attempt at a Staffordshire knot'.[22] The junction, which took three years to plan and another four to build, did not officially open to traffic until 1972. But as early as 1970 certain more adventurous and investigative members of the public were to be found inspecting its curlicues and arabesques in tourist-style awe. Barbara Castle, who took over the government's transport brief at the end of 1965 (and who has some claim to being the wisest of all the department's occupants these past fifty years), took to calling motorway junctions 'the cathedrals of the

---

* One refers to the length of the walk in miles because though the government decided Britain should go metric in 1965, this was surely the year's least effective piece of legislation.

modern world'.*[23] Soon enough coach trips were being organised for those curious to have a look at what the West Midlands Tourist Board were selling almost as an eighth wonder of the world. 'Four thousand years ago,' a spokesman for the board claimed, 'people would probably have gone to see the Pyramids for the same reason.'[24]

But if roads were the future, railways were the past. Such, at least, had been the view of Ernest Marples, the Transport Minister under Harold Macmillan and subsequently Sir Alec Douglas-Home from 1959 through to 1964. Marples and his fellow Conservatives had been helped to this conclusion, it should be said, by a brutally effi-cient strike by two of the rail unions back in 1955. Called mere days after the Tories' general election win under Anthony Eden, the strike, which was over pay differentials and lasted from 29 May to 14 June, had brought pretty much the whole of the country's industry to a standstill. After a fortnight and more of misery the government caved in and the British Transport Commission settled the pay claim. It was a sacrifice the government would not forget. From here on in, the Tories were adamant, cars would be the way forward. For trains there was only one destination: the dustbin of history.

As why, from the Conservative point of view, should they not be? In 1958 a Gallup poll found that 60 per cent of the country's 8 million or so car owners voted Conservative – more than three times as many as car-owning supporters of the Labour Party, and almost six times as many as voted Liberal. (Were the contemporary Conservative Party as assured of the motorists' vote as it was half a century ago their perpetual hegemony would be assured.)

---

* Almost simultaneously, the French writer Roland Barthes argued that 'cars today are almost the exact equivalent of the great Gothic cathedrals: I mean the supreme creation of an era, conceived with passion by unknown artists, and consumed in image if not in usage by a whole population which appropriates them as a purely magical object'. Roland Barthes, *Mythologies* (1957), translated by Annette Lavers (1957; Vintage edition, 1993), p.88.

But the Conservative love of the car went beyond the diktats of practical party politicking. The boxed-off, hemmed-in, sealed-up and thoroughly atomised individuals the car inevitably produced were far more amenable to the Tory imagination than the collectives it was certain it saw on the railways.

So it was that a couple of years into the transport job, Marples took a look at the railway finances and pronounced himself shocked. Given the state of play, the government's suggestion that by 1962 the railways could be making £85 million in profits was, he decided, nonsense. In 1961, after all, they had recorded a loss of £87 million – £2 million more than they were meant to be *banking* the next year. Worse, the 1961 loss had been bigger than the 1960 loss by some £19 million. And given that both passengers and freight were increasingly moving away from using rail transport and on to the roads, all the signs were that such losses were going to go on rising. Something, Marples said, must be done. It was vital, he argued, that the railways begin to make a profit. At the same time, he announced the freezing of pretty much all government investment into the rail network. From now on, the trains were on their own.

On their own apart from Dr Richard Beeching. Beeching was the man Marples appointed to head British Rail (as the British Transport Commission rapidly became known after his accession to the job) at the then astonishing salary of £24,000 per annum – a sum so astonishing (it was more than five times greater than Marples's own pay as Minister of Transport) that it was to be a key factor in the loathing so much of the general public were to come to feel for Beeching.

The proud owner of the least fetching moustache since Himmler, Beeching was a scientist who had been working as the technical director of the chemicals giant ICI. He had no experience of the rail transport system and even less interest in it. Still, his task as chairman was clear enough. He was to do whatever it took to make the railways profitable by 1970. In his search for profits, he was to give no consideration to any social benefits that the railways might be thought to bring to the populace (both users and non-users). If a line was not making money, then that line's closure was up for discussion. If a station was used by very few people, then that station's continued existence would have to be considered.

Hence Beeching's claim that it would be necessary to close fully one third – 2,363 to be precise – of the nation's railway stations with the concomitant loss of around 70,000 staff. A bigger fraction came into play for the lines themselves: half of British Rail's 18,000 or so miles of track should not be modernised because they were used by just 4 per cent of traffic. In terms of freight transport, things were worse still, Beeching said. Almost half of the nation's stations accounted for a mere 4 per cent of the railways' parcels business. More, rail consignments took an average of two days to arrive at their destination – and sometimes rather longer than that. It was, one wag claimed to have proved, quicker to walk across London to deliver a parcel than to have it sent by train.[25] As to the passenger coaches, well, 9,000 of them stood idle for nine months of the year, coming into use only during the summer holidays. Some 2,000 of them were in use fewer than ten times a year. That just wouldn't do.

Passengers, though, were the last thing on Beeching's mind. Why? For the simple reason that according to Beeching the railways would soon have none of them to serve. Members of the public increasingly wanted to transport themselves from A to B, and only one in ten personal journeys was being made by train. (This percentage is undeniable, though it is worth pointing out that while today, half a century on, fewer than one in fifty journeys is made by train, the actual number of train journeys is still roughly the same – and still the same, incidentally, as those made at any time since the Second World War.)

There was, of course, some truth to Beeching's claim about the public's blooming love affair with the car. But there was just as much truth to the suggestion that that love was being fed and watered by

Beeching's pruning of the railway system. For Beeching's essential aim was to find wanting any rail service that was less cost-effective than those that served the London commuter belt. And since pretty much every rail service outside London was nowhere near as busy as the commuter lines into the country's capital, there would seem to be something to the claims of those critics, who have argued that Beeching and the government he worked for had decided what they wanted their report to say before sitting down to write a word of it, might have been on to something.[*]

And so it came to pass that overnight, dozens of tiny stations and charmingly winding branch lines ceased to function. Not that Beeching gave anything but short shrift to those many Britons who lamented the loss of their local halt or nearby junction. These people, he lectured, should stop acting as if they were a nation of Hardyesque rustics, and ponder the fact that the only areas of the country that really mattered to the wider economy were London and a couple of other big cities. It was a lecture forever memorialised in Flanders and Swann's delightful song 'Slow Train':

At Dog Dyke, Tumby Woodside
And Trouble House Halt.
The Sleepers sleep at Audlem and Ambergate.
No passenger waits on Chittening platform or Cheslyn Hay.

There is poetry there, not just in Flanders and Swann's rhythms and rhymes but in the very names of the stations they are writing about. It was the kind of poetry Edward Thomas had spotted almost half a century earlier, in 1917, and memorialised in a poem every schoolchild of the post-war generations had to read, 'Adlestrop'. In

---

[*] Now the Royal Mail has been privatised, something similar will surely happen to deliveries outside the London area. There is as little direct profit to be made from delivering mail to out of the way places as there was in providing them with train services.

it, Thomas documents in wondrous reverie the 'willows, willow-herb, and grass/ And meadowsweet, and haycocks dry,/ No whit less still and lonely fair/ Than the high cloudlets in the sky' he spied 'one afternoon/ Of heat the express-train drew up there/ Unwontedly'. Needless to say Adlestrop station in rural Gloucestershire was high on Beeching's hit list – as were such delightfully named stations as Bassenthwaite, Melton Constable, Tinker's Green Halt, Pampisford, and Evercreech Junction.

And yet, and yet . . . for all the bucolic ache of such names, it was Beeching's closure of the branch lines that was his most catastrophic error. Leaves fall off trees every year, after all, but cut off their branches and even the mightiest oaks can die. Beeching's argument was that the bulk of the rail system's lines and stations simply weren't used that much – and were therefore unprofitable. Which is undeniable enough, though so is the fact that the driveway to Beeching's garage was rather less used than the roads in his town – and those roads rather less used than the country's motorways. All journeys diminish in usage the closer their makers get to home. (As David Henshaw has argued, had the road system been subject to a cost-benefit analysis on the terms Beeching set out for the railways, they would have come up short, too.[26]) And yet even that highest of High Tory poets, John Betjeman, who loved trains and the British countryside – and was to be seen extolling their virtues on television screens throughout the sixties – was won over to the Beeching cause. 'I love the branch lines,' he said, as the Beeching axe bagan to fall, 'because they are little quiet worlds of peace and seclusion. But in order to try and preserve them, we have got to be what is called practical!'[27]

But practical implies logical, and Beeching's plan was very far from that. It argued, for instance, that the establishment and maintenance of stations in seaside towns were a drain on the system as a whole because so few people bought tickets to travel from them. True enough, but only because the great majority of people who use the trains at seaside stations have arrived there – and will eventually leave there – by means of the return ticket they bought at the station in their home town. The same applied to stations on the branch lines – lines that while they could never justify themselves financially as individual units were essential if the main lines were to pay.

Which is why, to compound the problem he had set out to address, Beeching's cuts actually resulted in fewer monies coming into the rail system's coffers. The local routes he was so fond of closing down frequently functioned not merely to transport people around their own area but to connect them with main-line services to the major cities. Hence, one of the first results of the cuts was that the main lines themselves found themselves in financial trouble as fewer and fewer people used them. As Labour's Lord Hughes put it, if the railways were an orchestra, then Dr Beeching was like an efficiency expert telling the conductor that he could save money by losing the oboist because he played only a couple of notes per symphony.[28]

There was precious little music in 'The Reshaping of Britain's Railways' (as Beeching's report was titled). Still, the report had at least the distinction of being the work of the first – and the last – man to ever sit down and ask himself what our railways are for. His answer was written in impeccable bureaucratese: 'The railways should be used to meet that part of the total transport requirement of the country for which they offer the best available means ... they should cease to do things for which they are ill-suited.'[29] A lot turns on how you interpret 'best available' and 'ill-suited', of course, which is why we could argue until the 10.47 from never-never-land comes in that Beeching arrived at the wrong answer to the wrong question. Still, we do both him and the Macmillan government he was working for a disservice if we accuse them of being bent on nothing but vandalism. For all the wrongheadedness of their conclusions, they were asking serious long-term questions about one of the country's most important public services.

Hence there is some logic to Beeching's confession, when asked how he felt about being remembered as the mad axeman of British Railways, that he felt pretty good about it because most men weren't remembered at all. He knew that he'd been engaged in something momentous. All the men who've tinkered with public transport since have merely been playing political games. Would that someone in John Major's government of the nineties had had the same sense of public responsibility about our railways as they were being privatised. After all (to quote an MP who had no truck with Major's vision), 'So long as the railways are in private hands they may be used for immediate profit. In the hands of the state, however, it might wise or expedient to run them at a loss if they developed industry, placed the trader in close contact with his market and stimulated development.' Thus that famous left-wing ideologue, Winston Churchill.*[30]

Which means that one of the abiding mysteries of Harold Macmillan's long political career is why he allowed Marples and Beeching their heads over the railway modernisation programme. For the Beeching axe was nothing more than an exercise in market-driven ideology – one of the most naked in the history of post-war Britain – and one that was bound to disappoint. In an increasingly post-industrial age, the railways were never going to be profitable.

As such, it was entirely out of character for Macmillan who was all his life a pragmatic, One-Nation Tory. Throughout the eighties, he let it be known that he detested the Thatcher revolution, likening her government's privatisations of British Telecom, British Gas, British Steel and sundry others to selling off

* Despite the claim that Churchill only once in his life got on a bus (the joke is that when the conductor asked him where he was going he said '66 Kensington Church Street'), he had form on preferring public to private transport. Back in the 1920s he had dismissed the idea that the monies collected from Lloyd George's 1909 Road Fund should be spent only on roads. See Plowden, op. cit., pp.199–200.

the family silver. Yet Macmillan oversaw a revolution in transport policy that was not only economically unsound, but that also wrecked what he undoubtedly conceived of as this green and pleasant land. And he licensed all this, moreover, while himself remaining an inveterate user of public transport. Mrs Thatcher famously declared that any man over the age of twenty-five who didn't own a car could call himself a failure. Macmillan couldn't have agreed less. The MP for Stockton-on-Tees (one of the birth-places of the railway), he had also been at one time a director of the Great Western Railway – and all his life used his gold pass that granted him free rail travel around the country. His late-night train journeys from London to Haywards Heath were an almost daily routine.

To cap it all, Macmillan's transport revolution wasn't a big hit with the public. Partly this was down to the air of wilful brutality that hung around Beeching – what Richard Crossman called his ability to 'make [. . .] every cut in a local service look like a piece of deliberate cruelty, and every closure of a station like an act of class war'.[31] But mostly it was down to practicalities. Almost 90 per cent of people still relied on public transport for getting around, remember, and though many of them undoubtedly hoped that they would one day be able to afford a car, hope is pretty much all they were doing as the Beeching axe fell.

So it was no surprise when Harold Wilson jumped on the anti-Beeching bandwagon. In the run-up to the 1964 election, Wilson took to promising a thoroughgoing review of the Beeching pack-age. Partly this was electioneering, of course. It was plain from even the most cursory glance at the map of the railway lines that Beeching was proposing to close, that the people who would most suffer as a result were those in the countryside furthest from major towns and cities – just the kind of people most likely to vote for the Conservatives. As the placard that local Labour activists secreted on to the last train to pull out of Silloth station in what is now

Cumbria read: 'If you don't catch this, there'll be another one if you vote Labour at the next election.'

How many votes the strategy won for Wilson we shall never know. What we do know is that once elected (with only the smallest of majorities – four, to be precise) he quietly but quickly turned his back on any notion of reworking Beeching's plans. Plainly, not even the most up to date of trains fitted in to Wilson's white-hot Britain – a Britain, he said, where there was going to be 'no place for restrictive practices or outdated methods on either side of industry'. No indeed, and there are no prizes for guessing what was soon seen as restrictive and outdated. In March 1965, after five months in office, Wilson made his first public statement on the railway closures. He was, he said, powerless to stop the thirty-eight line closures that 'The Reshaping of Britain's Railways' had recommended the previous government embark upon. Not all that powerless, though, for Wilson and Transport Minister Tom Fraser actually speeded up the rate at which the Beeching axe fell. Over the course of 1964, Marples had authorised the closure of some 991 miles of rail track. Over the course of 1965, Fraser closed 1,071 miles.

Confused? So was the government. After rejecting Beeching's second report of February 1965 ('The Development of the Major Railway Trunk Routes') and electing not to renew his tenure at the Railways Board, it nevertheless insisted on going ahead with further drastic cuts and closures – just as Beeching wanted. Indeed, his second report not only called for further reductions to the rail network, but also suggested that all future investment in it be focused on the key city-to-city routes. Only 3,000 of the 7,500 miles of track that were to have been retained in the first report (published, be it remembered, a mere two years earlier) should continue having money invested in them, he now argued. The rest should be left to deteriorate and dwindle away. And even then, Beeching said, he couldn't guarantee that the railways would turn a profit.

In the event, some 10,500 miles (out of the country's total of 18,000 miles) survived Beeching, though their continued existence owes little thanks to the Wilson government. Closures went on throughout the sixties – and not just to the structurally non-economic lines. The result was (and is) a rail system famous for its incoherence and which serves a far smaller proportion of our towns and cities than comparable networks do in any other European country.

Compounding the chaos caused by such cuts was the chaotic nature of the cutting itself. Under Macmillan, for instance, the Tory government had in 1962 decided to triple the population of Haverhill in Suffolk. A year later, Beeching earmarked Haverhill station for closure. Anything the Conservatives could do, though, the Labour Party could do just as well. Throughout its first years in office, for instance, Wilson's government was pressing ahead with plans to establish a new town at Milton Keynes in north Buckinghamshire. It was there that one of Wilson's greatest achievements, the Open University, was established. One of the reasons the town was selected was that it lay equidistant between the cities of London, Birmingham, Oxford and Cambridge – and yet even as plans for the Open University's development were being drawn up it was decided that the Oxford–Cambridge train line should be closed. (*Plus ça change, plus c'est la même chose.* Half a century on, in 2011, a Conservative MP was arguing that the Cameron government could give the flagging economy a kick-start by building a road between the two university towns.)

It was this haphazard approach to line and station closures that has left Britain with the disconnected abstraction that is our rail service. While ensuring that isolated villages in Mid-Wales or the Scottish Moors – places where people haven't worked in industries which require logical, connected-up commuting for years – were still catered for, Beeching's cuts left many of our major towns with neither links to each other nor, just as important, to London. It's a measure of the absurdity of the Beeching cuts that pretty much since they were made the rail authorities have been trying to reinstate the lunatic gaps in the network.* And yet the Labour government, whose core belief in the social collective might have been thought to ensure its faith in the future of public transport, oversaw this madness with nary an eye even to its putative economies.

Putative they were. The blunt fact is that Beeching's cuts were never going to justify themselves in fiscal terms. Beeching's own estimates of the savings to be made from closures and the cuts in stopping services were some £30 million – less than a third of the overall annual deficit. And as Wilson had sagely pointed out in the run-up to the 1964 election, the closure of some 19 per cent of track mileage in the ten years previous had resulted in a saving of only 7 per cent of British Railways' working deficit. If the closure of a fifth of the system saved so little, how much less would the closure of a further third?

And lo and verily, according to the official historian of British Rail, while the average annual losses made on the rail system in the fourteen years preceding Beeching (1949–53) were some £40 million, over the ten years that followed the Beeching cuts (1963–73) that figure rose by almost 100 per cent to a startling £77.5 million a year at the same prices. Beeching's insistence that cuts to the rail system would increase profitability turned out to have been utterly oxymoronic. Indeed, as more than one wag has pointed out, the logical conclusion to Beeching's calculations was that the railways would stop losing money only when the whole system had been closed down. Especially since

* The finest example of this thoughtless strategy is Stratford-on-Avon, the birthplace of William Shakespeare, home to the Royal Shakespeare theatre company and one of the country's top five destinations for both foreign and home-grown tourists. Getting there on the train is far from easy though. I was once a student at the University of Warwick – which is located just south of Coventry and therefore a spit from Stratford. But try getting there via rail without having to connect to Birmingham (ten miles and more in the opposite direction) and linking up with the West Midlands suburban system. Now try getting to Stratford from London. Or Exeter, or Manchester or York.

it had been decreed that it was the duty of the Railways Board to sub-sidise those bus operators whose buses were replacing closed branch line services to the tune of £100,000 a year. (By 1966, incidentally, that figure had quintupled to some £500,000 annually.)[32]

Never mind. Remember that what mattered most to the origi-nal architects of the rail closures was that cutting services would mean the train unions could no longer hold the country to ransom by going on strike. And yet they had quite failed to foresee that the increased emphasis on public transportation by road would only embolden the men who worked on the buses. So it was that in February 1965 several of the regional bus driver unions, confident in their new-found power, embarked on a series of one-day (Saturday) strikes. The fight promised to go national a few days later when the Transport and General Workers Union said that if talks didn't proceed on their demand for a pay hike of 16 per cent and a two-hour cut in their working week. Public transport, the public can be forgiven for having concluded, was falling apart. That same month, the Ministry of Transport was obliged to hire 150 new driv-ing examiners – not only to help clear a backlog of 430,000 driving test appointments but to cope with the unprecedented rise in demand for tests that had come about as a result of the rail closures and the busmen's strikes.

How had it come to this? The essential problem was that Beeching had taken his inspiration from the United States, where the government had begun to run down train services back in 1960. In such a vast country, though, there were what at least looked like sound economic reasons for cutting rail services. (But only looked like: by the 1970s, America's bankrupt railways were, as the late Tony Judt pointed out, 'de facto "nationalised"'.[33]) The sheer size of America, the distances involved in getting around it, meant that domestic flights were in competition with the railways in a way they could never be in Britain. A traveller from, say, the south-eastern corner of England has to be wanting to get to

Aberdeen – or even Inverness – before air travel becomes a viable alternative to the service the pre-Beeching railway system offered.

Not, of course, that much was available by way of domestic air travel in the Britain of 1965. The alternative here to transportation by rail was transportation by road – but build up our roads though we might, we would still have no chance of travelling on them with the speed and ease that people in America could. Although by the mid-sixties a far bigger percentage of Americans were driving cars than were Britons, the two countries' different population densities meant that traffic congestion – and traffic pollution – was already a lot worse here than over there.

No less significant than the car's environmental impact are its existential effects. The car has a profound effect upon personality. It's not just that, as we have seen, getting behind the wheel can transform even the most mild-mannered into seething, envious monsters. It's that being sealed off in a speeding glass and steel box, a box increasingly filled with the sounds of one's own choosing, blunts you to the lives and needs of others. Cars dehumanise their drivers – and in doing so they render everyone outside their driver's domain less than human too. The car, that is, alienates us not just from ourselves, nor just from our fellow man: it alienates us from the very idea of men as fellow beings. That is why the rise of the car and the demise of the train served notice of the strains the social democratic post-war settlement would increasingly be subject to as the sixties wore on. Indeed, despite the Conservative Party's fretful bellow about how everything went wrong in the sixties, the fact is that it was that decade that made the party's neo-liberal revolution of the eighties and since possible.

One of the great myths about Britain in the sixties is that it was a decade of collectivist activism. In fact, it was the decade in which the great mass of people finally abandoned the Judaeo-Christian emphasis on deferred gratification and began to live in and for the here and now. The great expression of this new lifestyle (itself a

1965 word) was consumerism. And what was consumed more and more during the decade were labour-saving devices such as washing machines, telephones, TVs hi-fi systems and, of course, cars – each of which had, for all their undoubted benefits, the effect of privatising and individualising experience.

Certainly there can be no doubt that the Conservative Party regarded cars not only as emblems of freedom but as a highly practical means of avoiding the great unwashed. As late as the turn of the millennium, an early Tory hopeful for the London mayoralty, Steve Norris, was to be found delivering himself of the opinion that the problem with public transport wasn't the transport but the public.

But as we have seen, the Labour Party wasn't much better. It went along with the motoring revolution because it saw cars as aspirational objects that would aid its own aspiration of electability. Only deliver a motor to every voter and they would be yours. As Tony Crosland was to say a few years after Beeching had trashed our trains: 'all of us want the car and the greater freedom of mobility it brings.'*[34] Alas, it turned out that if all of us have that freedom we are all a little less free. 'People love cars,' the poet and critic Randall Jarrell† once observed. 'Looking at them driving off fast in every direction, a Thoreau or an Emerson might ask: "From what are they all escaping?" The answer is themselves.'[35] But as the sixties went on proving, there can be no such escape. Sometimes, not even a jet pack is good enough.

---

* Crosland, incidentally, was the transport minister who signed off the building of the M25.
† Who loved sports cars – and who likely committed suicide by walking into the path of a car on highway 15-501 in the United States on 14 October 1965.

5

SOMETHING IS
HAPPENING HERE

In which pop goes modern,
and classicism rediscovers melody

'Nothing is capable of being well set to music that is not nonsense.'

Joseph Addison

Bongos. That's what you'd have heard had you been at the Southern Cathedrals Festival concert in Chichester Cathedral on 31 July 1965. Bongos. And not only bongos. A xylophone, a glockenspiel, blocks and a rasp – such were just a few more of the elements in Leonard Bernstein's *Chichester Psalms*. In any setting, Bernstein's arrangement of sounds would have been arresting. Inside a cathedral they were startling. In *Farewell My Lovely* Raymond Chandler describes one of his more colourful heavies as being 'about as inconspicuous as a tarantula on a slice of angel food'. Dissonant, deranged and at times foot-tappingly catchy, Bernstein's *Chichester Psalms* were similarly unobtrusive. They still are. Whatever you think about their place in church, they deserve their place in the orchestral canon.

Bernstein had been commissioned to write the *Psalms* just before Christmas 1964 by the Dean of Chichester Cathedral, Dr Walter Hussey. Hussey had a reputation as one of the Church of England's more avant-garde aesthetes. While Vicar at St Matthews in Northampton he had commissioned Benjamin Britten to write his 'Rejoice in the Lamb' cantata to mark the church's fiftieth anniversary. At Chichester, meanwhile, he had altarpieces painted by Graham Sutherland (*Noli Me Tangere*), tapestries designed by John Piper, and even ordered a stained-glass window from the hands of the Jewish atheist Marc Chagall. 'I always say my west window has all the charm of Chaucer with none of the concomitant crudity of the period,' says Alec Guinness's Reverend Lord Henry D'Ascoyne in *Kind Hearts and Coronets*. Hussey, one suspects, never had a qualm about a concomitant in his life.

The pointing out of technical constraints aside, he certainly gave Bernstein absolute licence when it came to writing *Chichester Psalms*. 'I hope', Hussey wrote to Bernstein as he was getting his ideas in shape for the score, 'you will feel quite free to write as you wish and will in no way feel inhibited by circumstances. I think many of us would be delighted if there was a hint of *West Side Story* about the music.'[1]

In the event, they got more than a hint. Mournfully lyrical though parts of *Chichester Psalms* are, the piece is more often characterised by a writhing, jazzy mood (predominantly in 7:4 time*), undercut by some punkily bombastic percussion, that cannot help but put you in mind of Bernstein's revolutionary Broadway musical. Indeed, the choral section midway through Bernstein's second movement (a setting of Psalm 2, verses 1–4) was reworked from a chorus written for but discarded from the 'Prologue' to *West Side Story*. The phrase in Bernstein's melody that accompanies the

---

* The beat Stravinsky had used at the end of *Firebird* – and which the Beatles would use for the verses of 'All You Need Is Love'.

line 'Why do the Heathen so furiously rage together?' had first been written to accompany 'Mix!', *West Side Story*'s invocation to let battle commence between the Sharks and the Jets. Yet by some secular miracle, phrases written as components of show tunes turned out to fit precisely the rhythms of ancient Hebrew texts.

As for the rest of the piece, most of its melodies were taken from a score Bernstein had been working on the previous year (with the lyricists Betty Comden and Adolph Green and the choreographer/director Jerome Robbins) for a musical version of Thornton Wilder's *The Skin of Our Teeth*. Fifteen years earlier, Bernstein, Comden and Green had written the musical *On the Town* – like *West Side Story* (which Robbins had also choreographed), a hymn to the hustle and hum of New York City – and their plans for the Wilder musical were no less daring. Bernstein told Comden and Green he wanted the show to have a 'Brechtian/Pirandello' feel, with actors and singers stepping out of their characters and addressing the audience directly. Among the questions Bernstein wanted his stars to ask the audience was whether Wilder's essential theme – a humanist, optimistic faith in the gradual improvement in the conditions of life throughout the course of history – might not by now be a busted flush. Wasn't it time, the musical's characters were going to suggest, to give up on the idea of progress – to ask not only whether the show must go on but whether life itself could go on. Whatever else it was, such Cold War eschatology was a far remove from Psalm 100's invocation to 'Make a joyful noise unto the Lord all ye lands' in the first movement of *Chichester Psalms*.

Still, there was no doubt that Bernstein's noises were joyful. As the *Sunday Times*'s Desmond Shawe-Taylor remarked of the *Chichester Psalms* debut, Bernstein was a religious composer 'of the kind Luther must have had in mind when he grudged the devil all the best tunes'.[2] Though Bernstein had written the piece after spending more than a year noodling around with twelve-tone figures, the end result had, he said, 'an old-fashioned sweetness' checked by some more 'violent moments'.[3] The *Chichester Psalms* were, he believed, 'as simple and tonal and tuneful and pure B flat as any piece you can think of'.[4]

Which doesn't mean that the piece is a breeze for performers. Like *West Side Story*, a show which requires its leading man to hit a high C – a full octave above the top note in the standard tenor range, and therefore well into soprano territory – Chichester Psalms makes some daunting demands on its interpreters. It's not so much the range or pitch relations that are effortful here, though, as the tricky rhythms Bernstein chose to structure his melodies around – the seven-beat bars we have previously noted, along with several no easier to count five-beat bars. It is these irregular pulses that give the music a slinky, syncopated feel* that is quite at odds with its ostensibly liturgical content.

Written in the early months of 1965, just as President Lyndon Johnson was escalating the American bombing campaign in Vietnam, *Chichester Psalms* was Bernstein's attempt to politicise the putatively ideology-free arena of classical composition. (On 24 March, midway through writing the score, Bernstein abandoned his manuscript paper in his Manhattan apartment and flew to Alabama to help Harry Belafonte mount a show in support of the civil rights marches from Selma to Montgomery.) Just as *West Side Story* had dreamed of an end to the ethnic tensions of the modern city – and embodied that vision in the astonishing resolutions it found for its often Schoenbergian discords – so *Chichester Psalms* openly pleaded for peace among men – a plea it makes manifest in its movement from clashing dissonance to unified grandiloquence. So one way of labelling the piece the London Philomusica string

---

* A feel is all it is; nowhere in the piece will you find any actual syncopation.

orchestra and the choir of Chichester cathedral ended up performing is as a kind of choral version of the protest songs that were elsewhere all the rage.

Or had been all the rage, anyway. For even as Bernstein was turning Hollywood show tunes into hallowed texts, another New York musician was in London forsaking the sacred poetry of protest for the secular pleasures of pop. Four years earlier Bob Dylan had made his name as a Greenwich Village folkie, singing cover versions of songs by the likes of Woody Guthrie and Leadbelly. Since then he had taken to writing his own songs, heavily politicised numbers about the various forms of oppression people suffered under American capitalism. In 'The Lonesome Death of Hattie Carroll' he bemoaned the licence and liberty that wealth can buy a cold-blooded murderer. In 'Oxford Town' he evoked the wilful blindness to class conflict that underlay southern racism. In 'Masters of War' he advised those titular villains with their 'big bombs' and 'death planes' that 'Jesus would never/ Forgive what you do'. 'Anger', James Baldwin once argued, 'can only with difficulty, and never entirely, be brought under the domination of the intelligence.'[5] He hadn't heard Bob Dylan sing.

Not that Dylan ever pretended to have any solutions for the age of anxiety his songs so precisely delineated. Indeed, in 'Only a Pawn in Their Game' he faced up to the terrifying, Kafkaesque prospect that there was nothing that could be done to change things because the game in question was always bigger than any one person could understand. The answer, as he intoned repeatedly in the song that did most to seal his reputation, was 'Blowin' in the wind'.

As far as his fans were concerned, though, the answer wasn't blowing in the wind. It was blowing out of Dylan's mouth with every glorious word he sang. They saw him as a new messiah. His songs held the wicked to account, spoke the truth to power, and pointed the path to redemption. They were visions of a better world served up by a man who knew that world back to front because he was closer to it than any mere mortal could ever be.

It was a hard act to live up to, especially since Dylan denied ever wanting to have put it on in the first place. Folk songs, he started letting it be known, weren't really his kind of thing. Born in 1941, he had spent his teens listening to rock and roll, and rock and roll would always be his first musical love. The decision to write political songs, he let slip, had been a purely pragmatic one. He wanted to make a name for himself, and thought they would afford the quickest way of doing so. 'I never wanted to write topical songs,' he said in 1965. On the other hand, he had soon enough realised that it would help his career if he did so because 'in [Greenwich] Village there was a little publication called *Broadside* and with a topical song you could get in there.'[6]

But economic logistics underlay the form of Dylan's early work, too. Like an artist who makes his name with charcoal drawings because he can't afford to experiment with oils, Dylan had become a folk singer because folk songs were cheaper to perform than rock and roll songs. The folk tradition of one man and his guitar meant that you could put on a show with the minimum of assistance. 'It was easy,' Dylan explained. 'You could be by yourself, you didn't need anybody. All you needed was a guitar. You didn't need anybody else at all.'[7]

You did need some other people, of course: people who were willing to make up a paying audience. But now Dylan had them on board, he felt free to experiment in the form hitherto closed off to him. 'I'm in show business now,' he told Robert Shelton (the journalist who would become his first serious biographer).[8] From now on, he said at a press conference in San Francisco in December 1965, he would like to be thought of as 'a song and dance man'.[9] It was a line that got a big laugh, not least because Dylan delivered it from behind one of those boyishly embarrassed cute grins he was, at twenty-four, still capable of. The laughter got in the way of a serious message, though: Dylan wanted it known that he didn't deal in serious messages.*

Like all true moralists, Dylan believes humour is the only kind of seriousness that counts. Back in April, when he had arrived in London for a UK tour holding in his hand a large industrial light-bulb he claimed to take with him wherever he went, he had responded to a question about what his 'real message' was with a variant on Teddy Roosevelt's advice on speaking soft and carrying a big stick: 'Keep a good head', Dylan said, 'and always carry a light-bulb.'[10] Alas, few of the attendant journalists spotted the joke. Too busy looking for the voice of a generation their editors had ordered them to meet, they took Dylan far more seriously than he ever did himself.

As for the fans, they just couldn't get a handle on their hero's Wildean refusal to accept the importance of being earnest. For them, Dylan's folk songs were the latter-day equivalent of the Manichaean sermons their parents and grandparents had grown up on. The Dylan they loved was a hellfire and brimstone preacher full of eloquent, grandiose, certitude. They thought of him as an angry young man with an acoustic guitar, a hanging judge with a harmonica, a man who dealt in the truth and nothing but. Now here he was, putting on an act. And so the dread thought reared in their adoring minds: perhaps the protest music he used to write (and is still singing to us) was an act, too. Perhaps he's been putting us on all along. Perhaps he's only been pretending to care about all the things we care about.

'I was singing a lot of songs I didn't want to play,' Dylan would say of that UK tour. 'I was singing songs I didn't really want to

---

* Paradoxically, one learns from Martin Scorsese's characteristically vivid documentary *No Direction Home* (2005), the suits in head office were worried that by abandoning his political stance for what they called a more commercial sound, Dylan would make himself a less saleable artist.

sing ... I knew what was going to happen.'[11] What was going to happen was that the audience would applaud the moment Dylan sang the opening line of any number whose sentiments they could congratulate themselves for sharing. Dylan need only play the opening chords of 'The Times They Are a-Changin'' or sing the first line of 'The Lonesome Death of Hattie Carroll' and whatever venue he was in would erupt with applause. He could have muffed the chord or sung off-key and the applause would still have erupted. That was because the applause was less for Dylan than it was for the audience itself. They loved the fact that they were *bien-pensant* liberals, and loved even more the fact that Dylan had confirmed the rightness of their stance.

Dylan hated it. Like any good preacher, he didn't want to preach to the converted; he wanted to undermine the certainties his last lesson had hardened into. 'He is not so much singing as sermonising,' one more than averagely insensitive journalist claimed during Dylan's UK tour. 'His tragedy, perhaps, is that the audience is preoccupied with song.'[12] Nothing could be further from the truth. It was Dylan's audience rather than Dylan himself that was preoccupied with his sermonising. His fans wanted to hear the same sermons over and over again – hence their applause at the start of a song rather than merely at its end. They were telling Dylan what they wanted him to tell them. The converted were preaching to the preacher even as the preacher was undergoing a crisis in faith.

Predictably enough, the fans were having none of it. They couldn't believe Dylan's about-turn, couldn't believe that their prophet had become a profiteer, couldn't believe that their fierce and fiery preacher had turned into a knockabout comedian. As a gaggle of Liverpudlian schoolgirls told Dylan during his UK tour, they didn't like 'Subterranean Homesick Blues' and the other songs of electrified surrealism that appeared on his first album of 1965, *Bringing It All Back Home*, because 'it doesn't sound like you. It sounds like you're having a good old laugh.' 'Well, don't you want me to have a good old laugh?' Dylan asked back.[13] No, they made clear, they didn't. Such laughter, Dylan's fans believed, represented not just an abandonment of the faith but an abasement of it.

The faith was authenticity. Folk music was defined, its worshippers held, by its authenticity of feeling and moral passion. Folk's subject matter was demarcated by social need and political demand. Folk songs were ineluctably transgressive and rebellious because life – at least as it was lived under capitalism – demanded transgression and rebellion. In formal terms, too, folk music was authentic. Its sound was made up of acoustic instruments accompanying a human voice addressing listeners one on one. Intimacy, the sense of a personal relationship between performer and listener, was what counted. It followed that live performance was the essence of folk, live performance that gave you access to what the philosopher Jacques Derrida was contemporaneously describing (and disparaging) as the 'full presence' of a writer (or singer).[14] Recordings, on the other hand, were untrustworthy because they might not be direct reproductions of the sound of a soul expressing itself. They could have been tampered with, rearranged, burnished, improved upon.

So for the fans, *Bringing It All Back Home* was a betrayal of all that they and Dylan had hitherto held to be true. Only one of the LP's two sides – and the second side at that – had been recorded on acoustic instruments. The first side was made up of what Dylan's denigrators called electric music – music played on instruments that needed amplifiers to make their sounds audible. For the folkies, amplification made for a barrier between artist and audience. Inheritors of the romantic tradition, they clung to a Luddite belief in the inherent evil of all things technological. As far as they were concerned, the electric guitar was capitalism – and capitalism was all that folk music had been created to destroy. Like the German musicologist and philosopher Theodor Adorno before them, they loathed the idea of 'contemporary musical life [being] dominated by the commodity form'.[15] (Not that Adorno would have been over-impressed with the sixties folkies. He would have thought them no more the real thing than all those jazz players he so dreaded hearing.*)

Dylan, though, couldn't get enough of the electric guitar. One of the first things he did when he arrived in London in 1965 was check out the music stores for the latest designs and models. 'Will you look at this,' he points to the camera in D. A. Pennebaker's documentary account of Dylan's UK tour, *Don't Look Back*, as he stands, goggle-eyed, in front of a Denmark Street window full of outrageously stylised electric guitars. 'We just don't get this kind of thing in the States.' Maybe not, though they certainly heard the noises such instruments were capable of making. In early 1964, just a few weeks after Dylan had released his third album, *The Times They Are a-Changin'*, the Beatles had arrived in New York city for their first US gigs. Overnight, rock and roll, a moribund form pretty much since Elvis had been conscripted into the army six years earlier, rendered acoustic music history. Dylan loved the Beatles' sound. 'It's great!' he said of their first American chart-topper 'I Want To Hold Your Hand'.[16] 'They were doing things nobody was doing. Their chords were outrageous, just outrageous, and their harmonies made it all valid. You could only do that with other musicians . . . I knew they were pointing the direction of where music had to go.'[17]

Certainly they were pointing the direction Dylan believed his own music had to go. And not just his music. Dylan's jokey,

---

* Nor would he have been entirely wrong. The fact is that the whole folk thing had been a put-on – not just by Dylan, but by the bulk of young men and women who were involved in the movement. (More than 200 folk albums were released in the United States in 1963.) Genuine folkies, after all, were also Okies – people who hailed from Oklahoma. It followed that non-Okie folkies were putting on an act. At the time Dylan arrived on the scene, one of the key folk figures in New York was Ramblin' Jack Elliot, a cowboy-ish singer who also happened to be the son of a Jewish surgeon from Flatbush, real name Elliot Adnopoz. If he was authenticity incarnate, then so were Herman's Hermits.

bantering, tensely tetchy press conferences on which we have already touched owed a lot to the Beatles' gently mocking take-downs of journalists in their own PR-defying interviews. Yet the fact of Dylan taking his inspiration from the Fabs would only inspire the Beatles to borrow from him. Over the next few years, he and the Beatles would engage in a kind of charitable com-petition, an aesthetic tussle to see who could write the most outrageous, drug-drenched songs. (When Dylan met the band, in New York in August 1964, he thanked them for reintroducing him to the delights of amplified music by introducing them to the delights of marijuana.)

One of the things Dylan most loved about the Beatles' songs was that nobody felt the need to comb them for meaningful messages. The lyrics to numbers like 'I Wanna Hold Your Hand' and 'Please Please Me' were as direct as highway hazard warnings. 'We're not the preaching sort,' Paul McCartney told a reporter from the *New Musical Express* in 1965, 'we leave it to others to deliver messages.'[18] And anyway, he warmed to his theme, 'Protest songs make me con-centrate on the lyric, which I don't like.'[19] Like Sam Goldwyn, McCartney believed that if you wanted to send a message you should send it by Western Union.

So too the new Dylan. 'What I'm going to do', he said within weeks of McCartney's critique of consciousness-raising pop, 'is rent Town Hall and put about 50 Western Union boys on the bill. I mean, then there'll really be some messages . . .'[20] From now on, Dylan said, he had 'stopped composing and singing anything that has either a reason to be written or a motive to be sung'.[21] Just as T. S. Eliot had insisted he didn't know what he was up to whilst writing *The Waste Land*, so Dylan was now adamant that he didn't care whether he understood what he was singing. The sounds the songs required him to make were enough.

The first fruits of this new, message-free songwriting were to be found on the electric side of *Bringing It All Back Home*, which opens to the sound of a wiry, twanging guitar, a thudding drum and a nonsense lyric abundantly amused at its own inanity. 'Subterranean Homesick Blues' is a good old laugh indeed – and one topped off by the visual comedy Dylan contrived to extract from it while in London. Here, in May 1965, shooting *Don't Look Back* in an alley next to the Savoy Hotel where he was staying, Dylan and Pennebaker effectively invented the pop video. A more calculated affront to those few folk fans Dylan had yet to offend it would be hard to imagine. Authentic this performance is authentically not. The gentleman doth not protest enough.

Just look at him, this skinny young Dylan, stone-faced yet surly, with thighs like a jockey and eyebrows like Lauren Bacall in *The Big Sleep*, as he holds up and then discards a series of poster-sized boards with some of the key words to 'Subterranean Homesick Blues' emblazoned on them. Given the joyous raucousness of Dylan's band – as well as the wheezing, burst bagpipe drone of Dylan's voice – it is difficult (even after half a century of being able to listen to them) to hear the words to the song, so it was nice of him to let us read them for ourselves on these huge prompt cards. But Dylan is not dexterous enough with the cards, and he struggles to change them in time with the music. A given word or phrase is rarely shown us at the same time as we hear it. The effect is to suggest that Dylan (whose moody, downturned mouth doesn't move throughout the whole video) isn't singing so much as being sung.

Certainly these lyrics are not the heartfelt outpourings of a man angered at injustice, much less the sounds of a soul in torment. Indeed, as the video version of the song ends, an automaton-like Dylan walks lazily out of the frame, the music still playing in the background, as if he's no more than a workman who's been hired to do a job and has now done so and is clocking off. A couple of days earlier, after a gig in Leicester, one of Dylan's fans delivered himself of the opinion that 'what made it for us was that he sang the words of his songs as if they had meaning. You see so many artists who perform like zombies, as if they're there for the money and that's all.'[22] Oh, dear. Soon enough Dylan was to be found telling an interviewer that yes he did make a lot of money and 'I spend it all. I have six Cadillacs. I have four houses. I have a plantation in Georgia.'[23] *Don't Look Back*, in which Dylan comes across – to nonconformists, at least – as petulant, arrogant, surly and cliquish, would do nothing to improve his new image.

Albert Grossman, Dylan's manager, had come up with the idea for the movie after the big-screen success the Beatles had enjoyed the previous year with *A Hard Day's Night* (1964). Pennebaker, meanwhile, had been ruminating on the possibilities of shooting a picture about 'an artist trying to stay on top of an extraordinary talent in the face of adulation and disapproval'. Both men, it seems fair to say, thought they were going to make a documentary film.

And indeed, *Don't Look Back* looks a lot like a documentary. It was shot on fast, grainy, black and white film stock. The photographer worked with a lightweight, hand-held camera that allowed him to go anywhere his subject went without the need for elaborate lighting set-ups. The movie had no script and no story to tell. And yet, as the tour progressed, it became clear to the director that his film was actually tracing the familiar arcs of a classical narrative. Far from being the arid slice of cinema-vérité Pennebaker had envisaged, *Don't Look Back* shaped itself into a drama in front of his lens. By the time Pennebaker had finished shooting, his movie had a beginning, a middle and an end – and, *pace* Jean-Luc Godard, whose maverick spirit otherwise informs the whole movie, they appeared in that order.

Underneath its ramshackle surface, *Don't Look Back* is as tightly structured as a farce. The editing links time and space in ways the documentary habitually eschews. When in a swish London hotel a BBC interviewer asks Dylan, 'Where did it all start for you, Bob, how did it all begin?' Pennebaker cuts to some footage of a much shorter-haired Dylan at a Mississippi civil rights rally of a few years earlier. People who walk on seemingly purposelessly in the early stages of the film reappear with very good reason as things move to a close. The entrance of other characters (for let us call them what they are) is built up to in what we must accordingly refer to as dialogue. For a shapeless record of a chaotic tour, *Don't Look Back* drives itself on like a whip does a horse. The movie is always going somewhere, and the somewhere it is going is the mock conflict at the heart of its leading man – is he Bob Dylan or 'Bob Dylan'? Is he Bob Dylan pretending to be 'Bob Dylan'? Or is he 'Bob Dylan' pretending to believe in the existence of a Bob Dylan? As he quips when he reads a tabloid report of his eighty-a-day cigarette habit, 'I'm glad I'm not me.'

As usual with Dylan, though, the gags take you to the heart of the matter. Dylan isn't simply playing a role in the movie. Rather, he uses the movie to play around with the whole notion of roles. As Pennebaker has said, the film 'may not be so much about Dylan because Dylan is sort of acting throughout the film ... He needs some protection in a sense against the process.'[24] And so we get charming Dylan, shy Dylan, aggressive Dylan, ironic Dylan, angry Dylan* – rarely, though, do you feel you are getting anywhere near real Dylan. At one point in the picture Alan Price defends the British Dylan imitator Donovan (who has shown up at Dylan's hotel desperate to sing the great man one of his own inconsequential numbers) to the man himself by saying 'he's not a fake'. No, indeed, though to Dylan's ears this need not be unadulterated praise. He for one was perfectly happy to play the phoney.

Certainly that was how he approached his interludes with the press on this tour. Believing – doubtless correctly – that the journalists sent to interview him would want to turn him into just another cardboard caricature, Dylan plays up the play-acting with

---

* Such actorly variation was only one of the reasons Todd Haynes's Dylan biopic *I'm Not There* (2007) felt redundant even before you saw it.

them. Their questions bounce off him like rocks off a jellyfish. Dylan turns the tables on his interlocutors, and they end up revealing far more of themselves to the camera than he does. (In 1966, Dylan turned the tables on press photographers, too. Debouching from a newly touched down plane during a tour of Scandinavia, Dylan whipped out a camera and proceeded to take pictures of the people paid to take pictures of him.) Dylan turns every chat and interview into a philosophical investigation, his tough-guy strut and wise-ass scepticism a sour cocktail of Bogart, Brecht and Bertrand Russell. Like all good logical positivists, Dylan is forever asking people to define their terms. There is much comedy to be had as these ill-briefed hacks attempt to analyse their stock of clichés. The laughs come from the fact that by joking with them Dylan is in fact answering their basic question – what's your message? His message was and is and has always been that you should think for yourself.

The worshippers weren't convinced, *hélas*. It didn't help that Dylan's arrival in England had coincided with one of his last protest songs, 'The Times They Are a-Changin', making the UK chart – fully eighteen months since he'd recorded it (as the title track to his third album), eighteen months in which he'd regretted giving voice to such passionate intensity and had decided that the best did indeed lack all conviction. Yet it was perhaps this song more than any other that summed up the Dylan his fans adored – an earnest, caring visionary with a weather eye on the trials of youth and the harbingers of doom. That is why to watch him open each show with it during *Don't Look Back* is to watch a man pained by the shame of younger certainties.

If certainties they were. Dylan had written the song in the autumn of 1963, shortly before the assassination of President John F. Kennedy. It was, he has said, 'definitely a song with a purpose. I knew exactly what I wanted to say and for whom I wanted to say it to [*sic*] ... I wanted to write a big song, some kind of theme song . . . the civil rights movement and the folk music movement were pretty close and allied together for a while at that time. Everybody knew almost everybody else. I had to play the song the same night that President Kennedy died.'[25]

He didn't have to play it that night, of course, any more than he had had to write it. And yet, as his fellow musician – and sometime stage companion – Tony Glover has remembered, Dylan all but said that he *did* have to write it. In September 1963, Glover says, he visited Dylan in his New York apartment and found among other things a sketch for a lyric that included a line about the need for senators and congressmen to heed a call. Having read the line out loud, Glover turned to Dylan and asked him 'What is this shit, man?' Dylan shrugged. 'You know,' he said, 'it seems to be what the people like to hear.'[26] (And would go on wanting to hear. As the protest singer Phil Ochs said when asked whether he thought Dylan wanted to disown his political songs, 'I don't think he can succeed in burying them. They're too good. And they're out of his hands.'[27])

By 1965, though, the times they really were a-changin'. Giving people what they wanted to hear was what Dylan wanted to get out of. 'I don't want to write for people any more,' he said, much less 'be a spokesman' for anyone. Having lost faith with what he called 'finger-pointing songs', he was adamant that 'from now on I want to write from inside me.'[28]

Part of this protest against protest originated in the despair Dylan felt at seeing how vanishingly little change political numbers had brought about. 'Songs', he told a reporter in 1965, 'aren't gonna save the world.'[29] From now on, like many an avant-garde artist before him, he would be committed to the notion that art could (and sometimes should) work to uproot settled mores and moods without feeling the need to set out an alternative agenda. And so, far from being the moral treatises on the state of the West his fans had been expecting, the two albums that Dylan released in 1965 were acts of musical insurrection. As well as making protest songs history, *Bringing It All Back Home* and the yet more revolutionary *Highway 61 Revisited* – recorded just two weeks after Dylan's return from Britain – rendered the idea of rock and roll as mindless fodder fit only for sex-starved adolescents redundant, too. From now on, rock would be as susceptible to serious discussion as any other art form.

Ezra Pound (who turns up in a lyric on *Highway 61*) called literature news that stays news. Half a century on, these two albums seem as fresh and new as the day they came out, their wacko mix of beat poetry and blues patterns, country twang and cut-up tangle, rock and roll and rococo surrealism still dauntingly inventive. Fans weaned on the certitude and assurance of early Dylan, his songs' insistence on right and wrong, good and evil, found themselves all at sea with the wilfully incoherent visions on offer here. Like the deadpan, double-taked vision of the video for 'Subterranean Homesick Blues', all Dylan's new songs were perfectly, beautifully meaningless. It had taken painting more than 500 years to abandon the idea of ever-greater verisimilitude as its defining feature, fiction and poetry longer than that, but within a decade or so of its being named, rock and roll had overnight gone modernist.

How had Dylan arrived at this new aesthetic? Boredom, partly: no intelligence as fecund and fickle as his could have ignored what else was going down in the New York he had arrived in five years earlier. The folk music movement he quickly tied himself to was, as we have seen, founded on a return to traditional – or at least traditional ideas of – form and content in songwriting. But Dylan was a painter as well as a songwriter – 'In writing songs', he once said, 'I've learned as much from Cézanne as I have from Woody Guthrie'[30] – and he was alive to the great experiment in American art that had been going on, largely in New York city, over the past twenty years.

He had, for instance, soaked up the great lesson of Robert Rauschenberg's work – that two or more found objects (literally found, in Rauschenberg's case: every day of the week he searched the streets around his Manhattan studio for detritus) yoked together by the artist's eye – or merely by the fact of their being in a gallery – could add up to considerably more than the sum of their parts. Rauschenberg's 'junkyard angel' aesthetic was a key component in Dylan's new armoury of techniques, its ceaseless marriages of magpie gleanings ushering in one line of visionary balderdash after another. The whole of the psychedelic experience of two years later was to be found in these songs, though nothing written in 1967 or 1968 was as pregnant with delirious dread as Dylan's work of 1965. Philosophy, some philosophers say, is just footnotes to Plato. The hippie-drippy experiments of the late sixties were just footnotes to Dylan.

Unlike the hippies, though, Dylan was open to a multiplicity of influences. Around the time Dylan was writing *Bringing It All Back Home*, Rauschenberg's friend and fellow painter Jasper Johns said that his artistic technique was to 'Take an object. Do something to it. Do something else to it. Do something else to it.'[31] It might have been Dylan's dictum, too. Where once he had looked at the world and made sense of it through moralistic storytelling, now he looked at the world and saw 'Chaos, watermelons, clocks, everything'.[32]

Johns famously said that the idea for the paintings that made his name – his paintings of the American flag – came to him in a dream.[33] So too Dylan's new songs. One of them, indeed, is called 'Bob Dylan's 115th Dream' and no amount of laboured exegesis could extract from it anything like a singular, coherent meaning. Whatever else they were, these weren't songs of commitment (though many among Dylan's critics thought they merited committal – to the lunatic asylum that their erstwhile hero now so frequently descanted on). As he told *Playboy* magazine at the end of the year, 'I do know what my songs are about . . . some are about four minutes; some are about five, and some, believe it or not, are about eleven or twelve.'*[34]

Dylan had limbered up for the jittery gibberish of his new songs with the composition of *Tarantula*, his first and thus far only attempt at fiction, which he completed – indeed, largely composed – in the spring of 1965. Actually, to label the baggy and hypnotically inconsequential tract that is *Tarantula* as fiction is to dignify it with a logic and sense of order it wholly lacks. Better, perhaps, to think of it as Dylan's first foray into the kind of automatic writing the French Symbolist *poète maudit* Arthur Rimbaud (whom Dylan had been reading with pleasure ever since his arrival in New York) had invented a century or so earlier. Yet although more than one critic has inventoried the references in and influences on *Tarantula* – from Nietzsche to Brion Gysin, from Yeats to the Beats – there is no hiding from the air of tiresome malarkey that hangs about it. 'I wrote the book', Dylan said, 'because there's a lot of stuff in there I can't possibly sing.'[35] Right enough, though there's also a lot of stuff in there you can't possibly read. Nobody, one feels safe in saying, ever read the book at a sitting. Nor have more than a handful of people ever read it in its entirety.

But everybody has heard the songs that Dylan was freed up to write by *Tarantula*. The book had loosened him up verbally, and given him the confidence to believe that the yowling whorl of names and images that floated around the modern consciousness could be pasted onto the collage-like abstractions he began to write in 1965. Parking meters, Egyptian rings, hypnotist collectors, Napoleon Bonaparte, Santa Claus, Captain Kidd, the Pope of Eruke, the President of the United States, Paul Revere's horse,

---

* Three years later Tom Stoppard would steal the gag: 'Mr Stoppard, what is [your hit play] *Rosencrantz and Guildenstern are Dead* about?' Stoppard: 'It's about to make me a lot of money.'

John the Baptist, Ezra Pound, T. S. Eliot, Columbus, Captain Ahab (almost): such are just a few of the characters – or 'found objects'* – who crop up in Dylan's songs of 1965. None of them had hitherto featured overmuch in the iconography of rock and roll.

Not, it should be said, that this cast of gargoyles and gewgaws featured in Dylan's work as anything like themselves. Their names were picked not for their accretions of meaning but in order to root Dylan's flights of fancy in something approximating the empirical world. Like the painted nails and glued-on oilcloth Braque and Picasso introduced into mid-period cubism, they functioned as concrete emblems of the real, challenging you to deny the truth of what you were seeing or hearing by reminding you that what you were looking at or listening to had its place in a world external to yourself.

Dylan wanted his new art to be both difficult and exemplary. Part of his purpose was to send you scuttling off to the encyclopaedia to check on just who or what it was that he had been cawing about in that last verse. David Bowie once self-mockingly suggested that he 'had been responsible for whole new schools of pretentiousness' in the pop world. It was a fair cop, but the arresting officer would have had every right to point out that actually, sir, he'd seen this kind of thing before. That fellow Dylan had been doing similar stuff for ages. Indeed, a couple of years after he'd kicked the game off, Dylan himself showed up on the cover of the Beatles' *Sgt. Pepper's Lonely Hearts Club Band*, which was only fitting, because Peter Blake's kaleidoscopic, cut-up assemblage of portraits was surely inspired by the deluge of references in the Dylan lyrics John Lennon, if not Paul McCartney, took increasing inspiration from as 1965 became 1966.

Those proper names were also integral to Dylan's new vision of

---

* Copyright Marcel Duchamp, to whose influence on Dylan we shall return.

his art, because their solidity – their clunking, non-poetic clusters of consonants – represented a challenge. Hard and lumpy against the harder and lumpier rhythm of Dylan's new music, it was a struggle to fit them into verse lines. Gone was the porcelain-smooth perfection of Dylan's early work – say hello to the impacted facture of modernity. Not that there wasn't poetry here as well. Dylan's reputation as a lyricist could never have endured without its joyously clanging concatenations of sound. James Joyce, Picasso once told Gertrude Stein, was an 'incomprehensible that everyone can understand'. So too, Dylan's mid-sixties nonsense. True, many of the lyrics read like clumsy, first-year Latin translation exercises, with object and subject and verb and pronoun seemingly thrown together any old way. On the other hand, there is beauty in the way Dylan's voice unifies these often highly wrought inversions with the rough, wheezy-sounding blues figures his melodies fool around with.

But Dylan wants us to have fun listening to these songs, wants us to laugh at the seedy doctor in 'Leopard-Skin Pill-Box Hat' who counsels the number's narrator that his girlfriend is sick – only for the narrator to find that the doc is using his absence to put the moves on the girl in question himself. Laughter, the habitually didactic Dylan was out to prove in these songs, can be serious too. By all means find something Kafkaesque and alienated about the window that is made out of bricks in 'Maggie's Farm'. Remember too, though, the brick wall that is exposed by Magritte's 'Empty Picture Frame' – and try telling me you did so without smiling.

The same goes double for 'Desolation Row', the putatively apocalyptic threnody that closes *Highway 61 Revisited*. Putatively, because Dylan sings this heavily *Waste Land*-influenced number with such laid-back, Warholian affectlessness that one laughs rather than recoils at its imagery. You don't have take me so seriously, Dylan seems to say. Indeed, at the start of 'Bob Dylan's 115th

Dream' he breaks down and guffaws himself after the first few bars. Even in the mordantly disparaging 'Ballad of a Thin Man', Dylan almost blows the first verse by half chuckling a line.

There was, though, no humour to be found in the first great masterpiece of Dylan's post-political work, 'Like a Rolling Stone', a hectoring, haranguing, humiliating diatribe that is less a song of protest than it is a song of detestation. Certainly it takes no prisoners. One does not have to agree with Charles Shaar Murray's suggestion that the lyric is aimed at 'a spoiled rich girl whose ways are acutely offensive to ... Dylan's (fictitious) proletarian integrity' nor that the song posits as female 'the reactionary stagnation of the social order' to acknowledge that this is as 'sneeringly and contemptuously sung' song as has ever been committed to vinyl.[36]

So abrasive in sound is 'Like a Rolling Stone', so violent and wrenching in imagery, that Dylan could have had no expectation his audience would go on following him once they had heard it. Far from reassuring them that all was right with the world because God – and, of course, Dylan – was on their side, the song told everyone that they were alone in a universe more hostile than anyone bar a few philosophers had ever dare let on. 'Like a Rolling Stone' was a kind of aural judgement day, a howling threnody from an Old Testament prophet counselling – decreeing? – that none shall survive. And yet, among the many ironies of Dylan's career, one of the nicest is that it was with this litany of tantrum, petulance and spite that he really hit pay dirt. By writing a song that comprised an attack on everything Dylan's then fans held sacred, he won himself a whole new army of admirers.

What makes that success all the more remarkable is the song's length. Recorded on 16 June 1965, just five weeks after Dylan's last gig in the UK, 'Like a Rolling Stone' clocks in at a full six minutes – roughly double the length of the average single. Indeed, when it was released as a 45, it was cut into two three-minute halves – an act of cultural vandalism that engendered such volumes of hate mail from incensed radio listeners (who would often hear the song being faded out midway through by DJs who rarely listened to more than a bar of any record) that it was soon re-released with the song intact on one side.

Who was the villain of Dylan's song? Not merely Shaar Murray's poor little rich girl, nor simply Mike Marqusee's 'someone raised in privilege who finds herself fallen among the dispossessed'.[37] Indeed, 'Like a Rolling Stone' doesn't just evade such surety – it is about the very act of evasion. Its enemy is certainty, its target anyone who affects to know what life is definitively about. Which means, of course, that at least in part it is about Dylan himself – about the fact that Dylan could no longer write songs that would reassure either himself or his audience with their conviction. For all its declaratory, accusatory emphasis, though, the song's repeated hook line was as autobiographical as any Dylan has ever written.* It was Dylan himself, after all, who had cut the ties to everything that hitherto held him stable and afloat, Dylan himself who had come to believe that giving his fans what they wanted was bad for both parties.

It is easy to forget – given the song's barbarous reputation – that this is joyous music, music that was originally conceived in waltz-time, music that for all the hellfire and damnation histrionics of its lyric never strays out of the key of C major. (Long after the event – and perhaps wise after it, too – Dylan would call C major 'the key of strength, but also the key of regret'.[38]) Joe Macho Jr.'s bass line hops and bounces gleefully along, while Al Kooper's organ – astonishingly, a last-minute addition to the mix – is so offhand and blasé, so honeyed and viscous, it oils much of the grind and friction out of Dylan's cawing invective.

* In which he sounds, not for the last time, like the man he has said is his favourite singer – Peter Lorre.

So it is that far from being a take-down of anyone, the song ends up sounding like an invocation to freedom – the same kind of freedom Dylan himself was enjoying as the long struggle to make the sounds he had been hearing in his head coalesce in the studio and on vinyl came to an end. Once 'Like a Rolling Stone' was written, Dylan said, he would no longer sing 'words I didn't really want to sing'.[39] Hence Martin Scorsese's use of a line from the song for the title of his documentary about the revolutions in Dylan's art in 1965. After this artistic volte-face, Dylan really did have 'No Direction Home'. Moreover, the song had freed him from any more authentic overreach. 'I didn't care any more after that about writing books or poems or whatever. I mean it was something that I myself could dig. It's very tiring having other people tell you how much they dig you if you yourself don't dig you.'[40]

Not that many people dug Dylan the day 'Like a Rolling Stone' made its live debut. Bombed out of his brains, and wearing a shiny black leather jacket, he couldn't have been more of an affront to the down-at-heel denim look folk musicians were meant to affect. As the guitarist Michael Bloomfield, who organised Dylan's band for what was to become his legendary gig at the Newport Festival on 22 July 1965 said, Dylan 'looked like someone from *West Side Story*'.[41] Except that *West Side Story* was never booed, whereas Dylan and his band were heckled and hectored through-out their set. Opinions differ as to what exactly prompted the booing. There are those who say Dylan's fans were disappointed that his set was made up of only three songs – an inarguable fact, though why then the booing all the way through the set and not just at its end? There are those who say that Dylan's fans were hacked off not by the fact that he was playing rock and roll but by the fact he was playing it badly. And there are those who maintain that it was merely the lousy sound quality that irked ticket-holders.

The late Pete Seeger, the folk singer who had helped organise the Newport Festival, was among these last. He was, he said, 'ready to chop [Dylan's] microphone cord',[42] and not because he disapproved of the cacophony of rock and roll but merely because the cacophony was so distorted. Well, maybe from where he was standing. Still, anyone who has seen Murray Lerner's recently released film of the gig, *The Other Side of the Mirror*, which features not only the performance but also footage of Dylan and his band warming up, will be unconvinced. To be sure, their rendition of 'Like a Rolling Stone' was scrappy, its rhythm lumpy and lacklustre (Dylan's band had been pretty much assembled on the spot), its vocal ragged, its meaning rendered more strident, less forgiving, than on the record. There is, though, no doubt about the sound quality, which is as clear as it could be given all the booing.

Dylan was said to have been stunned by the reception he got at Newport. There are reports of his crying backstage after the show. Those reports may even be true, though the fact is that the controversy over his appearance only went to prove the old saw about there being no such thing as bad publicity. Whatever the real feelings behind the uproar at Newport, they did Dylan's career no end of good. To have the likes of Ewan MacColl decrying what he saw as this 'youth of mediocre talent' and his attack on 'the disciplines of traditional music'[43] didn't half play well with a new generation of fans who were determined to like anything amplified. Only a couple of weeks later Dylan was to be found rueing the fact that an audience for a gig at Forest Hills Stadium in New York had not been displeased with his band's performance. When drummer Levon Helm told Dylan how nice it was to perform in a friendly atmosphere Dylan told him he 'wish[ed] they had booed. It's good publicity. Sells tickets.'[44]

It also gave him some ideas for new songs. Among its many other distinctions, 'Ballad of a Thin Man' was Dylan's most vituperative assault on anyone not hip enough to go with his new aesthetic flow. Indeed, legend has it that at Forest Hills Dylan had the band play the (to my ears thrillingly) dissonant B minor intro to the song over and over until the audience shut up.

Who was this Mr Jones Dylan was singing about? For Robert Shelton, there was no mystery: he was Pete Seeger, the man who had been 'thrown for a complete loss by Dylan's electric music' debut at Newport.[45] Dylan himself was rather less definitive. 'He's a real person,' he told Nora Ephron, a few days after the Forest Hills gig – though maybe not all that real: 'I saw him come into the room one night and he looked like a camel. He proceeded to put his eyes in his pocket.'[46] So unlike Mr Dylan then who preferred to put his tongue in his cheek, as well as some cheek in his tongue. For the fact is, of course, that 'Ballad of a Thin Man' was a response to nothing so particular as one individual. Rather, the song's enemy is as diffuse and unfocused as the guerrillas US forces were contemporaneously fighting in Vietnam. Hence the name Jones, which Dylan pounced on for its sheer ubiquity. It is the second most common surname in Britain, and the fourth most common in America. Smith is more common still, of course, but myth, pith and herewith aside, few words rhyme with that name. And Dylan wanted a name he could rhyme with, the better to give his invective the stinging, clamorous logic of form.

Not that that has stopped amateur private eyes fingering one after another real-life Mr Joneses as the inspirational fall-guy behind Dylan's glorious invective. One of them, the journalist Jeffrey Owen Jones, certainly seems stupid enough to have deserved it. Here is a man who actually put himself forward for the honour of being the song's subject, a man who proudly declaimed to the world that he had interviewed Dylan immediately after the Newport gig and had hacked him off mightily with his inanely literal line of questioning. 'I was thrilled', he said, 'in the tainted way I suppose a felon is thrilled to see his name in the newspaper. I was awed, too, that

Dylan had so accurately read my mind.'[47] But whatever treatment Dylan meted out to Jones can have been as nothing compared with what he gave *Time* magazine's Horace Freeland Judson (again in London). A journalist and science historian of some repute, Judson was subject to one of the positivist, anti-intellectual rants Dylan specialised in in 1965. During their interview, which can be seen in all its triumphalist horror in *Don't Look Back*,* Dylan not only pours scorn on Judson and *Time*, but on an imaginary figure, one 'Mr C. W. Jones, on the subway going to work'. Like Dwight Macdonald, who once said that just as cigarettes are what we turn to when our hands have nothing to do, so *Time* is what we turn to when our minds have nothing to do, Dylan had no time for *Time*.

And yet it was minds concerning themselves with too much that were the real subject of 'Ballad of a Thin Man'. Attack Dylan's first set of fans though it did, it also put the knife into his new fans – the ones who were keen to subject the wilfully impenetrable tomfoolery of his recent work to the kind of analysis they had been taught in Eng Lit 101. For all the modernist enigma of his recent work, Dylan was a dab hand at coming on like a populist. When he told one of the reporters in *Don't Look Back* that he could sing just as well as Caruso he was being facetious, but he was being deadly serious when he called Smokey Robinson America's greatest living poet. In the sleeve notes to *Bringing It All Back Home* he tells us that 'the fact that the White House is filled with leaders that've never been to the Apollo theatre amazes me ... I would rather model harmonica holders than discuss Aztec anthropology/english literature or history of the united nations.' In 'Desolation Row' he sings of Ezra Pound and T. S. Eliot being laughed at, and in 'Ballad

---

* How one hopes Dylan is still haunted by his shameless maltreatment of a bright man having to do a dumb job. Incidentally, critics of the anagrammatic school might like to note that the name Jones is all but contained in the name Judson.

of a Thin Man' he chastises whomever the titular character is for being well read while seeming to understand nothing of life as it is lived outside the pages of a book.*

Not that Dylan reserved all his scorn for what he called 'the literary world'. There were 'museum types', too, 'which I also have no respect for ... In my mind, if something is artistic or valid or groovy ... it should be out in the open. It should be in the men's [sic] rooms'.[48] And maybe it should, because the men's rooms were certainly entering the museums. Only a few months earlier, one of the twentieth century's most influentially fertile avant-garde artists, Marcel Duchamp, had licensed the manufacture of eight replicas of his notorious 1917 work *Fountain* for sale to the highest bidders. *Fountain*, it should be said, was no more than a porcelain urinal (signed 'R. Mutt') that Duchamp instructed must be hung upside-down on a gallery wall. At least three of these replicas ended up being bought with American money. Their accession to such hallowed institutions as the Philadelphia Museum of Art and the San Francisco Museum of Modern Art had prompted just the kind of media controversy Dylan enjoyed – even as he was trashing the kind of people who'd take the time to look at a urinal in a museum.

Dylan himself had dropped out of the University of Minneapolis in his freshman year. Universities, he said, 'are like old-age homes – except for the fact that more people die in college'.[49] It's another great gag, though laughter shouldn't blind us to the fact that we are none too distant from the ludicrous public schoolboy rant about the pointlessness of education that is Pink Floyd's 'The Wall'. Certainly Dylan's attitude to formal schooling was a key influence on the

---

* By a cosmic irony not even Dylan could have foreseen, his work is now the subject of much intense discussion and analysis in the academy. Whole courses now revolve around Dylan studies. The late Frank Kermode once contemplated writing a study of Dylan's work, and Sir Christopher Ricks has said he hopes Dylan might enjoy his book-length study, *Dylan's Visions of Sin*. Hmmm.

bravura know-nothingism of the 'tune in, turn on, drop out' culture for which the late sixties became famous. Dylan would go on to disparage the psychedelic era for ensuring that 'everything became irrelevant',[50] but his own omniscient nihilism played its part in the great dumbing-down, too. In a way, Dylan's music, like Duchamp's ready-mades, was *too* liberating. By conjuring up an aesthetic space where anything went, they played a part in ensuring that *everything* went. Dylan wouldn't thank me for saying so, but like Robert Moog, whose synthesiser was being introduced to the world just as *Highway 61 Revisited* was released, he has to shoulder some of the responsibility for our increasingly standards-free culture. By proving – as Bernstein had with *Chichester Psalms* – that popular music was worthy of sacred attention, he helped usher in the aesthetic free-for-all of the postmodern era.

But while it is true that rock and roll has largely failed to live up to the tests that Dylan – and, as we shall see, the Beatles – set it, it is also true that for a brief while it abandoned its seemingly preordained role as either mindless fodder for mindless teenagers or mindless fodder for mindless ideologues, and threatened to rival the more rarefied arts as an arena for sensuous intelligence. Just as Leonard Bernstein had shown that abrasive, demanding music could be made from and for Broadway show tunes, so Dylan proved that the pop song was capable of far more than priapic brashness and/or saccharine dogma. Seriousness, the songs Dylan began writing in 1965 argue, isn't the same as solemnity. Lightheartedness needn't mean levity. Pop can be vital for more than just its vitality. Nobody said that before 1965. Nobody has tried to deny it since.

6

CLASS ACTS

In which the establishment is disestablished –
but so are standards in schools

'O let us love our occupations,
Bless the squire and his relations,
Live upon our daily rations,
And always know our proper stations'

Charles Dickens, *The Chimes*

'What is the first part of politics? Education. The
second? Education.
And the third? Education.'

Jules Michelet, Le peuple

One day in July 1965 the Conservative Party did the unthinkable and decided that since the country around it was changing it was time that it changed too. An increasing number of Tory Party members believed that in what was by now undeniably the century of the common man, the party looked out of date. 'We are sick of seeing old-looking men dressed in flat caps and bedraggled tweeds strolling with a twelve-bore,' read a letter to Conservative Central Office from a senior industrial manager distraught that he could no longer bring himself to vote for the party he had hitherto always supported.[1] In the age of denim and dayglo he surely had a point.

One of the main problems with the party, it was thought, was the long-standing – not to say pre-democratic – method by which it chose its leaders. The party as a whole simply didn't come into it. What happened, whenever a new leader was needed, was that he (in those days it always was a he) would simply be deemed to have 'emerged' from a smoke-filled room of Tory grandees – or 'magic circle' of Old Etonians as Iain Macleod labelled them in a damning *Spectator* article on the succession[2] – after what Harold Macmillan called 'the customary processes of consultation'. Eighteen months earlier, while the Conservatives were still in government, the customary processes had ushered in the leadership of Sir Alec Douglas-Home. Why Home, who had never sought the job, let alone the prime-minister-ship? Simply because unlike those two men who had put up against him and who really had wanted the job – Reginald Maudling and Rab Butler – he hailed, as so many previous Tory leaders had, from the landed gentry.

Across the floor on the opposition benches, Harold Wilson and his team were 'ecstatic with pleasure'.[3] As Richard Crossman, Labour's shadow education spokesman, had confided to his diary a few months before illness forced Macmillan's resignation from Number 10, 'the contrast between Harold's character and Macmillan is an overwhelming advantage to Harold and the Labour Party.'[4] With the man Wilson took to reminding the public was 'the fourteenth Earl of Home' at the helm, things wouldn't change much.

Certainly Home enabled Wilson to go on painting the Tories as being out of touch with the modern meritocratic Britain he wanted to promote. 'We are living in the jet age,' he said, 'but we are governed by an Edwardian Establishment.'[5] Like Macmillan, whom Crossman had characterised as an 'old, effete, worn out ... cynical dilettante',[6] Home was the Establishment incarnate. Indeed, to Crossman's charge sheet of Home's aristocratic inadequacies, the fourteenth earl added another of his own: economic illiteracy. When reading documents containing lots of numbers, he said, he found it a great help to have at hand 'a box of matches ... moving them into position to simplify and illustrate the points to myself'.[7] Alas, the little match boy would be no match for the Promethean, quick-witted Wilson who as an economics student at Oxford had taken what has been called 'an outstanding first'.[8]

But if Home the Prime Minister had been unable to dodge Wilson's blows, he seemed even slower on his feet in that thankless role of leader of the opposition. And since the Labour Party had won power by promising to put an end to the 'stop-go' cycle of inflation/deflation/inflation that had come to characterise the Tories' thirteen years in office, the mathematically challenged Home was likely to find things got tougher rather than easier if (as they always are) the new government's own economic policies came to be called into question. So it was that within three months of their election loss, the Tories had both adopted a formal proce-dure for choosing a new leader and were plotting to install one.* This time, the more meritocratic members of the party were adamant, there would be no 'magic circle' doing the installing. This time there would be a secret ballot of the party's MPs. This time there would be democracy.

Three candidates put themselves forward, though one of them, the radical free-marketeer and serial resigning hot-head Enoch Powell, entertained no serious thoughts of victory. A two-horse

---

* One stresses the speedy nature of this plotting because these days we are apt to forget that the idea of former prime ministers quitting the leadership of their party as soon as they have lost an election is a very new one, inaugurated, in fact, in 1997, by John Major.

race, then, between the former Chancellor and now shadow Foreign Secretary, Reginald Maudling, and the party's new shadow Chancellor, Edward Heath. If the polls were to be believed, Maudling should be the natural successor. An NOP survey for the *Daily Mail* found that fully 44 per cent of the general populace supported him, with only 28 per cent backing Heath's candidacy. Among Tory voters, too, Maudling was favourite, with 48 per cent support against Heath's 31 per cent.

Among Tory MPs, meanwhile, the marks against Heath were several and varied. As chief whip to Eden and Macmillan he had had a famously brusque manner and rough tongue. As chief negotiator of the Macmillan government's vetoed application to join the European Community he was counted a failure. As Home's president of the Board of Trade he had pushed through the abolition of resale price maintenance – a triumph for consumers, but a minor tragedy for the shopkeepers who relied on it to keep their profits up (and whom the Conservative Party relied on in turn for electoral support). Many MPs, indeed, blamed the loss of the 1964 election on what they saw as the 'common little oik's'[9] retailing folly. And as if all that weren't enough, Heath was that pretty unusual figure in adult life (and downright weird figure in public life) – a bachelor. Anyone who believes the sixties was one long swinging party needs to remember that for a goodly portion of the decade the Conservatives were led by an asexual prig who preferred sailing to sex and Berlioz to the Beatles.

Not that all – or any – of this meant Maudling was a shoo-in for the leadership. Like David Cameron and George Osborne today, the Labour government that took office in 1964 was forever bemoaning and blaming its problems on the (£800 million) deficit Maudling's 'dash-for-growth' chancellorship had bequeathed it. Whether or not such charges were fair, there could be no doubt that Maudling had done little to boost his chances by having accepted thirteen private directorships* since his departure from 11 Downing Street. Whatever else such extra-curricular work spoke to, it hardly smacked of commitment to the task of opposition.

If anything, Maudling's approach to the leadership election itself was even less committed. As front-runner he was too ready to sit back and let Heath's team do all the work. His record, he believed, spoke for itself, and to embark on a campaign of high-octane canvassing would only annoy his party colleagues who were quite able to see who was the right candidate for the job. Let Heath amuse himself with such pestering if he wanted. He would find out soon enough that it hadn't amused anyone else.

Nor, perhaps, had it, but Heath's rather more effortful efforts to win the leadership did have the effect of painting him as the fighter a party in opposition needs. Maudling didn't seem to realise that the Tories, having just overthrown the tradition of a leader's magical emergence, weren't in the mood for someone who, however able and experienced, wasn't prepared to actually make it known that he wanted the job. As the BBC's *Panorama* put it on the eve of the election, Maudling was 'the man for those Conservatives who want the driver at the wheel to be steady, sound and shrewd'.[10]

But the Conservatives weren't at the wheel, and they wanted someone who at least seemed willing to have a go at wresting it from the party that was. They wanted someone who could come across on TV, someone aggressive enough to take on the wily, witty Wilson, someone ambitious enough to know that even if it were true that all things come to he who waits it's better to get there ahead of everyone else just in case. They wanted someone who, unlike the party's four previous leaders, was neither the nephew of a duke nor the son of a seventh baronet, neither the son-in-law of another duke nor that aforementioned fourteenth earl of Home. They wanted someone who not only wasn't chosen in secret by an

---

* Heath had accepted only one such directorship.

Old Etonian cadre but who had never been anywhere near Eton. Someone who, like so many of the strivers and achievers of the era, hadn't been to a public school at all.

To be fair, Reggie Maudling was hardly your standard-issue public schoolboy turned Tory MP. Though he had attended Merchant Taylors' School in Hertfordshire, he had done so on the back of a scholarship win – and subsequently won another scholarship to read Greats at Merton College, Oxford, where he developed a lifelong interest in the philosophy of Hegel.* Heath was an Oxford man, too, though he had failed to win the Balliol scholarship he had tried for and was forced to find £220 a year in fees. No easy task given that his father was a jobbing builder and his mother a housemaid. True, with a consulting actuary for a father, Maudling was hardly that much grander, but his schooling and his scholarships had had the effect of smoothing down any rough edges the more patrician Tories might have been offended by. Heath, on the other hand, abraded by the rough and tumble of his slightly rockier ascent, looked more like a man of the age. For what really marked him out to the Conservative Party of 1965 was the fact that he was a grammar-school boy made good. Who better to take on the grammar-school boy heading up the team on the benches opposite?

For all that, Heath can hardly be said to have stormed to victory in the leadership election. Though Maudling pronounced himself shocked by the final result (he got 133 votes to Heath's 150),† it was hardly a wipeout. On the other hand, there is no gainsaying the importance of Heath's ascendance to the top of the Tories. Heath

---

* Whatever you think of Hegel, it has to be said that for an MP of any suasion to have any thoughts about him seems near miraculous in our age of designer ignorance. One of the effects of the cultural revolution that 1965 ushered in was the excruciating sight of prime ministers palling up with the likes of Oasis and affecting a fondness for the work of Snow Patrol.

† Powell scored a mere 15 votes, even fewer than he had expected.

wasn't, as is often suggested, the first non-aristocrat to lead the party. But as an ex-grammar-school boy he was certainly the first man of lower-middle-class origins to head the party of nobility. (Even Bonar Law had been to an independent school.) Nor was he the last. For fully forty years after Heath's accession, the Conservatives were led by men – and, of course, a woman – with backgrounds which would have been unthinkable to earlier versions of the party: the builder's son, the grocer's daughter, the shopkeeper's boy, the son of a trapeze artist turned garden gnome manufacturer. Thanks to what these and the men and women on the benches opposite were about to do, though, the grandees' time would soon enough come again.

Harold Wilson always denied saying that Britain's grammar schools would be destroyed 'over my dead body',[11] which is just as well because the fact remains that it was on his watch that the kind of education that had made possible his and Heath's high-flying political careers began its long, slow death. For the past twenty years, Britain's state education system had been modelled on a three-rung ladder. Up at the top were the grammar schools, which educated the around one in five children who were deemed, having taken the eleven-plus exam, to be the brightest in their area. Below them were the secondary moderns, which educated the vast majority of children, and on the lowest rung the so-called technical schools, which educated no one very much. It was, of course, an avowedly elitist system, a system predicated on the utilitarian idea that education was a public rather than a personal good – that you educated people not so that they could make the most of themselves but in order that the state could make the most of them.

As such, it might sound like just the kind of system the proudly statist Labour Party would have been in favour of. Yet early in 1965, Wilson's new education secretary, Tony Crosland, made it known that he saw his main aim as being the destruction of 'every fucking grammar school in this country'.[12] That was in the privacy of his home, of course. In Parliament it was all put rather more politely:

> This house, conscious of the need to raise educational standards at all levels, and regretting that the realisation of this objective is impeded by the separation of children into different types of secondary schools, notes with approval the efforts of local authorities to reorganise secondary education on comprehensive lines which will preserve all that is valuable in grammar school education for those children who now receive it and make it available to more children; recognises that the method and timing of such reorganisation should vary to meet local needs; and believes that the time is now ripe for a declaration of national policy.

In the subsequently infamous Circular 10/65, Crosland 'request[ed] local education authorities, if they have not already done so, to prepare and submit to him plans for reorganising secondary education in their areas on comprehensive lines'. The request was accompanied by a little judicious strong-arming. From now on, applications for grants for school improvements and new buildings would be looked upon favourably only if the authority in question had agreed to go comprehensive. And given the numbers of children born in the post-war baby boom, many schools did indeed need such improvements and add-ons.

But if Crosland can be said to have been forcing the authorities' hands, he was doing so not just because he felt it was the right thing to do. He was also doing it because it was the popular thing to do. In 1964, opinion polls ranked education second only to the cost of living in the public's litany of worries.[13] The now Labour peer Giles Radice has remembered that as a humble campaigner during the 1964 election 'the eleven-plus was an important doorstep issue'.[14] Indeed, Margaret Thatcher, who as education secretary during the first half of the seventies oversaw the conversion of more schools into comprehensives than anyone else, was convinced that the Conservatives' insistence on the retention of the eleven-plus in the 1964 campaign had been a major factor in their losing the election.[*][15]

As early as the mid-fifties, the Tories had been wise to the grammar schools' problematic place in the public consciousness. While the party continued to praise the idea of grammars and selection, it also began to talk of delaying the age at which selection took place, of finding the money to upgrade the secondary moderns, of encouraging experimentation with the comprehensive idea, and of merging and even doing away with some of the smaller grammars. By 1963, the Conservative's education minister Edward Boyle was to be heard railing against the tripartite structure of the nation's schools, and suggesting that 'none of us believe in pre-war terms that children can be sharply differentiated into various types or levels of ability'.[16]

No indeed. Because while the great majority of parents were against the abolition of the grammar schools, they were also very much *for* the abolition of the eleven-plus – the exam that children took at primary school in order to determine whether or not they got to grammar school. Ostensibly an IQ cum comprehension and arithmetic test, the eleven-plus was really, Crosland had argued in opposition, no more than a means of finding out whether or not you were middle class and thereby fit to benefit from an elite education. All the exam really did, he said, was separate 'the unselected goats and the carefully selected sheep on the basis of tests which measure home backgrounds as much as innate ability'.[17] Essentially, Crosland argued, you passed the test by knowing your Mendelssohn

---

[*] In point of fact, comprehensive schools had been increasing in number during the Tories' long reign prior to the Wilson accession. In 1951, when Labour had last left office, there had been a mere ten comprehensives in existence. Thirteen years later, when it returned to power, there were 175 of them, educating some 6 per cent (168,000) of the nation's 2.8 million secondary school children. A further 700,000 children were at grammar school, with the rest in secondary moderns and techs.

from your Mozart – and since the majority of families were working class, how many children would have heard of either, especially in the age of the Moptops?* All of which is as it may be, but the key point to remember is that it was the middle classes who wanted rid of the eleven-plus. They lived in fear of their children failing the exam and being relegated to the secondary modern with the great unwashed.

None of this might have mattered had that post-war tripartite system, which had been set up with the best intentions, been delivering the goods. But twenty years on it was clear that it wasn't. The technical schools, which were meant to be modelled on those German institutions that were equipping that country with all its engineers and technicians and craftsmen, were, where they existed at all, mere sumps for the troubled and troublesome. As for the secondary moderns, being in the main housed in old and unsuitable buildings, they were rather less modern than secondary, and almost entirely devoid of aspiration. Certainly they educated very few children to the stage where they were deemed fit to sit an external exam. The great majority of their pupils left at fifteen.

Many of the grammars, on the other hand, offered pupils an education that gave the most expensive public schools a run for their money. Add to that their strong links with the worlds of higher education and the professions and there is no mystery as to why so many parents wanted their children to attend one of them. But if wishes were horses beggars would ride, and the fact remained that very few educational beggars could ever think themselves suitably saddled up under a system predicated on selection. Hence the idea of comprehensive schools – selection-free institutions that would, it was claimed, give all children a proper start in life. Once

---

* Another of the tabloids' names for the Beatles. Incidentally, I have in front of me a collection of IQ tests from the 1950s, and can see no evidence of a class bias in the half dozen papers I have just worked my way through.

through their portals, children would find that 'the expectations which teachers have of the majority of their pupils are better [than in the secondary moderns] – and their pupils, sensing and responding to this higher regard, in turn achieve more'.[18] Tony Crosland went so far as to suggest that the comprehensive system would be so good that only the most unreconstructed snobs would want to waste money on paying for their progeny to attend a public school.*

Well, it sounded like a nice idea. So did the suggestion that the new schools would assist in 'the forging of a communal culture by the pursuit of quality with equality, by the education of their pupils in and for democracy, and by the creation of happy vigorous local communities in which the school is the focus of social and educational life'.[19] For the move to comprehensive schooling was expected to be as much of a sociocultural revolution as an educational one. Twenty years after the war, twenty years after an election which had promised an egalitarian New Jerusalem, there were precious few signs of the class system breaking down. Comprehensive schools would be the final nail in elitism's coffin.

Some hope. The truth was that, in the educational arena at least, what signs there were of social mobility – of working- and lower-middle-class people moving up the social ladder – were to be found coming out of the grammar schools. To be sure, the secondary moderns and tech schools were too often grossly inadequate for children's needs, but that didn't mean there was any point denying that the grammar schools did the job they were designed to do. They took the brightest people from homes that could not afford to pay for a private education and gave them one, free of charge. They were postwar Britain's great engine of social mobility and they offered even the poorest the chance to escape from their poverty. Without his grammar-school education Harold Wilson would have been lucky to get elected to Parliament, let alone make

---

* As, it is worth noting, his own parents had done for him.

it to Number 10. Yet the government he led took it upon itself to dismantle the one component of the state education system that was indubitably functioning as it was intended to. Instead of working out how to improve the often dismal educations on offer in the secondary moderns and tech schools, instead of removing the public schools' ludicrous charitable status (which helped – and still helps – them keep down fees for the rich at the expense of the general taxpayer) the government went to war on the one area of schooling that was doing what was required of it.

Still, given that so many parents were against the eleven-plus, the news that the comprehensive schools would provide, according to Wilson, 'a grammar school education for all' was bound to sway them – even though it was patent nonsense. How could schools that admitted everyone regardless of ability hope to compete with those that very carefully selected who would study there? As well ask if Manchester United would have such a record of success if, instead of spending vast amounts of money on building up the best team possible, it worked only with people who hailed from the streets around Old Trafford. Education, like life, is unfair, and it is not the job of a government, even a genuinely egalitarian government, to pretend otherwise. There will always be those who take to French irregular verbs more quickly than others, always some who grasp quadratic equations and some who don't. (There will also, of course, always be some who are more able to work wood than others, some who are better at physical education than physics.) This hard truth could and can be tough on children – and tougher on their parents, whose aspirations often enough outstrip their offspring's abilities. So it is important to grasp that what Wilson and Crosland believed they were offering is what most parents have always wanted: schools that offer a solid, disciplined education from which their children emerge knowing more than when they went in.

Could it have been a success? We'll never know. The comprehensive experiment might have worked on its own terms. The trouble is, it wasn't tried in isolation. At the same time as our schools moved away from their demarcated tripartite structure, they moved too towards the progressive, child-centred learning techniques that might have been designed to ensure pupils came out of school knowing no more than when they entered. The progressive arguments were brutally summarised (though hardly lived up to) by Muriel Spark's titular heroine Miss Jean Brodie, when she railed against her headmistress for regarding school as a place where facts are thrust into pupils. The word education, she pointed out, has its roots in the Latin *ex duco* – to lead out. Hence to educate is to lead out into the world what is all already inside the pupil.

Children, according to this line of reasoning, weren't Lockean blank slates just waiting to be written on. They were walking encyclopaedias that just needed a little help in accessing their inbuilt information. They might have been savages, but they were savages pregnant with nobility, and all that was needed to bring their nobility to gestation was that they be left free to play. For play was learning without the pain. Which is why so many of our classrooms abandoned their Hobbesian model of seeing little children as wild beasts to be tamed and became instead experimental labs modelled along the lines Rousseau put forward in *Emile*, places where rote repetitions of verbs and times tables were dismissed and what counted was teasing out the inherent creativity of the individual. Such creativity was repressed by – indeed, *in the very name of* – grammar schools: for what could be more repressive to creativity than the arbitrary system of rules and regulations that is grammar? Fifty years on, the arrogant, ignorant certitude still takes your breath away. For let us say it loud: this was nonsense – nonsense akin to the nonsense of telling a promising young tennis player that it doesn't, after all, matter that he serves in front of the line or returns the ball within the court, or even hits it with his racquet. All that matters is that he's having fun! Forgive them, for they know not what they do . . .

There is no reason to doubt that Crosland really did believe that the new comprehensive schools would raise overall educational standards and in so doing render null and void the fee-charging public schools which were the real objects of his loathing. Nor is there any denying that the advocates of the child-centred approach had the best interests of children at heart. Yet, within ten years of the comprehensive/progressive experiment any parent with the wherewithal to buy their children out of state education was doing so. Britain's universities have ever since been trying to compensate for the fact that prospective students from fee-paying schools are so much better equipped for higher education than their state-school counterparts. The effect has been to put history into reverse. Our country has retreated from the social and intellectual meritocracy bequeathed it by the post-war settlement to a new version of the socially selective system that had obtained hitherto: just as in those pre-grammar school days, if you have the money, you can buy your family an education denied to those who, however much they – and, perhaps, society as a whole – might benefit from it, can't.

For proof, we need look no further than the politicians whose fault the sorry state of our education is. The grammar school educated elite that climbed its way right to the top began with the election of Harold Wilson in 1964 and ended with the accession of John Major to Downing Street a generation – twenty-six years – later. The present government has a cabinet with more privately educated graduates in it than has been the case for decades past – and in David Cameron the first Old Etonian prime minister since Wilson's predecessor, the infamous 'fourteenth Earl'. This isn't, emphatically isn't, because Britain has embraced class distinctions again. It's because in 1965 our education system became once again one of the bulwarks of class division in our society.

7

TAKING OVER THE ASYLUM

In which sanity is challenged and
the family falls apart

'The world is so full of madmen that one need not seek them
in a madhouse.'

Goethe

The naked man, who had taken to painting himself to look like the withered whore his speech and body language increasingly suggested, was standing at the kitchen sink dusting his genitalia with talcum powder when the guy who wore a flat hat topped off with a big dead bird walked in, took out his Luger, and shot him in the balls.

Welcome to Kingsley Hall, the psychotherapy 'community centre'[1] set up by the radical psychiatrist R. D. Laing and his Philadelphia Association in London's East End in June 1965. Within its walls, which rang to the sounds of the Beatles and Bob Dylan, and into which dropped such luminaries as the theatre critic

Kenneth Tynan, Sean Connery* and the playwright David Mercer,[†] many of the key fantasies of the sixties were dreamed and enacted. For a few years, madness reigned here.

Laing believed that what the man in the street calls madness is in fact sanity – the sanity of a mind that has admitted it cannot cope with the strictures of a lunatic society. It followed that madness was not a biological phenomenon but a social one – and that by changing societal structures we would do much to ease its depredations. Accordingly, Laing transformed Kingsley Hall into a kind of psychotic arena – a living, breathing theatre of the absurd in which derangement was treated not as an illness but as an all-too comprehensible reaction to a world out of joint. The Hall became home to people who would otherwise have been sectioned, a place where men and women suffering from severe psychoses could coexist in something approximating equality with their carers. While there, Laing said, they could use LSD and other drugs to hallucinate their way back through their traumatic histories in the hope of being able to eventually slot themselves back into normal daily life.

Kingsley Hall was an attempt to re-imagine the idea of asylum – to return to the original meaning of such institutions as places of sanctuary, places where people were protected, where they could be made safe. Hence the Philadelphia Association was named after the city of brotherly love. Its founders – Laing, David Cooper, Aaron Esterson, Sidney Briskin, Clancy Sigal, Joan Cunnold and Raymond Blake – were all committed to the idea that far from being a symptom of a nervous disorder or a genetic abnormality, a psychotic breakdown is the result of a crisis in existential self-belief.

---

* Whose then wife, Diane Cilento, had introduced him to Laing in the hope that he might get some help with what she thought of as his issues.

[†] Whom Laing helped with the writing of his screenplay for Ken Loach's harrowing film about schizophrenia, *Family Life*.

Nor is it a dead-end down which the afflicted are destined to travel on sufferance. Treated properly, such a crisis could be an avenue to freedom.

For Laing the shooting of the man he called the 'collapsed harlequin' was precisely the kind of existential epiphany that Kingsley Hall existed to engender. Among other things, Laing had been treating this 25-year-old schizophrenic for castration anxiety. After the shooting (which it quickly became apparent wasn't for real; the gun had been loaded with blank cartridges), the man lost a goodly portion of his worries. After four largely unproductive years of analysis with Laing, he was never so fearful again. 'Completely unpredictable and unrepeatable' as it had been, Laing said, no amount of psychiatric interpretation 'could be as primitive as that dramatic action'.[2]

But the people who lived in the streets around Kingsley Hall, in Bow, were rather less convinced by what went on there. After closing time at the local pub, the rougher elements took to smashing the Hall's windows with stones. One night they took an axe to the front door. The morning after, others among the neighbours (and perhaps some of the wreckers themselves) would complain to the Hall's trustees about the eyesore the building was becoming. They complained to Laing in person when one of his patients, Francis Gillet, took to walking around the area without wearing shoes and socks. And they called the fire brigade the day that another of the residents, Mary Barnes, went out on the roof to perform a sundance while wearing nothing but the abstract expressionist patterns she had daubed on her naked body using her own shit. To be fair, Laing himself subsequently claimed that he had 'always found Mary Barnes a bit of an embarrassment'.[3] Nonetheless, by the time his experimental psychotherapeutic arena closed, in the early seventies, he had been accused of being perpetually drunk there, high on drugs and of 'fucking everyone' in sight.[4]

It was all so very different from how things used to be in this respectable working-class area. The older neighbours remembered the pacifist sisters who had built Kingsley Hall as a community centre back in the 1920s, how it had been a soup kitchen for the unemployed in the Great Depression, and how, in 1931, while attending a conference on Indian independence, Mahatma Gandhi had stayed in one of its rooftop rooms. Not that the locals were up in arms only at the depravity Laing and his radical psychiatrists were bringing to their area. They thought the patients in an insane asylum should be better treated and looked after than they were at Kingsley Hall. 'It's an absolute disgrace,' Laing would remember more than one of them telling him. 'These poor people are suffering from some tragic disease and they ought to be given proper treatment and attention, given a bath and kept clean and not allowed to disgrace themselves.'[5] Now it was Laing's turn to disagree with them.

For Laing was deeply unhappy with the traditional models of psychiatric theory and disturbed by the putative therapies those models licensed and relied upon. Certainly he had no time for the idea of the psychiatrist as guardian of acceptable societal values and of the hospital as microcosm of the larger world. Like Michel Foucault,* he had come to believe that madness was no more

---

* In April 1965, Laing recommended that his publisher, Tavistock, bring out an English edition of Foucault's first book, *Madness and Civilization – a History of Insanity in the Age of Reason*. It was published a couple of years later, during the so-called Summer of Love.

Laing's endorsement of Foucault is something of an oddity in his career. There can be no doubt that the two men were in agreement on what they thought to be the socially constructed nature of madness – but stylistically they were miles apart. Laing is on record as believing – and all his published work attests to the belief – that the writer's job is to be as clear as possible. Clarity of expression, he old-fashionedly held in the free-for-all of the times, equates to clarity of thought. Not even Foucault's wildest fans could accuse him of clarity. And to his detractors, he is one of the great obscurantists of the late twentieth century. So what did Laing see in him? A similarly panoptic-seeming scholar, one surmises, whose thought appeared to offer a unified-field theory for both the humanities and the sciences.

than a post-enlightenment nomenclature for anything the age of rationalism deemed irrational. To be sure, he said, all cultures have produced individuals whose behaviour is regarded by the great mass of mankind as different or even unusual. Annoying as these people could be, though, they could also be seen – and often enough had been – as amusing or even saintly. At worst, they might have been called possessed; at best visionary. It was only in the eighteenth and nineteenth centuries, Laing argued, after the Christian categories of sin and salvation came to be replaced by scientific terms of health and illness, that madness came to be designated as a sickness.

Laing acknowledged, of course, that the nineteenth century had brought forth much physical evidence that established links between certain forms of madness and lesions on the brain. But his specialism was schizophrenia – the most common form of mental illness, and the one for which no physical indexes, genetic defects, or biochemical abnormalities had ever been isolated. And yet traditional psychiatry treated people that it labelled schizophrenics as if they were diseased. Thus labelled, such patients could be hospitalised for treatment – by means of tranquillisers, electroshock therapy or even going under the surgeon's knife for a lobotomy. This was dangerous hooey, said Laing, and in his 1965 bestseller, *The Divided Self*, he argued that it takes a lunatic to call another man insane. The book, an ambitious yoking together of philosophy and literature with psychiatry and psychoanalysis was intended, Laing said, 'to make madness and the process of going mad, comprehensible'.[6]

Relying more on thought derived from the phenomenological existentialism of Martin Heidegger and Jean-Paul Sartre than on the tenets of straight psychoanalysis, Laing argued that schizophrenia was not a biological phenomenon but a social phenomenon brought about by disturbed interpersonal relationships. It was, he said, the result of a breakdown in an individual's ability to police the border between his outer false self and his inner true self. In what Laing called the 'sane, schizoid state' a fictional carapace is established around the real person, the better for him to deal with the world outside. But problems can kick in when the inner self, the real existential being, is brought up against the unreality of its dealings with the world – when it is forced, that is, to admit to the existence of the phoney alter-ego it has conceived in order to accommodate itself to everything that is not it.

For Laing, an acute schizophrenic episode (or nervous breakdown) is brought about by the sudden removal of the mask of the false self, a removal that calls time on the ostensibly normal behaviour the sufferer has hitherto felt obliged to perform. 'Then', writes Laing, 'the self will pour out accusations of persecution at the hands of the person with whom the false self has been complying for years.'[7] Far from wanting to cure the sufferer of such afflictions, though, Laing wanted to celebrate them. He believed that a psychotic episode could offer its victim a chance of doing away with the horrific division between true and false selves, unifying them once more into the unadulterated wholeness of innocence. 'Madness', he wrote in an infamous phrase, 'need not always be breakdown. It may also be break-through. It is potentially liberation and renewal as well as enslavement and existential death.'[8] (Not for nothing did Laing's fellow Scot, the novelist Alisdair Gray, quip that Laing was all too tolerant of the mad while being intolerant of the sane.[9])

The forcing house of all these strains and stresses, held Laing, was the repressive regime that was bourgeois life. 'By far the most important channel of transmission of culture remains the family: and when family life fails to play its part, we must expect our culture to deteriorate.'[10] Thus one of Laing's favourite poets, T. S. Eliot. Not that Laing had any time for this particular sentiment. He wanted done with the family. Like Sartre, Laing was adamant that liberation from the mental shackles of family life

Only after the deaths of two great patriarchal protectors of the old Britain – war-time Prime Minister Winston Churchill (above) and the reactionary modernist poet T. S. Eliot – could the cultural revolution of 1965 begin.

Peter Cook and Dudley Moore's *Not Only . . . But Also* (above), like
Roman Polanski's *Repulsion* (with Catherine Deneuve, below right),
introduced surrealism to the mainstream. Meanwhile, Deneuve's then
husband, David Bailey (below left), was making an art-form of photography.

Bridget Riley's op art abstractions
(main picture), *Ariel* by
Sylvia Plath (inset), and Mary
Whitehouse (right) and her
campaign against pornography
– all in their different ways
revolutionized the life of women
in 1965.

'No well-dressed man should be without one,' says James Bond (Sean Connery) of the jetpack he wore in *Thunderball* (above) – and in the year when the millionth of Alec Issigonis's Minis rolled off the production line (below), and Britain was witness to a record number of road accident casualties, he surely had a point.

Grammar school boys actor Michael Caine and future prime minister Edward Heath, both hit the big time in 1965. Alas, no sooner had they made it than the selective education system that had made them was destroyed.

Emma Peel (Diana Rigg) hurls another hapless villain through the air in *The Avengers* – an espionage drama more spaced out than the acid trips the radical psychiatrist R. D. Laing (below) recommended his patients embark on.

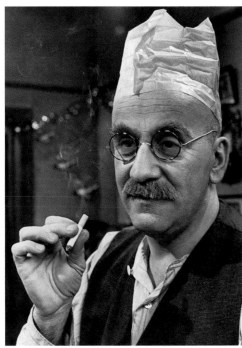

Thanks to the joyously creative foul language of TV's Alf Garnett (Warren Mitchell, above right), and despite the horrific murder spree of Ian Brady and Myra Hindley (below), 1965 was the year Home Secretary Roy Jenkins (above left) decided to abolish censorship – part of his mission to 'civilize' Britain.

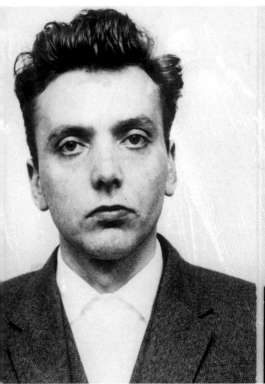

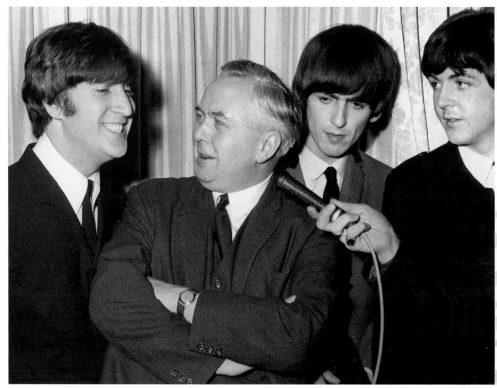

The Beatles' fifth album, *Rubber Soul*, turned pop music into high art. For their efforts, Prime Minister Harold Wilson (second from the left) had them made MBEs in 1965. A few weeks earlier, Albert Johanneson (left) made history – as the first black man to play in an FA Cup Final.

was the first step on the route to individual stability. As he told an audience at the Institute of Contemporary Arts a few months before *The Divided Self* soared up the bestseller lists, 'when the stone-age baby first confronts its twentieth-century mother, the baby is subjected to these forces of outrageous violence, called love . . . These forces are mostly concerned with destroying most of its potentialities . . . By the time the new human being is fifteen or so, we are left with a being like ourselves. A half-crazed creature, more or less adjusted to a mad world.'[11] A couple of years later, he warmed to his theme in book form: 'The family is, in the first place, the usual instrument for what is called socialisation, that is, getting each new recruit of the human race to behave and experience in substantially the same way as those who have already got here. We are fallen Sons of Prophecy, who have learned to die in the Spirit and be reborn in the Flesh. This is also known as selling one's soul for a mess of pottage.'[12]

Family life was nothing to do with life proper. The family was false consciousness made flesh, and worked as a kind of barrier between the individual and real, lived experience. 'The family's function is to repress Eros,' Laing wrote. 'To induce a false consciousness of security; to deny death by avoiding life; to cut off transcendence; to believe in God, not to experience the Void; to create, in short, one-dimensional man; to promote respect, conformity, obedience; to con children out of play; to induce a fear of failure; to promote a respect for work; to promote respect for "respectability".'[13] Little wonder that 'A child born today in the UK stands a ten times greater chance of being admitted to a mental hospital than to a university, and about one fifth of mental hospital admissions are diagnosed schizophrenic. This can be taken as an indication that we are driving our children mad more effectively than we are genuinely educating them.'[14]

The core problem, Laing argued, was the unwillingness of parents to let children pursue life as they themselves saw fit. Parents infantilised their infants, in other words, and having done so interpreted any (to Laing utterly natural) change in behaviour or attitude not as fledgling steps en route to individuation but as evidence of disturbance – even of insanity. Time to call in a shrink.*

Still, Laing was keen to point out, he wasn't anti-parents per se. 'I'm not against families,' he once said. 'I have a very nice one here. Although I have tried to show how families go wrong, I think they are one of the best relics of a crumbling system we have to hang on to.'[15] Not that he ever made much effort to hang on to his own families. By the end of his life Laing had fathered some ten children by four different women. But his relationships with them were largely tortured and distant. Once Laing had abandoned a wife or lover he largely abandoned the children he had produced with her, too. 'We've got too many problems for him,' his daughter Susie once said. 'He can solve everybody else's but not ours.'[16] Such gripes are common enough among the children of the rich and famous, of course; still, there does seem to have been something to Susie's disenchantment. A few years later, when she was diagnosed with

---

* Even as Kingsley Hall was opening its doors to Laing's non-patients, a few miles to the west those of the Aldwych Theatre were opening to admit audiences to Harold Pinter's *The Homecoming*. The play was an astonishing assault on the family, a demolition job that imagines hearth and home as no more than the venue for territorial wars in which no peace can ever be brokered, no victories ever won.

It is also full of Laingian divided selves. The much-discussed, long-dead mother, of whom her husband Max recalls that 'Even though it made me sick to look at her rotten stinking face, she wasn't such a bad bitch', was also 'the backbone to this family . . . with a will of iron, a heart of a gold and a [strangely modifier free] mind' *and* 'a slut-bitch of a wife' who presided over a 'crippled family, three bastard sons'. Two of those sons, Lenny and Joey, the first a monstrous, misogynist bully, the second a rough-and-tumble idiot, look like the complementary halves of a split personality, while the other brother, Teddy, functions in the play as a kind of counterpoint father-figure – the sagacious and worldly wise half to Max's bullying senility.

lymphatic leukaemia, Laing stood alone against her mother, her fiancé, her brothers and sisters and even her doctors in insisting that Susie be told of her condition and informed that, since it was untreatable, she would shortly die. He wanted, he said, 'to give her a chance to prepare for her own death'. After all, no 'fully fledged human being ... [should be] deprive[d] of their own death'.[17] Susie's boyfriend was less certain, almost coming to blows with Laing over what he saw as a horrendous invasion. Susie's mother (and Laing's first wife), Anne, was no less distraught. After Laing went ahead with his announcement of Susie's death sentence, Anne said she hoped that Laing would 'roast in hell for eternity'.[18]

None of this invalidates his theories and beliefs, of course (just as Laing's attack on Marx as 'an enormously alienated man. One of his children died of pneumonia and starvation because he wouldn't deign to spend a few hours a week writing articles'[19] does nothing to invalidate the theory of alienation). And Laing surely spoke the truth when he said that his 'attack on the family [was] aimed at the way ... many children are subjected to gross forms of violence of their rights, humiliation at the hands of adults who don't know what they're doing'.[20] After all, Laing had been one of those children. He was, he once said, a 'symptom of the times'.[21]

Nobody, not even Dickens, could have imagined the childhood and upbringing that R. D. Laing endured. He was born in Glasgow, in 1927, to a mother who had done her best to hide the fact of her pregnancy from neighbours and what passed as her friends, and to a father who was mystified as to how a couple who never had sex might, nine years after their marriage, have come to conceive a child.*

---

* Jesus, who it will be remembered, urged his followers to abandon their families for an authentic spiritual community not unlike that in Kingsley Hall, was conceived in similarly immaculate style.

So baffled was he that several days went by before David Laing announced to the world that his wife Amelia had given birth. The suspicion that David might not have been the father of baby Ronald (named for the matinee idol Ronald Colman) likely did the rounds. And doubts as to his real origins must have occurred to the preternaturally bright young Laing, too. Years later, when Laing was well into his thirties, his father hiked up a trouser-leg to show that he, like his son, had a birthmark on his right knee. Even allowing that this is any kind of proof of paternity, what kind of family lets such doubts hang in the air for three decades and more?

'Everyone in the street knew she was mad,' Laing's school friend Walter Fyfe once said of Amelia.[22] All day, all year, she kept the curtains of the family flat drawn. Every week she burned the household rubbish lest her neighbours look through it – the only time many people remember seeing her. Certainly few visitors ever came to the Laings' apartment, and nobody recalled Amelia venturing out into the world much, either with or without the young son with whom she shared a bedroom. Her husband had been relegated to a small back room that Amelia lovingly referred to as 'the dog kennel'. Stranger still, he wasn't allowed to use the same crockery and cutlery as his son, which Amelia insisted were Ronald's alone. When, a few years later, Amelia made a present of a red braided dressing gown to Ronald, David threw it on the fire, accusing her of favouring her son over her husband. Not to be outdone, Amelia once decided that Laing was getting too fond of a wooden horse on wheels he had been given – pretending to feed it and talk to it and so on – and threw that on the fire, too. Much later on in Laing's life, his mother would tell one of his daughters that she had constructed a wooden doll of her son into which she stuck needles and pins. Partly this was because she was ashamed of his being a psychiatrist. Far from evidencing his caring nature, she said, his career only proved that he had a fixation on 'all the filth in people's minds'.[23] Who could be surprised, then, that at her husband's funeral she declaimed herself embarrassed by the fact of her son's mournful weeping? This time Laing got his own back. When Amelia died, Laing announced to the world that he wished he'd hurt her more than he had.[24]

As well as not wanting to hug or kiss or even, on occasion, touch her son, Amelia seems to have wanted to not let Ronald be contaminated by any contact with the world outside his immediate family. He was frequently beaten by his father, on his mother's orders – once for swapping a morsel from his school lunch box for a taste from another boy's pack. Yet school, Laing would remember, came as a blessed relief from the claustrophobia at home. Certainly at the end of the school day, when Laing had walked home with one or other of his friends and paused for a chat outside the family's flat, it was always a painful moment for him to leave the boy. He had been given the sign to do so by his mother, who would appear at the window above them, beckoning him in with a gloved hand.

And like the Miss Havisham her behaviour recalls, Amelia had great expectations of the boy in her charge. Not, it should be said, without reason. Though his grades would not always prove the point, Laing was likely the brightest boy in school – an autodidact who spent much of his schooldays in libraries, working his way alphabetically through encyclopaedias and keeping always at hand a dictionary of his own devising. Such self-improvement went on throughout his life. He taught himself German, he once said, by reading Heidegger's *Being and Time* with no more help than that provided by a German dictionary. With characteristic cheek, he claimed that Heidegger, by some measure one of the most dauntingly unreadable philosophers of the twentieth century, was 'very simple basically if you're not German'.*[25]

---

* Sceptics might remember the speed-reading course that enabled Woody Allen to get through *War and Peace* in ten minutes: 'It's about Russia,' he said.

Laing's critics, of whom there would be many over the years,* ascribed what they saw as his off-the-wall theoric to his lack of proper training in the many fields he claimed authority in. There is something to this, of course, as there is something to the suggestion that Laing's idea of himself as the lone visionary scholar mirrored his vision of the all-seeing lunatic sage a little too perfectly. Nonetheless, by the time he left secondary school, he had been told by a teacher that his wide reading in the classics meant he was already at PhD standard. Given what Laing would go on to write, with its impressively broad range of cultural reference, there is no need to doubt this judgement – even though we know of it, like we know so much else of Laing's childhood, only from his own (phenomenally good) memories of the time.

As well as his undoubted intellectual prowess, the young Laing demonstrated exceptional musical talents at the piano. At ten he was thought to have perfect pitch, passing his Royal Academy of Music exams years earlier than anyone else at school. By his teens he was playing Chopin and Liszt and Beethoven, reputedly with great skill and feeling. Whenever he could, he would play with the windows open, in the hope that some passing impresario would sign him up on the spot and book him on a world tour. He might have gone on to read music at university had he not broken his wrist shortly before decision time.

Music wasn't Laing's only artistic leaning. He was a great reader of poetry and philosophy – he had worked his way through Kierkegaard, Nietzsche, Marx and Freud long before he took his highers – and he toyed, too, with the idea of studying English literature at university. Having learned from his studies in the *Dictionary of National Biography* that Havelock Ellis had published

---

* Not until 1982, fully twenty-two years after its first publication and more than fifteen since its accession into the bestseller charts, was *The Divided Self* granted a review in the pages of the *British Journal of Psychiatry*.

his first book before he turned thirty, he vowed to do the same. In the event, things took a little longer than that, but it is vital to grasp that Laing's immense popularity in the sixties owed a great deal to his background as a reader of books seemingly irrelevant to the medical world in which he ended up studying and subsequently working. It is difficult to overestimate how central to Laing's success was his way with the English language. Even his greatest psychiatric opponents would have been hard-pressed to call him a bad writer.

Once at medical school, at Glasgow University, Laing went on reading far beyond the parameters of his studies. (He had decided to read medicine rather than philosophy or literature, he said, because those were the subjects you kept up with anyway.) He lapped up every new issue of Cyril Connolly's *Horizon*, that monthly monument to aesthetic despair and disdain, and was particularly taken with an article by Antonin Artaud (who invented the theatre of cruelty that Kingsley Hall was so often taken for) on Van Gogh's suicide. Artaud, who had himself been a patient at a French lunatic asylum, used the piece to launch an all-out attack on psychiatry and the 'vicious society [which] has invented [it] to defend itself from the investigations of certain visionaries whose faculties of divination disturbed it'. Lunatics, Artaud went on, are men 'society does not want to hear but wants to prevent from uttering certain unbearable truths'. It was not they 'but the world that [had] become abnormal'.[26] The band Pink Floyd, which was just starting gigging as Laing's work made famous his own libertarian sentiments, have built a half-century long career carolling about similarly unbearable truths.

What most struck Laing about Artaud's essay, though, was its belief that while 'It is almost impossible to be a doctor and an honest man', it is 'shamefully impossible to be a psychiatrist without bearing the stigma of the most indisputable insanity at the same time'.[27] Since psychiatry was the medical field Laing felt most drawn to, he began to wonder whether he might be able to humanise it. At the Psychiatric Unit in Glasgow's Duke Street Hospital he came into contact with patients rendered immobile by crippling catatonia. Other than when it came to feeding and medicating them, these people were largely shunned by the medical staff. Yet Laing found that he could identify with their predicament only too well. He was determined to use his seemingly rare empathetic powers when he had qualified.

After graduating (he failed his exams first time around, but did very well at a resit six months later), he took up a position at a Neurosurgical Unit at Killearn, 15 miles or so north of Glasgow, where he would gain hands-on (as it were) experience of the central nervous system and insights into the brain/mind interaction. From there, Laing was conscripted into the forces, where he was posted to the British Army Psychiatric Unit at Netley, near Southampton. It was to this bleak, end of world outpost that the poet Wilfred Owen had been brought for electroconvulsive therapy (ECT) after suffering shell shock during the First World War. By the time Laing arrived, ECT had been supplemented with insulin shock therapy, a practice that worked by drugging schizophrenics into comas for days- and often weeks-on-end in the hope of jolting them out of their suffering. Here Laing began the work – both theoretical and empirical – that would lead to the development of the ideas and intuitions that underlay *The Divided Self*.

It all began one night when he was doing his round of the wards. From one of the hospital's padded cells could be heard some crazed screechings. Laing went into the cell, took one look at the patient, John, who was naked and surrounded by his own excrement and urine, and asked for a sedative injection to be brought. But while waiting for the syringe, he listened to John who, though he had been incarcerated because of his habit of taking head-first running-jumps at brick walls, began to calm down. Laing changed his mind about the need for a sedative. The next night he heard the same furious noises, and followed the same listening strategy. Soon enough, Laing was spending chunks of each evening with John, 'almost "hanging out" there', he once recalled, and feeling 'strangely at home there ... I could *almost* understand him, I could *almost* follow'.[28] After a few nights of this Laing had become 'a sort of Sancho Panza to his Don Quixote'. Soon enough 'he nominated me Horatio to his Hamlet'.[29]

But what did Laing nominate himself? To the outsider, the striking thing about John's troubles is how closely they mirrored Laing's own. Like Laing, John came from a troubled home (he was the son of an army officer and a prostitute). Like Laing, he had been perhaps too close to his mother in childhood. Like Laing, he was deemed to have disgraced his parents by failing his university exams. John's problems – he was an acute psychotic – were, of course, far worse than Laing's. But what Laing saw as John's central, defining problem, the fact that he had not been allowed to grow up believing that he was his father's son, that he was estranged from his own identity, surely chimed with Laing's feelings about his own broken-backed upbringing. Hence Laing's admission that what he was doing was 'beyond the line of duty', and that John's 'padded cell had become a refuge for me and his company a solace'.[30] If Laing was the Horatio to John's Hamlet then it is also true that John was the Hyde to Laing's Jekyll.

Such role-playing was central to John's conception of himself. Having been placed in the untenable position of having his self-image denied by the only people who could validate it, he had sought to liberate himself by means of the existential invocation to 'be anyone he cared to be'.[31] And what, Laing wanted to know, was wrong with that? 'Why should he return to a world where he is unable to satisfy every one of his fundamental desires?' he asked in a letter to his then girlfriend, Marcelle Vincent. 'Why indeed? I find it very difficult to give him an answer ... we are "free" to choose insanity or suicide. And more and more people

are exercising their freedom in this direction.'[32] It was for suffering such subversive thoughts that Laing's fellow psychiatrist
Anthony Clare once wondered whether Laing might be 'too sensitive to be a doctor'.[33]

Certainly shortly after John was discharged from Netley, Laing
began to question his own sanity. 'I was beginning', he recalled, 'to
suspect that insulin and electric shocks, not to mention lobotomy
and the whole environment of a psychiatric unit, were ways of
destroying people and driving people crazy if they were not so
before, and crazier if they were.'[34] Warming to this theme on Swiss
Radio, Laing made plain that he had come to feel at Netley that he
hated the 'misery, absurdity and humiliation' of its regime. He had,
he said, decided that far from improving the lot of its patients, 'psychiatry was largely making matters worse . . . was itself part of the
social disease'.[35] Such was the thinking that underlay the experiment at Kingsley Hall.

Laing and his fellow Philadelphians believed that the traditional
doctor–patient relationship was not at all conducive to engender-
ing improvement in, much less curing, the sufferer. Indeed, by
undermining any sense of a one-on-one relationship twixt analyst
and analysand, traditional psychiatry only worked to confirm the
schizophrenic in their sense of desperate solitude. At Kingsley Hall,
by contrast, the professional demarcation lines between doctors and
patients and nurses were abolished. Laing, who had charmed its
owner, Muriel Lester, into letting him have the place for a pep-
percorn rent of just £1 a year, envisaged it as a refuge from the
world, a safe house wherein the distressed and disorientated could
embark on an inner journey to find their true selves. The Hall's residents weren't just what a more traditional hospital would call its
patients – they were what would be called the staff, too. Absent the
traditional hierarchies of such institutions, there would never be any
question about who might need help and who might offer it, who
might manage and who might be managed.

Early-morning yoga sessions aside, days at the Hall were all but unstructured. Sceptics won't be surprised to learn that basic tasks like shopping, cleaning and cooking were soon enough being carried out shoddily, sporadically or not at all. During the day people painted, sang, danced, played ping-pong, or just talked. In the evening, though, most people convened for a late supper and later debates and discussions that frequently went on into the small hours. Laing spoke often, of course, holding forth on a variety of topics, from the philosophical and scholarly to the lewd and jocular.

Who came to stay? People who wanted to avoid being locked up in a traditional mental hospital; people worried they were about to have a breakdown; people who had, perhaps, read Laing's books and were fascinated by the idea of his experiment in communal living. Once the community was established, it was the residents who decided who should be allowed to move in next. (Providing, of course, that there was room: the Hall had space for fourteen people, each of them inhabiting tiny rooms, though they could share these if they chose to.) Laing was adamant that the decisions were never his alone. He never insisted that space be made available for a specific patient. All decisions were those of the community. Priority was given to those people who appeared to be most genuinely in need of the experience.

One of the first to move in was the aforementioned Mary Barnes, a 42-year-old qualified nurse and presently an assistant matron at a hospital. She came from what she called an 'abnormally nice' Southampton family, but a couple of years earlier, in 1963, she had suffered a mental breakdown. She had been consulting Laing ever since – perhaps not just because he once told her that she needed therapy twenty-four hours a day. As far as she was concerned, all her problems arose from the dynamics of life among that abnormally nice family. Everyone, she once said, 'thought we all lived happily together ... Mum and Dad were always considerate and polite to each other ... They never shouted.' None of which sounds too bad. Alas, 'Violence lurked beneath the pleasantries . . . Life was like ice' and 'the whole family wanted the ice to melt . . . but we feared if the ice broke, we would all be drowned.'[36]

Not that things were much drier when Barnes was around Kingsley Hall. 'Life became quite fantastic,' she once recalled. Though still working at the hospital for the first few weeks of her sojourn at the Hall, she would come home each evening and tear 'off my clothes, feeling I had to be naked. Lay on the floor with my shits and water, smeared the wall with faeces. Was wild and noisy about the house or sitting in a heap on the kitchen floor.'[37] Soon enough she quit work and moved in full time. Once resident there she stopped eating solids and insisted on being fed milk from a bottle by Laing or Joe Berke (her favoured analyst), or whoever else was around. The idea was that by reverting to childhood, Barnes could live her life over, and grow up again, though this time in a manner more conducive to contentment.

Then she stopped drinking the milk. As she lost weight, she grew weaker and weaker, yet unlike in a normal asylum, nobody had any powers to intervene. The community met and took the decision that they couldn't allow her to carry on in this way. On the other hand, they felt uneasy about the idea of the catheters and feeding tubes that would have been inserted without a thought in that traditional asylum. Eventually Mary was persuaded to resume eating and drinking, though that didn't put an end to the problems she caused. The 'shits' she had smeared on the walls of her room (which was next to the kitchen) stank the whole place out. This time the residents decided to do nothing.

Thankfully, Mary eventually 'came up' out of her madness and began to do things she'd never been allowed to do as a child – wear trousers, play ball, dance. When Berke made her a present of a packet of wax crayons she took to scribbling black breasts on the walls of the Hall. And her condition began to improve. Over the next few years – indeed, for the rest of her life (she died in 2001) –

Barnes made her living as a painter. In 1971, a year after the dissolution of the Kingsley Hall community, she and Berke collaborated on a book, *Mary Barnes: Two Accounts of a Journey Through Madness*, whose title suggests the liberation she felt she had achieved through her residency at the Hall. The book and the paintings brought her a measure of fame. So much that in 1977, David Edgar wrote a play about her that transferred from its original production at the Birmingham Repertory Theatre to the Royal Court.

It was this fame that did so much to fan the flames of controversy around Laing through the seventies and eighties. Perhaps in part because Edgar's play was almost conventional in its three-act redemptive structure – it shows us Barnes as an emblem of the stresses and strains the soul must endure under bourgeois capitalism before it is released from such shackles by the insights of Laingian psychiatry – there were those who remained sceptical of Barnes's achievements. The radical psychiatrist Thomas Szasz, for instance, who agreed with Laing on many key principles, was unconvinced by Mary Barnes's experiences at Kingsley Hall.[38] He thought both her disorder and her cure were imaginary – that she had been encouraged, or even hypnotised, into believing she was in the throes of hysteria in order to be cured by a couple of men who wanted to make a name for themselves and their theories. Not, he insisted, that Laing and Berke were hucksters. Genuine hucksters knew they were gulling people. Laing and Berke had somehow contrived to kid themselves into believing in the efficacy of their treatment. Everybody was deceiving everybody else. But it was worse than that, argued the literary critic Mary Showalter. She thought Laing's treatment of Barnes (which 'drew upon his own heroic fantasies: a male adventure of exploration [and] conquest') was significant only in that it was symptomatic of the oppression of womanhood under capitalist patriarchy.[39]

Not everybody saw it that way, of course – including not every woman. Shortly after the opening of Kingsley Hall an ad appeared in the classifieds of the *Village Voice* advising that 'Two chicks who dig Coltrane, the [Grateful] Dead and R. D. Laing are throwing a party next Saturday night for anybody into similar interests.'[40] Bliss was it in that dawn to be alive and well and partying through the night. Because despite all those doubters in his own profession, Laing was taken joyously to the heart of the burgeoning counter-culture. The hippies simply adored him.

They loved the idea that by forcing individuals to be cogs in the industrial machine capitalism causes madness. They loved the idea that the result was either a feelings-free automaton or a tormented soul in perpetual conflict with both the world and himself.* They loved the idea that conventional psychiatric treatment was no more than a means for seeing off the psychic pain that would be of such use in the coming revolution. They loved the idea of freedom that Laing's Rousseauian, romanticist take on psychiatry and existentialism embodied – and they loved the route to liberation that Laing was painting out at Kingsley Hall and in the pages of *The Divided Self*. They loved his claim that to be crazy was to be creative, if only because it licensed the idea that all you had to do to be creative was act crazy. Above all, they loved his belief in the indivisibility of knowledge, in the idea that scientific and medical 'learning and factual knowledge [are] of very limited value unless [they] are related to the rest of human wisdom'.[41] Such sentiments chimed with the everything-is-connected, lifestyle–Buddhism that was so transiently trendy in the sixties.

But it was the rhetorical power of Laing's prose – that elegant, coiling, beautifully timed mash-up of Eliot, Wordsworth, Artaud, Coleridge and Kierkegaard – that really entranced his fans. Laing was one of the great stylists of the sixties, his rhythmic sentences Nietzschean in their ambition if not always in their reach. To read

---

* I use the male pronoun self-consciously, man.

two lines of it is to know it was written by a musician. Its marriage of poetry and philosophy was hardly new – certainly a lot less new than Laing would have had you believe – but its incantatory pulse granted it a power its often abstract conceits would not normally have had any claim to.

It was this air of numinous mystery, along with Laing's disavowal of the catch-all explications of scientism and positivism, that spoke to the tuned-in, turned-on, dropped-out brigade of the sixties.* Indeed, though *The Divided Self* was and would remain his most conventional book, its sales took off in 1965 because in the new introduction Laing had written for it his sympathies for the counterculture were made subconsciously plain. 'This [book] was the work of an old young man,' he wrote. 'If I'm older, I'm now also younger.'[42] And perhaps he was, since in the preceding twelve months he had plainly forsaken the pleasures of Beethoven for those of Bob Dylan. A year earlier, in 'My Back Pages', Dylan had ended each verse of his song with the claim that he felt he was getting younger and more innocent as time went by. When Laing writes elsewhere in that new introduction about 'The statesmen of the world who boast and threaten that they have Doomsday weapons' being 'far more dangerous, and far more estranged from "reality" than many of the people on whom the label "psychotic" is affixed',[43] he was surely paraphrasing the peacenik sentiments of Dylan's 'Masters of War' and 'A Hard Rain's a-Gonna Fall'.

Yet like Dylan, Laing himself was adamant that he was no ideologue, and that whatever contributions he made to the general dialogic tug weren't intended to be anything more than personal

---

* Despite his long-haired romantic image, Laing could come on like A. J. Ayer when he wanted to. 'Schizophrenia', he once opined, 'is the name for a condition most psychiatrists ascribe to patients they call schizophrenic,' for all the world as if he'd just put down his copy of *Language, Truth and Logic*.

and individual. Though the New Left were keen to involve him in their debates, the man dubbed 'the Acid Marxist' steered well clear of them. Largely this was because Laing, for all the revolutionary impulse of his work, had little interest in the cut and thrust of politics proper. While his home was full of books, its shelves were largely given over to volumes of philosophy, poetry, the arts – along with yards of biography. Of political tracts there was scarcely a sign. A biography of Trotsky and a pamphlet by Lenin had somehow snuck under Laing's ideological radar, but otherwise he was adamant that solutions to man's predicament were not to be found in politics.

Certainly he had no time for the Marxism that was so fashionable in the sixties. Though in his youth he came to believe that Scotland was a colony owned by English capitalists, and though he made notes for the writing of a biography of the Glaswegian communist (and friend of Lenin) John Maclean, Laing couldn't countenance a philosophy founded on the belief that economics was central to human life. Indeed, while both one of his patients, the writer Clancy Sigal, and his fellow psychiatrist Joe Berke argued that he 'idealised madness' and conceived of the schizophrenic as 'a sort of emotional proletariat',[44] Laing never sided with the workers proper. If anything, he was a Nietzschean, a worshipper of the lordly and woe-bringer to the lumpen. 'The enlightened individual', he wrote in a prize-winning essay from his student days, 'despise[s] the mass.'[45] And if social tumult was what you were after, Freud trumped Marx every time: 'The Marxist imagines that a revolution in the Politico-economico structure of society will revolutionise man's mind. But it may well be that a change of mind can revolutionise society.'[46]

Perhaps, unsurprisingly then, Laing's deepest and most durable legacy has been felt on the right. Edmund Burke's belief in the madness of the wise is echoed in Laing's faith in the wisdom of the mad, after all, and as his biographer John Clay has argued,

Laing's essential philosophy was that 'it was up to each individual to take responsibility for himself'.[47] One can almost hear Margaret Thatcher's Amen to that. Certainly Laing's emphasis on the individual, on the let-it-all-hang-out nature of socially constructed madness, his insistence that one must be free from the influence of family and become authentically oneself, spoke presciently to the Thatcherite revolution. His suggestion that madness is not the product of genetics or of chemical confusion but of a simple existential choice is only the inverse of that strand of political thought that would damn anyone who dares to be different.

And what was the Thatcher government's lauding of so-called 'care in the community'[48] (so-called because the community very quickly made clear that it didn't care) if not an echo of the laissez-faire philosophy that underlay Kingsley Hall? Here was a Conservative government committed at least rhetorically to the hang 'em and flog 'em school of punishment advocating the release of mental patients from asylums the better to treat them in their own homes. In truth, the government's real interest in community care stemmed from its love of cost-cutting. Yet there is no denying that Thatcher and her cohorts saw in the policy a version of the libertarianism they sought to preach – precisely the kind of get-off-my-back libertarianism the sixties counterculture had been founded upon. Alas, the results of this government policy were a combination of the shaming and shocking, with far too many patients left to roam the streets, a danger both to themselves and to others, and a tragic rebuke to the naive romanticism of the decade from which Thatcher unwittingly took so much.

Nobody would argue with Laing's basic contention that the mentally afflicted and disabled have over the years suffered wanton intervention on the part of both state and psychiatry. Thanks at least in part to his teaching and example, though, what they now have to fear is simple neglect. The afflicted are the afflicted, after all, whether locked away in an asylum or not. Laing was right to see that the sufferings of the schizophrenic and otherwise deranged had been politicised by institutionalisation. Still, he couldn't bring himself to see that removing the institution would do nothing to remove the suffering. In large part this was because he refused to acknowledge the fact of the suffering. Like his beloved Nietzsche, he was almost envious of the mad. He saw them as visionaries, emissaries from an alternative world who could see through the deceits of this one. Since, he always said, you'd have to be mad to be normal, it followed that it was normal to be mad. But it wasn't and isn't, and the forces Laing always believed he was subverting have only grown stronger on the back of the confusion.

This doesn't, of course, confute the whole of his work. Some 113 people stayed at Kingsley Hall during the second half of the sixties – one of them for as long as four and a half years. (The average residency lasted three months.) None of those people who hadn't already spent time in a conventional mental hospital ever did so subsequently, and many of the residents were able to manage their lives much better after their stay. Moreover, those inmates who have spoken of their time there have all been very positive about their experiences of working with Laing. Best of all, none of them committed suicide, none of them died, and nobody was murdered. These are negative positives, certainly, but negative positives are better than positive negatives. It bears repeating that without the existence of the Kingsley Hall experiment its residents would likely have found themselves banged up in a mental hospital, where they would likely have been treated with drugs and electric shocks. Laing was honest enough to call his experiences there 'not a roaring success'[49]; but neither, surely, were they a crashing failure.

Laing's biggest influence was on the creative fields he at least

always half belonged to. The Dialectics of Liberation conference*
Laing helped set up in the summer of 1967 was as much an arts
festival as it was a debate on the marriage of Freud and Marx its
title (as well as the sixties as a whole) seemed to promise. Its
venue, the Roundhouse in London's Camden Town,† was one
generally reserved for rock gigs and theatrical happenings, and
despite the line-up of heavyweight thinkers (Herbert Marcuse, Paul
Goodman, Erving Goffman, Ernest Mandel among them) who,
along with Laing and his Kingsley Hall partner Joe Berke, spoke at
the conference's morning lectures, it was given over in the afternoon to screenings of arthouse movies and poetry readings by the
likes of Allen Ginsberg. Berke remembered it as a sixteen-day-long
gathering of people 'talking, fucking, fighting, flipping, eating and
doing nothing, but all trying to find some way to "make it" with
each other and together seek ways out of what they saw to be a
common predicament – the horrors of contemporary existence'.[50]

These lessons were not lost on rock and roll as the sixties became
the seventies. Over the next few years the Kinks' Ray Davies would
write 'Acute Schizophrenic Paranoia Blues'; the Who's Pete Town-
shend would write *Quadrophenia*, in which a putatively mad Mod,
Jimmy, would attend sessions with a 'psychiatrist ... [who] ...
never really knew what was wrong with me. He said I wasn't mad
or anything ... [that] ... there's no such thing as madness'; David
Bowie would call his character Aladdin Sane 'schizophrenic ... he
had so many personalities'.[51]

---

* It was actually called a 'congress', which was only apt since, just as at so many rock concerts of the time, much congress went on there. Thankfully Wilhelm Reich, whose
arguments for love and against war had done so much to inspire the counterculture, had
died ten years earlier and so was not around to see what he had presciently feared would
be a 'free-for-all fucking epidemic'.
† A measure of the area's salubriousness at the time might be suggested by the fact that
two of its local residents were Vivian MacKerell and Bruce Robinson. Twenty years later,
Robinson would write and direct an autobiographical account of their life there, *Withnail
and I*. An hilarious sight it is, though nobody could call it a pretty one.

But the earliest instance of Laing's influence on rock culture came in 1965, when one of the new students at the Camberwell School of Art tore pages out of his copy of *The Divided Self* and used them as part of a collage project. 'Fart Enjoy' was one of the first works of Syd Barrett, the founder member and leading light of the psychedelic band Pink Floyd (who played at the Roundhouse shortly before the Dialectics of Liberation conference). Alas, Barrett was too sensitive a soul for the ravages of the rock world, and within weeks of his band beginning to find fame he started to exhibit signs of mental instability. At first, Barrett's madness only fuelled his inventiveness. The joyous derangement of the songs he wrote during Pink Floyd's fledgling days – 'Arnold Layne', 'Interstellar Overdrive', 'Bike' – seemed to both embody and endorse Laing's theories of the liberating holiness of madness. Soon enough, though, the band's manager, Peter Jenner, who had worked with Laing on a community adult education project called the London Free School, began to worry that Barrett was suffering from a schizophrenic disorder. Jenner asked Laing to take a look at Barrett, though Barrett was less than communicative when they met. 'No therapy can ever take place unless the patient wants it to,'[52] said Laing.

Perhaps not, though this insistence on change coming from within did nothing to dissuade the counterculture as a whole from having great faith in the liberating qualities of LSD – a drug Laing had used as a psychotherapeutic agent at his Wimpole Street practice. This was not, it should be said, as off-the-wall a practice as Laing's reputation as the guru of hippiedom might suggest. Like one of his great heroes, Aldous Huxley, Laing believed LSD was a way of cutting through the defence mechanisms attendant upon traditional Freudian free-association dialogues, as well as a means of transporting oneself into the arenas of the preternaturally gifted or the schizophrenic. By making use of the drug, he hoped, he would be able to gain some insight into the experience of schizophrenia.

Nor was Laing the only psychiatrist using the drug on his patients. In America, Laing's counterparts Richard Alpert and Timothy Leary were both experimenting with LSD (both medically and shall we say socially*), and in Canada the CIA were funding research by the Scottish psychiatrist Ewan Cameron into the drug's effects. The hope was that it might serve as a truth serum or even as an instrument of mind control. Even Cary Grant, Hollywood's besuited paragon of taste and charm, who abandoned his career in the cinema just as the counterculture burgeoned, was using LSD. 'All my life', he said, 'I've been searching for peace of mind. I'd explored yoga and hypnotism and made several attempts at mysticism. Nothing really seemed to give me what I wanted until this treatment.'[53] Incidentally, none of this was in any way illegal. Throughout the fifties and sixties in the USA, LSD was the subject of a government-licensed experiment (Project MKUltra), which means that the great white hope of the hippie generation was introduced into polite society by the very suits the counterculture thought to overthrow.

Yet though Laing was not alone in his use of what he refused to call acid – like Albert Hofmann, who first synthesised LSD, he was fond of pointing out that it is in fact a base – and though he never advocated use of the drug as a lifestyle choice, the British psychiatric establishment demonised and sought to discredit him for his experimentation. In December 1965, just as the Beatles LSD-inspired LP *Rubber Soul* was released (of which more in chapter 10), Laing was told he had to resign his directorship of the Langham Clinic – a centre offering psychotherapy at reduced rates to people unable to afford private fees – because the rest of the staff disapproved of his use of the drug.

---

* Late in 1965, Laing pronounced himself appalled at their plan to distribute sufficient LSD for 300,000 trips within a twenty-four-hour period to school, college and first-year university students. See Bob Mullan, *Mad to be Normal: Conversations with R. D. Laing* (Free Association Books, 1995), p.222.

The Beatles – or at least two of them, John Lennon and George Harrison (along with their then wives, Cynthia and Pattie) – had first experienced the drug back in March, at the Hampstead home of the dentist John Riley. Riley, who believed the drug to be an aphrodisiac and had hopes of making the party swing, surreptitiously dosed a jug of coffee with a tab. Alas for him, the only results of his experiment were how-dare-you anger from Lennon and, later, dreamy and/or nightmarish fantasies on the part of all four victims. 'The walls moved, the plants talked, other people looked like ghouls and time stood still,' recalled Cynthia Lennon. 'It was horrific.'[54]

Not so horrific that her husband didn't soon want to try it again though. From now on, Lennon would attend vanishingly few recording sessions without having dropped a tab (often enough on top of the dope and drink he was already prone to ingesting). The title song of *Help!*, with its desperate plea about 'feeling down', was Lennon's first writerly response to the mixed emotions he felt for and about the new drug. Within eighteen months, though, he would go beyond mere reportage and find a way of transliterating the tripping experience into the distorted soundscapes of 'Strawberry Fields Forever'. This astonishing song, which attempted to both mimic and elucidate the relationship of the innocent child to a world he or she had yet to realise was indifferent to his or her fate, was a kind of aural embodiment of everything Laing had sought to bring about through his own practice.

George Harrison, meanwhile, who had driven Lennon and their respective wives back to his home in his Mini Cooper, was even more impressed with the cabinet of Dr Riley. Recalling the after-effects of his first LSD trip he said that, 'It was as if I had never tasted, talked, seen, thought or heard properly before. For the first time in my life I wasn't conscious of ego.'[55] There was, he said, 'no way back ... It had nothing to do with getting high ... It's shattering, as though someone suddenly wipes away all you were taught or brought up to believe as a child and says, "That's not it." You've gone so far, your thoughts have become so lofty, and you think that there's no way of getting back.'[56] This search for enlightenment – and not just a mindless desire for oblivion – would be one of the Beatles' key legacies to the counterculture.

The Beatles abandoned live performance within months of their beginning to use acid as an inspiration. Other bands, though, used the drug to transform their gigs into dizzying vortexes of visual and aural chaos that mimicked the sensory effects of tripping – and magnified those effects for anyone present who actually had dropped a tab. The results of this new aesthetic free-for-all were not always happy ones. In *Performance*, Donald Cammell and Nicolas Roeg's existential gangster cum psychedelia trip of a movie (which was released in 1971 but shot in the summer of 1968 and actually written during the Summer of Love itself), the zoned-out rock star at the story's centre, Turner (Mick Jagger), delivers himself of the opinion that: 'The only performance that makes it, that really makes it, that makes it all the way, is the one that achieves madness.' By the time of the movie's release, Jagger had made just such a performance – a performance that ended in death when a fan drew a gun and a bouncer, who also happened to be a member of the Hell's Angels motorcycling clan, took him down with a knife.*

Laing himself, it should be said, was somewhat less than pleased at having become identified as the psychedelic psychiatrist to the rock culture. He had never advocated the use of LSD as a lifestyle leisure drug, and when he talked of his wish that people would expand their horizons he meant they should do so in the same way he had done all his life – by reading poetry and philosophy and coming to see that the world might not be as you had been taught it was. No one was listening. Having decided that Laing really had

---

* The venue was the Altamont speedway track in California.

sung the praises of the mad over the sane, his worshippers concluded that he must also have been singing the praises of being bombed over being straight (to use the then trendy term). Before long even his fellow psychiatrists took to referring to Laing disparagingly as the idol of the 'bright young schizophrenics'.[57] Reviewing Laing's 1967 book, *The Politics of Experience* (by some distance his most lyrical and tripped-out work), the *British Journal of Psychiatry* dismissed it as the merest fashionable folderol: 'The authors, like other members of the "squared", older generation, are of the opinion that they know what is best, and this book is not good for [schizophrenic] patients.'[58]

Increasingly, this sceptical viewpoint came to be accepted more broadly, so that even Syd Barrett's long-time friend, the actor and writer David Gale, has come to regret the fact that the post-Laingian boosters of LSD never talked about 'the psychoanalytic implication[s]' of taking a psychotomimetic* drug.[59] All they wanted to hymn, Gale has said, was the drug's 'consciousness-expansion implication ... The idea you would have a bad trip, which would lead to more bad trips, which would unhinge you, was not popular, considered "uncool". [It was] a test of psychedelic manhood ... to take trips, survive and have a great time.'[60] As Barrett's sad example suggests, not everyone had a great time. Some of them, indeed, never survived – and there are those who would count Barrett, who wrote only a handful of songs after acid had its way with him, among their number.

So what survives of R. D. Laing? Not much, though in partial defence it should be said that he did himself few favours in the long-term reputation stakes. Write and sound and look like a visionary though he did in the days of the counterculture, in later years he often enough passed for just another Glaswegian drunk. In 1984, indeed, he was charged with disorderly conduct for hurling a bottle of wine through the window of the Bhagwan Shree

---

* A drug that mimics the effects of psychosis – delusions, hallucinations, etc.

Rajneesh Centre, just round the corner from his Hampstead home. When the police were called, they arrived to find Laing slumped on the pavement outside inveighing against what he called 'the orange wankers'.[61] There were those who thought Laing's dismissal of the Indian guru was prompted by the withering of his own fame. Five years later he was dead of a heart attack at the comparatively young age of sixty-one.

Does that mean, as Rosemary Dinnage has argued, that Laing was a victim of the decade that made his name? That the sixties merely chewed him up and spat him out? That the rest of his life was a struggle to keep up with the revolution he'd helped engender?[62] Was the novelist Doris Lessing (who consulted with him in the early sixties) right when she suggested that Laing's achievement was to have 'challenged extreme rigidities in psychiatry with alternate viewpoints and made more attitudes than the official ones possible. That is what he did. No more and no less.'?[63] Was Laing himself right when he wrote in his memoir that 'Fifteen years of study and research into wisdom, madness and folly have left me, it seems, none the wiser.'?[64]

Certainly at the medical level Laing is nowhere these days. As David Ingleby has remarked, 'British psychiatry trundles on as if [Laing] had never existed.'[65] For all the acolytes he won, there is no Laingian school of psychiatric thought and practice. Which is hardly surprising given that his claim that schizophrenia was the product of familial tensions and therefore insusceptible of chemical treatment has been thoroughly disproven. Subject to outrage at the time of their first utterance, such claims are now seen as the merest fantasy by the more biologically oriented psychiatrists of today. These days, genetics is all. And with reason. Heartfelt though Laing's ideas were, there is no gainsaying the fact that schizophrenia is best treated with the right drugs.

Perhaps unsurprisingly, Laing's reputation has proved rather more enduring among non-psychiatrists. Too often, Laing used to say, empathy was considered a flaw in a psychiatric trainee. And whatever the truth of his theories and treatments, he is still respected for having championed the cause of the mentally ill, for having refused to accept that just because these people behave differently from you and me they are somehow radically incomprehensible to us. Discredited empirically though they might have been, his theories and insights go on offering a valuable corrective to the random acts of violence the insane can be routinely treated to. Laing humanised an often dehumanised field. As Anthony Clare once suggested, he 'put the person back into the patient'.[66] That is a lesson psychiatrists – and other scientists, including political scientists – need constantly to be reminded of.

Because while Laing's theories on schizophrenia have been exploded, his essential shtick hasn't. Although he didn't have an answer for every question, neither do the biological determinists who currently rule the psychiatric roost. Certainly the antidepressants they're happy to dole out aren't always the solution to the trials of life. Why? For the simple reason that even if it could ever be proven that we humans are nothing more than the sum of our chemical and electrical impulses, we would surely go on acting as if we are emotional beings – as if we are something more than machines for living. How could we not? After all, even if you swallow the biological determinism that runs rampant through the contemporary mindset; even if you go along with the notion that your moods and feelings, your likes and dislikes, even your very self (divided or otherwise), are genetically and biochemically determined (and that therefore treating your distress with a pill is not only nothing to be ashamed of but eminently practical); even if you accept all that, who is the 'you' that is the doing the accepting? Is that 'you' merely an expression of biology and chemistry as well?

Or maybe you think it's wrong to find contentment, or at least peace of mind, through the mindless imbibing of chemical concoctions. Maybe you believe happiness is something to be worked for, or that unhappiness is another name for man's estate, and that it is one's duty to endure it. Not many of us fail to mourn the loss of a loved one, after all, and distressing and unpleasant though that mourning is, would you really thank a doctor for saying he could get you through it without the torment if only you'd take some pill?

These aren't questions the biological determinists can answer. If they were to respond, it would only be to say something about the questions not being relevant to biology. They'd say we were making a category error in believing that their field of science was susceptible of such a line of questioning. If they had some philosophical training too, they'd say we were talking metaphysically about matters that are purely physical. Rock-solid empiricists, they'd say we were talking nonsense in its purest sense, in that we aren't making meaningful statements about the world – or even our apprehension of it. They'd say that we've been beguiled by language into believing that we exist. And they might even be right, though the fact that so few of us are willing to accept ourselves as the sum of a bunch of random electro-chemicals suggests they're going to have a hard time getting their message across.

It may follow that the ease with which Laing got his message across is testimony to its simple-mindedness and his charlatanry. Or it may be that Laing's message got through thanks to the beauty of his medium. Regardless of the status of his scientific claims, R. D. Laing was one of the great prose stylists of the sixties, a writer who can hypnotise you into believing anything he says at least for the time it takes to read him – often against your better judgement. As Anthony Clare once said, it was Laing's poetic potency that 'dragged psychiatric illness and those who suffered from it right on to the front cover of newspapers and magazines where they have remained ever since and he gave the most powerful and eloquent of voices to those who until then had been mute in their isolation.'[67]

Thanks to the infantile bleatings of the hippie era that they helped usher in (and to the greed and self-centredness of the Thatcher era to which those bleatings gave birth), as well as to advances in medicine, there is no denying that certain of Laing's ideas have been discredited. But the emotions that underlay them could never be. Laing's heart was in the right place* – and we're in a better place because of it.

---

* Whether the rest of him was is rather more moot. When a letter appeared in the pages of *New Society* magazine purporting to be from one R. D. Laing, its putative author realised at once that he'd been the subject of a hoax. He hadn't written the letter. Alas, when he rang the magazine to tell them that they'd been conned, the man who gave us *The Divided Self* was asked: 'How do you know?' Laing didn't see fit to laugh at that story. Thanks to his example, the rest of us can. (See *R. D. Laing: A Personal View*, Bob Mullan [Duckworth, 1999], p.103)

8

CONDUCT UNBECOMING

In which our heroes find Queen
and Country wanting

'Men love war because it allows them to look serious.
Because it is the one thing that stops women laughing
at them.'

John Fowles, *The Magus*

At 3.30 a.m. one cold morning in February 1965 Harold Wilson rang US President Lyndon Johnson on the intergovernmental 'hot line' to discuss the war in Vietnam. The idea was about that the war, which had been ongoing for the best part of a decade by the time Wilson had come to office, had reached a hinge point. Both sides, it was feared, were ready to up the military stakes. Wilson was calling to tell Johnson that if, as the rumours had it, the Americans were preparing to use nuclear weapons in Vietnam, it might be a good idea for him (Wilson) to fly to Washington to discuss the political logistics. Johnson's answer was short and sour. 'If you want to help us some in Vietnam', he told Wilson, 'send us some men.'[1]

For more than one reason, Wilson couldn't say yes. For starters, it would have been to go against much of what he had said as an up-and-coming MP during the 1950s. Back then Wilson had regularly attacked US foreign policy, especially with relation to its activities in South-East Asia. During the 1954 Geneva Conferences on Indochina, he had argued that 'we must not join with nor in any way encourage the anti-Communist crusade in Asia.'[2] Later that year he had added the thought that 'a settlement is imperilled by the lunatic fringe in the American Senate who want a holy crusade against Communism.'[3]

But there were practical as well as political reasons for Wilson's inability to help Johnson out. With ongoing missions in Malaysia and Rhodesia, Britain's forces were already overstretched. Even had the Wilson government wanted to, it simply didn't have sufficient troops to assign any of them to Vietnam. Despite that, said Wilson's Foreign Secretary Patrick Gordon Walker, given our experiences in South-East Asia, we'd be happy to train US forces in jungle warfare and to help with medical operations. The offer made, he then restated that the country could not commit to putting forces on the ground in Vietnam.[4] Nor, added Wilson, would sending troops to Vietnam 'have been compatible with Britain's position as co-chairman' of the Geneva accords.[5]

And nor would it, though that doesn't mean that Wilson wasn't blustering. The fact was that with his government enjoying only the slenderest of majorities, Wilson wouldn't have committed troops to Vietnam even if he'd wanted to. The Labour Party, which had always been committed to building what it thought of as an international morality (half a century earlier, more than one party luminary – among them Ramsay MacDonald, the man who would go on to become Labour's first prime minister – had opposed Britain involving itself in the First World War), was violently riven over Vietnam. Long host to a pacifist wing, the party numbered many members who saw the war not as part of the West's struggle against communism (as the previous Tory administration had seen it), but as a war of national liberation against Western imperial oppression. And so while according to Britain's then Ambassador in Washington, Sir Patrick Dean, it was 'extremely important from the point of view of American standing with world opinion that the leading socialist-governed country in the world should support their objectives in South-East Asia', the bulk of the members of that socialist government weren't playing ball.[6] Indeed, a hefty number of Labour backbenchers attacked the government whenever it offered even the most minimal verbal support for the US position.

Some of its support was more than verbal. On Wilson's watch, Britain provided technical equipment for Saigon University, police advisers, teachers, technical experts and medical staff. Wilson also ensured that his Conservative predecessors' provision of military training to the South Vietnamese in Malaysia, and of intercepted signals intelligence from Hong Kong, was continued. And as well as providing $US2.4 million in economic aid to South Vietnam, Britain secretly sold arms to the United States for deployment in the war (among them napalm and 500-pound bombs, exported on the quiet from Hong Kong).

It should be said that the need for secrecy arose not merely because of the problems Wilson faced over Vietnam with his party. He faced similar problems with the country as a whole. The bulk of the British people were no more interested in being involved in the war than were the bulk of the Labour party's members. Around two-thirds of Britons thought the war wrong in principle, and almost half of the country thought that America should withdraw from combat. Far from being convinced by the claims made for the threat of international communism, these people believed that if the British government could be made to abandon the Americans, the Americans might abandon Vietnam in turn.*

But if Wilson couldn't bring himself to offer the Americans any active military help in Vietnam, nor did he feel he had the right to condemn them. As he told his Housing Minister, Richard Crossman, nobody should be under any illusions that the United States' 'financial support [of the UK] is not unrelated to the way we behave in the Far East: any direct announcement of our withdrawal, for example, could not fail to have a profound effect on my personal relations with [Johnson].'7 Or as he put it more bluntly to the trade union leader Frank Cousins, who had called Wilson out for what he saw as British subservience to America, 'we can't kick our creditors in the balls.'8 And doubtless we couldn't have, though neither could the tough-guy rhetoric of Wilson's realpolitik disguise the fact that the idea of Great Britain as a great power was now no more than the merest fantasy. The truth was that since the end of the war America had been propping the country up.

If it is to Wilson's credit – and it is – that he never stopped acknowledging that truth, we shouldn't forget that he deserves credit, too, for refusing to acquiesce in the sixties' big lie. The lie was the Domino Theory. The Domino Theory held that if one country fell under communist influence, then its neighbours – like so many tumbling dominos – would be bound to fall, too. This, it was argued, was what was happening in Vietnam, where the communist-ruled North was fighting to take control of the South. Were that to be allowed to happen, the Johnson administration argued, it would be the first step towards the whole region's 'going red'. Well, maybe, though the idea that America's propping-up of

* They were helped to these opinions by the fact that Vietnam was the first war of the television age. You had only to turn the box on during the mid-sixties to be confronted with imagery from this distant, bloody turmoil. Beyond the impressions of naked chaos, it was also easy to notice that America's part in the war was largely being fought by black troops and white officers.

Saigon's patently corrupt Thieu government would prevent South-East Asia from turning communist was the purest fantasy. It was a fantasy that grew out of another one: that the Chinese were set to intervene in Vietnam. No they weren't. The Chinese had neither the manpower nor the money to do more than a little cheerleading. Moreover, a divided Vietnam was less of a threat to a China that was only just beginning to recover from the devastation wrought by its so-called 'Great Leap Forward'. And anyway, the North Vietnamese had no intention of letting themselves be dominated by China.

The truth is that the war in Vietnam was essentially a civil war. Civil wars can be nasty things, as both the Americans and the British had reason to know, but that didn't mean that the West had any kind of right to intervene. The lie, that it did have such a right, resulted in the death of hundreds of thousands of people – 58,000 of them American troops, an unknown but far larger number of them their Vietnamese counterparts, as well as countless civilians. In 1975, ten years after US Marines were first dispatched to South Vietnam, America completed its withdrawal from the country – having achieved precisely none of its military, political or ideological aims.

From comparatively early on in the war, American writers and artists were coming to terms with the dislocating sense of hubris and loss Vietnam signified for their culture. With *Catch-22* and *Slaughterhouse-Five*, Joseph Heller and Kurt Vonnegut respectively cast a weather eye over the chaos engulfing the country. And the putatively mindless violence of so many American movies, from *Bonnie and Clyde* (1967) on, was in many cases precisely the opposite of mindless: violence resolutely mind*ful* of the crisis in confidence an unnecessary war was fuelling (a crisis reflected in so many marches and demonstrations).

Britain's cavils and doubts about the war were, of course, rather less empirical and concrete. For all their horrific repetition, television images of body bags being flown into American airports didn't have the same moral impact here as they did over there. Nonetheless, the fact that the country steered clear of any direct involvement in the war itself didn't prevent British artists from seeing through the Vietnam farrago. From 1965 on, the culture brought forth a slew of novels and movies and TV shows that sought, in far more subtle and serious and searching ways than the fatuous posturing of the counterculture's dopers and dropouts, to dramatise doubts about the war.

The price of this insight was what we might call the death of the hero. In 1956, Jimmy Porter, the lead in John Osborne's *Look Back in Anger*, had moaned that 'There aren't any good brave causes left.' That was before the fiasco of the Suez Crisis had taught the country that had been among those that won the Second World War how powerless it had become amid the peace. Now, in the shadow of Vietnam, and with the memory of the scandalous comedy of the Profumo affair* fresh in the public mind, it was as if the very idea of good brave causes was a nonsense. And without good brave causes, where are good brave heroes to come from? The answer, we learned in 1965 (and have been reminded of ever since), is that they're not going to come from anywhere. There were, we were repeatedly told by novelists and filmmakers that year, no more heroes any more.

In September, just a few months before his death, Evelyn Waugh published his *Sword of Honour Trilogy*, a reworked version of three novels written over the past decade and a half in which he lamented a lost Britain. The books (*Men at Arms*, *Officers and Gentlemen* and *Unconditional Surrender*) tell of the comic misadventures of the

---

* In 1963, at the height of the Cold War, John Profumo, the Secretary of State for War under Macmillan, was obliged to resign his post. In an attempt to cover up a two-year-old affair with Christine Keeler, a call girl who was also sleeping with a senior naval attaché based at London's Soviet embassy, Profumo had lied to the House of Commons. The scandalous comedy was, of course, what really did for him – and in the end for Macmillan.

highly autobiographical Guy Crouchback* during the Second World War, and their theme is that the twentieth-century burgeoning of a technocratic mass culture had annihilated age-old traditions of class-based courage and virtue. Not for nothing do the Crouchbacks – one of England's most ancient Catholic families – live in a house called Broome: for they know that once the war is over a new broom will be coming, a broom that will sweep them into the dustbin of history. Hence, the books suggest, it no longer follows that gentlemen make the best officers – and much less that officers are axiomatically gentlemen.

Waugh himself had done a good deal to prove this last point during his own war service. The black comedy of his own days in the military matched anything to be found in his pre-war novels. 'Everyone thinks meanly of himself for not having been a soldier,' said Dr Johnson, and despite having spent the bulk of his life thinking meanly of others Waugh was no exception to the rule. Not that he was a shoo-in for the army. Corpulent, half blind, and in his wheezy mid-thirties by the time the war broke out, he was no one's idea of soldierly material. Still, no less a figure than Churchill was impressed by the courage of Waugh's ambition to serve, and pulled a few strings in order to get him over the necessary hurdles.[9] The doctor who examined him passed a blind eye over his alarming medical report, and passed another over Waugh's own eyesight arguing that it didn't matter that he could barely see because most of what he'd be up to 'will be in the dark'.[10]

Nor did Waugh much look the part. As his friend Lady Mary Pakenham once remarked, he 'was one of the few people who was not made more distinguished-looking by wearing uniform'. But there is looking the part, and there is acting it, and Waugh acted it atrociously, contriving to be both loathed by the 'little boys'[11] in his

* Guy's wartime mishaps and cock-ups are in many cases identical with Waugh's own.

charge and despised by the officers above him who found him as rude and insubordinate as any turtle-necked peacenik of the fifties or long-haired sixties hippie.

He was uncaring, too. In May 1941, when Waugh's unit sailed into Crete's bombed-out Souda Bay aboard HMS *Abdiel*, they were confronted by what one of his biographers calls 'a vision of hell'[12] – abandoned vehicles and stores, sunken ships, ships on fire, wounded men and corpses here, there and everywhere. Once the *Abdiel* was docked, a soldier, deranged with terror and wearing nothing but shorts under his greatcoat, climbed on board. At first, says Waugh, 'We took this to be an exceptionally cowardly fellow', an insult not at all softened by his subsequent realisation that the poor man 'was typical of British forces on the island'.[13] Seven decades on, one would still like to put Waugh on a charge for insolence.

'I know that one goes into war for reasons of honour and soon finds oneself called on to do very dishonourable things,' Waugh had written to his wife Laura a year or so earlier.[14] Doubtless so, though in Waugh's case so many of the dishonourable things needn't have been said or done. Certainly it would be foolish to say that the *Sword of Honour Trilogy* in anyway atones for Waugh's vile behaviour during – and not only during – the war. Still, there is something to the suggestion that by transforming the insubordinate ugliness of his military career into the joyous comic antics of the trilogy, Waugh went some way towards making up for his otherwise dis-astrous service.

On the other hand, it is hard to forgive Waugh's suggestion in *Sword of Honour* that far from offering his country an opportunity for chest-beating pride, Britain's victory in the war (characteristically, he did not see it as a victory by and for the Allies) was in fact a cause for rue and regret. That victory, he believed, had prompted Britain to lay waste to a glorious past in favour of a glib present and in prospect of a glum egalitarian future. It was almost as if things might have been better had Hitler won. Britain's noble sacrifice, Waugh came to argue, had in reality been no more than a sacrifice of nobility. As Guy's unnamed Italian host says to him on the final page of the trilogy, 'For a chap who's on his way home you don't seem very cheerful.' But then, as far as Guy – and Waugh – was concerned, he wasn't: home no longer was home. For Guy, Waugh noted in the 'Synopsis of Preceding Volumes' he inserted at the start of the 1965 version of *Unconditional Surrender* in the trilogy, 'the just cause of going to war [had] been forfeited in the Russian alliance'.[15]

At least in fictional terms, this was a minority opinion that year. While it would be an exaggeration to say that many of the novels and films released in 1965 took precisely the opposite view to Waugh, it is certainly the case that there were plenty of writers willing to entertain the notion that the Cold War was a war that afforded none of its combatants anything by way of moral certainty. One of the comic engines of *Unconditional Surrender* was the frequency with which Guy Crouchback's scapegrace antics resulted in his being taken for a spy. It was a lovely joke, though by the time Waugh's reworked trilogy came out Guy looked about as mysterious and shady as a baby in a pram.

For 1965 was the year it became clear that nobody, whether officer or gentlemen, could withstand the chill blast of the Cold War. The bungle and muddle Waugh had so gleefully recorded in the fight against Nazism were as nothing when set against the malignant incompetence novelists and filmmakers were dramatising in the battles of the here and now. There was, we were told over and over again in the year's predominant genre of the spy thriller, no honour to be found in these battles – and what had once been an arena for the representation of unflinching loyalty and patriotism became, instead, a metaphor for duplicity and sedition.*

---

* Dozens of them were released or published. So predominant was the form that in October 1965 even that acerbic satirist Muriel Spark published a spy novel, *The Mandelbaum Gate*.

So much so that even that diehard reactionary Ian Fleming seems to have realised the chivalrous game was up. For a decade and more Fleming's fictional spy James Bond had been an almost pathologically nationalistic hero. So loyal was he to his commanding officer, M, that five years earlier, in the short story 'For Your Eyes Only', he had flown of his own volition to America with the intention of killing a man who had slaughtered some of M's friends. A few years before that, during a transatlantic telephone conversation in *Live and Let Die*, Fleming had written of 'the cold voice that Bond loved and obeyed'.

And here Bond was, in 1965, in what would turn out to be Fleming's last novel, *The Man With the Golden Gun*, neither loving nor obeying but druggily hallucinating like some bombed-out hippie – and fittingly keen to show how his espionage 'skills could be used in the cause of peace' if only the 'warmongers were eliminated'.[16] Chief among these last, it turns out, is the former father figure himself. And so, like Goldfinger and Dr No before him, M finds himself staring down the barrel of Bond's pistol. Fifty years on it is startling how much dramatic impact this moment of Oedipal crisis retains. Even the devil-may-care Bond that Sean Connery had for the past couple of years being bodying forth on movie screens around the world would have thought such insolence a touch de trop. But for the Bond of Fleming's previous novels, drawing a bead on the old man would have been akin to burning the carvings on the rood screen.

Bond being Bond, of course, he was soon enough back on the straight and narrow. And so for your genuinely insurrectionary secret agent anti-hero you had to look elsewhere.

Palmer: 'Er . . . is that my B107, sir?'
Colonel Ross: 'As if you didn't know. And it makes awful reading, Palmer. You just love the army, don't you?'
Palmer: 'Yes, sir, I just love the army [pause], sir.'

Thus Harry Palmer, the down-at-heel yet defiantly bumptious pro-
tagonist of *The Ipcress File*. By contrast with the hero of the average
spy movie or novel, Palmer was a joshing Cold War cynic who, like
the Michael Caine who incarnated him on screen, was unashamedly
on the make. A cashiered NCO with a shady past that allowed his
superiors to strong-arm him into work he would otherwise avoid,
Palmer was a man with no sense of moral rectitude, a hero who
believed heroism was for fools, a spy resolutely unconvinced that
Queen and Country come first. Unlike James Bond – who even in
Connery's effortlessly insurrectionary version was in no doubt that
he believed in his job because he believed that England was automatically in the right – Caine's Palmer made no bones about the fact
that he was out for himself and nothing but. Hence when, at the
end of *The Ipcress File*, he guns down his boss, he does so not
because the latter has been betraying his country but simply because,
as Palmer puts it, 'you used me.'

The Ipcress File made a star of Caine who became British culture's
ur-sixties icon of chippy outsiderdom. Indeed, Caine's presence in
Ipcress and it successors (*Funeral in Berlin* and *Billion Dollar Brain*)
worked to democratise the spying game. As the son of a navvy
turned truck driver, Sean Connery had undoubtedly brought a ple-
beian whiff to the movie take on Ian Fleming's patrician hero, but
Connery Bond's pleasures were still those of the high-living original – fine wines and languorous lunches. Harry Palmer's tastes were
somewhat down the scale – home-cooked omelettes, tinned mush-
rooms, mugs of tea. James Bond gave traction to the consumerist
fantasies of the sixties – effortless sex with sun and sand thrown in
for good measure. Harry Palmer chugged along on the down-at-
heel reality of post-imperial Britain. Like many a hero of sixties
British movies, he got around on London's red buses.

Not so Caine himself, a poor boy from the Elephant and Castle
who took great pleasure in the riches international stardom
brought him. Even today, half a century on, he can still be relied

upon to relate the story of how the manager of the Rolls-Royce showroom in Mayfair laughed at the Cockney upstart who came in wanting to buy one of his motors. Nothing daunted, Caine took himself off to another garage, bought the car he wanted and promptly drove back to the first showroom, raising two fingers at the manager as he passed. Did things really happen that way? We'll never know for sure. There can, though, be no doubt that within a year of the release of *The Ipcress File*, Caine was living high on the hog, yards from the US Embassy, in one of Grosvenor Square's grandest apartments. And while it is true that another year on Britain's new superstar steered studiously clear of the violent anti-Vietnam protests that made his new address more famous than ever, it is no less true that the suggestively subversive example of Caine's Harry Palmer had helped to make those protests possible.

But *The Ipcress File* was also the movie that began to open up the secret agent figure and his once sententious certainties to existential doubt and dread. Harry Palmer might not have been as culpable as the villains he was up against, but nor was he at all certain that what he was doing was all that defensible. There was no moral high ground in Palmer's version of the spying game, and from now on no fictional spy could be sure that what he was doing was axiomatically right and good.* Hence the fact that that year's Bond movie, *Thunderball*, was the first entry in the series to function solely as a technoporn fantasy. Unlike its predecessors, this was a film that had no purchase, however distant, on reality. One way or another, the first three Bond pictures, *Dr. No*, *Goldfinger* and especially *From Russia With Love*, had been able to claim some relationship to the goings on of the real world. (Scrape away his shiny

---

* It might be objected that Graham Greene had dramatised something similar in 1958's *Our Man in Havana*. But Greene was essentially a comic writer. He had none of the righteous indignation of the novelists under discussion.

patina and even that arch fantasist Auric Goldfinger was just a smuggler turned heist merchant.) Not so *Thunderball*, which began the Bond series' decline into hardware worship. Barely a minute of the picture goes by without some ludicrous gizmo or other being pressed into service.*

We have touched elsewhere on the use the movie's pre-credit sequence makes of both a military jet pack and – such a hit in *Goldfinger* – Bond's Aston Martin DB5, this time kitted out with a whole new arsenal of gadgets. And yet, these opening moments aside, Bond does very little driving in *Thunderball* – a worrisome synecdoche for a movie in which our patently bored hero is chauffeured around from one set-piece to another in order that he might react to whatever gargantuan gewgaw is now being passed in front of him. Far from being the man in charge, James Bond is here the man being told what to do by a series of mechanised inanities. 'We've reached the limit as far as size and gimmicks are concerned,' a characteristically astute Sean Connery told an interviewer during the shoot. 'We have to be careful where we go next ... What is needed now is a change of course – more attention to character and better dialogue.'[16]

He might have been talking about John le Carré's 1965 novel, *The Looking Glass War*, or Martin Ritt's *The Spy Who Came in from the Cold*, a movie based on le Carré's previous hit thriller of 1963. Certainly nobody coming to these two stories should do so in expectation of non-stop adventure. A great deal of both their narratives is taken up with philosophical debates on the finer points of the morality of spying. Of guns and gadgets there is no sign. What little action there is in *The Spy Who Came in from the Cold* is to be found in the scene in which its drunken hero, Alec Leamas, contrives to behave so badly that he is thrown into jail.

---

* Only fair to point out that for all its tedium, the fourth Bond movie turned out to be the biggest money-spinner in the series.

Quite why Leamas wants to be in jail need not detain us. Sufficient to say that the machinations of le Carré's double- and triple-crossed plot require all manner of betrayal and bluff and counter-bluff. It is not long before the reader is lost in this fictional maze. Which is exactly the point. By making us unsure of what is going on and uncertain of who we can trust, le Carré is ensuring that his readers come to know the moral and metaphysical quicksand his spies are forever crossing within what is left of their soul.* The spymasters, meanwhile, are exposed as mere pullers of puppet strings, players of games in which nothing save the odd human life is at stake. As Leamas asks his girlfriend, 'What do you think spies are: priests, saints, martyrs? They're a squalid procession of vain fools, traitors, too, yes; pansies, sadists and drunkards, people who play cowboys and Indians to brighten up their rotten lives.'[17]

He knew of what he spoke. While Sean Connery's James Bond was necking Martinis at the Nassau Junkanoo in *Thunderball*, the Leamas of Ritt's picture (Richard Burton) was to be found foraging for battered tins of bully beef in a run-down corner shop. The world inhabited by le Carré's characters – heroes they most decidedly aren't – is a dank and drab one, its shoddiness redolent not just of communist dystopia but the privations of home-grown post-war austerity too. When Leamas flies back to London at the start of the novel, even the landscape of the garden of England is described as 'the grey-green fields of Kent'.[18] Subtract the green and you have director of photography Oswald Morris's vision of Cold War Europe in Ritt's take on *The Spy Who Came in from the Cold*.

Just as Michael Caine's presence in the film version of *The Ipcress File* had democratised the world of international espionage, so le

---

* Le Carré had worked for MI5 and MI6 during the fifties and sixties, so may reasonably be supposed to have been writing about what he knew.

Carré's attentiveness to the textures of lived experience humanised it. There are no goodies and baddies in *The Spy Who Came in from the Cold*. The novel is careful never to take sides, and even Ritt's movie version of it, which, thanks to the populist strictures of cinema, might have been expected to come down harder on the evils of the East, remains scrupulously even-handed. It is true that the presence of the 34-year-old Claire Bloom as Leamas's communist girlfriend, Nan Perry, adds a touch of glamour; but as played by Bloom – numb and affectless – Nan is hardly a point of identification for the audience.

Much less does the casting of Richard Burton as Leamas mean we instinctively think of him as a hero. Rather, Burton's notorious off-screen presence as a shambling drunkard – concretised here in those beer-bleary eyes and that pumice-stone complexion – ensure we feel rather less pity for Leamas's tumble into alcoholism than we otherwise might. (Like the real-life Burton, Leamas is at the bottle from the moment he wakes up.) Meanwhile, Burton's magnificent contempt for what he always saw as the farcical business of thespianism helps us remain stolidly unmoved when it is revealed that Leamas's own theatrics have all along been part of a grander sham performance. Spies, le Carré makes plain, are actors playing parts, and the casting of Burton – who a few years earlier had been one of the greatest Hamlets of his generation – points up the self-loathing at the heart of the spying game.

Exposing sham performances was what le Carré was about, of course. A silky yet severe moralist, he had no time for the adolescent fantasies the spy thriller genre traditionally turned out. Certainly he had no time for the antics of James Bond, who, he said, existed in a world far removed from reality where he 'spends what he likes, keeps a stable of cars, fornicates by proxy for six million commuters. He is indifferent to pain (particularly other people's), and is fortunate in one respect: the nearer he gets to the enemy, the more horrible the enemy becomes.'[19] Not so le Carré's protagonists, who get nearer to the enemy the nearer they get to the mirror.*

The Looking Glass War (1965) took an even more twisted view of the world of espionage. On their own terms at least, the chess-move antics of *The Spy Who Came in from the Cold* made a kind of sense. Not so those of *The Looking Glass War*, a novel which abandons its predecessor's faith in the idea that spies of whatever hue might know what they're up to. Instead, it takes the view that none of them has a clue what they're doing. Or, rather, that all they're doing is amusing themselves with private yet deadly entertainments. *The Looking Glass War* might have been named after a novel aimed at children but it is very much a novel for adults.† What heroics there are here are patently fanciful. As le Carré writes of the very Bond-style training programme his game-playing spymasters put their latest puppet hero through, 'the first day ended, setting the pattern for the days that followed: carefree, exciting days for them both, days of honest labour and cautious but deepening attachment as the skills of boyhood became once more the weapons of war'.[20] Carefree, exciting, boyhood – far from fighting a battle for the forces of good, le Carré's men are engaged in nothing more than schoolboy tomfoolery. What is worse, they know it.

Hence the mournful mood that hangs over the novel's none-too fictional agency (anonymously named The Department), its members vying with each other over ministerial favours – bigger budgets, rides in limos, etc. Hence, too, the fact that its operatives,

---

* This Pirandelloesque conceit was taken to the highest pitch by the first-time novelist Derek Marlowe, who was labouring on his debut, *A Dandy in Aspic*, as *The Looking Glass War* was published. (Though written in 1965, Marlowe's novel wasn't actually published until May 1966.) The novel tells of a British Intelligence agent, Alexander Eberlin, who is tasked with tracking down and assassinating a Russian spy called Krasnevin. There's just one problem: Eberlin is a double agent and is in reality the man he has been told to kill.
† Rather more adult, in fact, than the aforementioned *The Mandelbaum Gate*. As Angus Wilson pointed out in his *Observer* review of *The Looking Glass War*, le Carré's novel was a far more serious work than Muriel Spark's novel.

nostalgic for the certainties of earlier wars, are desperate to convince themselves that a cache of out-of-focus twelve by nine photos really do show that the East Germans are setting up a secret rocket base. They *need* these to be pictures of concealed weapons in order to justify their own and The Department's existence. 'You could see it if you looked quickly,' le Carré's anonymous narrator notes when confronted with one of these blurry snaps. 'Something hid in the disintegrating shadows; but keep looking and the dark closed in and the shape was gone. Yet something was there; the muffled form of a gun barrel.'[21] Seek and ye shall find whatever you want to find . . . Picasso used to say that the camouflage techniques used on warships and tanks and uniforms during the First and Second World Wars owed a great deal to the illusionistic techniques he had developed in his cubist period.[22] John le Carré, by contrast, paints the Cold War as a kind of Bridget Riley abstract – an image that projects evanescent, and perhaps imaginary, patterns onto the retinas of people bent on seeing what they want to see.* Hence Leclerc, the spymaster who hands out those glossy twelve by nines, is 'smiling a little' as he does so, 'like a man looking at his own reflection'.[23] Which, of course, he is. Like the White Queen of Lewis Carroll's *Alice Through the Looking Glass*, Leclerc is someone capable of believing 'six impossible things before breakfast'.

But if spying came across as little more than childish posturing in le Carré, it seemed nothing less than playful pointlessness in the 1965 season of *The Avengers*. It wasn't that there was nothing to choose between the goodies and the baddies in the fourth season of what had hitherto been a standard-issue espionage thriller series. It was that there was no clue given as to what the goodies represented, much less what they wanted to achieve. Though our heroes,

* A few months later, Michelangelo Antonioni would come to London to shoot *Blow-Up*, a movie whose entire plot revolves around le Carré's idea of self-serving image-reading. For more on the picture see Chapter 10.

John Steed (Patrick Macnee) and Emma Peel (Diana Rigg) are in theory secret agents attached to some undercover government ministry, the plots they find themselves tangled in have no relation to anything going on in the real world. Rather, they are motiveless, Kafkaesque traps in which unseen powers are bent not – *à la* the villains of the Bond movies – on world domination, nor – *à la* both sides of the Cold War in le Carré's novels – on minuscule triumphs of one-upmanship, but merely on bending Steed and (more particularly) the lustrously leather-clad Mrs Peel to their will for the purpose of some kinky, camped-up thrills. Of ideas of right and wrong there is no sight – which means that as a metaphor for the air of chaotic amorality that hung about the Vietnam War the show couldn't be bettered.

The Avengers hadn't started out like this. When the show had launched, some four years earlier, it was as a straight-down-the-line meat-and-potatoes actioner. Back then it starred Ian Hendry as Dr David Keel, a man determined to avenge the murder of his fiancée at the hands of a drug-smuggling ring. Along the way, he teamed up with John Steed (Patrick Macnee), an undercover agent for a shadowy, unnamed organisation. As the series progressed, though, it became more and more interested in Steed and less and less in Keel – less and less interested, that is, in the character whose motivation for vengeance was plausible and realistic, and more and more focused on the character whose involvement in crime solving was (however enigmatically) professional.

For all its increasing emphasis on cowboys-and-indians style action, though, that first series of *The Avengers* remained down-to-earth in its design and concerns. Steed and Keel both sported the belted trenchcoats private eye figures had been wearing since Humphrey Bogart's turn as Philip Marlowe in *The Big Sleep* (1946). And none of the misdemeanours our heroes were called upon to oversee would have troubled Marlowe over much. Over the course of their twenty-six-week run, the Avengers found themselves pitted against an assortment of more or less commonplace forgers, black-mailers, smugglers, kidnappers – the staples of a thousand movies and TV shows before and since.

Things began to change in the second season. Hendry, ambitious for stage and film work, left the show, and his character was replaced – at least in some episodes – by that of Cathy Gale (Honor Blackman). A martial arts adept fond of leatherwear, Miss Gale was a far remove from the suburban naturalism of Dr Keel. More than that, though, she was a new kind of TV heroine – a woman who could hold her own in male company, and hold that same company down on the floor in a judo grip should the need arise. This wasn't, it should be said, because of any radical beliefs about sexual politics on the part of *The Avengers'* (almost wholly male) writing and production team. Rather, it was because the constraints of budgeting meant that scripts that had been written for Hendry to play were not changed one jot when they were thrust into Blackman's hands instead. Her tough-guy dialogue was just that – dialogue written for a guy whose job it was to seem tough.[24]

Not that Cathy Gale was the iconoclastic emblem she is often claimed to have been. While it is true that Honor Blackman wasn't actually a graduate of the Rank Charm School (she had in fact attended the Guildhall School of Music and Drama), nor is there any denying that her acting style owed a great deal to that factory for the production of nice middle-class gels. Like the Charmers proper, Blackman's posture was never less than perfect, her vowels never cut from any but the purest crystal. (For her sixteenth birthday, Blackman has let it be known, her father had offered her either a bicycle or elocution lessons. There are no prizes for guessing which option she went for.[25]) All of which is a way of saying that Cathy Gale looked backwards as well as forwards. Though she had been created as a compound of the cultural anthropologist Margaret Mead (Gale's husband, a Kenyan farmer, had been killed in the Mau Mau rising: like Dr David Keel, she too had cause for feeling vengeful), the *Life* magazine snapper Margaret Bourke-White, and that definitive Hitchcock blonde Grace Kelly, the fact was that the seductively husky-voiced Blackman was so sultrily sexy that it was only the Kelly accretions that stuck. Handle herself well in a fight though she might, there was no getting away from the fact that at heart Cathy was just another cracker.

Certainly she wasn't the bra-burning suffragette of sixties legend. As one critic pointed out at the time, Blackman's Gale was 'all bosom and black leather' and she 'herald[ed] the coming of the Swinging Dolly' quite as much as she inaugurated any notion of girl power.[26] Liberated and independent Cathy may have been, but as a certain future female prime minister might have told her, liberty and independence aren't the same thing as signing up to a programme of radical feminism. *Pace* Patrick Macnee's insightful suggestion that *The Avengers*' essential subversion rested on the fact that 'I was the woman and she was the man',[27] Cathy's independence went only so far. She had been married – and likely would have remained so had her husband not been killed.

Something of the same went for Emma Peel, the heroine invented to replace Cathy when Miss Blackman went on to grander things (playing Pussy Galore in the third Bond movie, *Goldfinger*). She too was married, this time to a man presumed dead after the plane he was flying had gone missing somewhere over the Amazon rainforest. In other words, those feminists who have claimed Mrs Peel as one of their own are slightly wide of the mark.[28] If anything, she was a post-feminist before the fact – a woman who lived in a world in which men neither ordered her about nor lusted after her. (Nor, in the John Wyndham-inspired *Avengers* episode 'Man-Eater of Surrey Green', do they look askance as she sinks a pint of ale in the taproom of the local pub.)

Because while it goes without saying that Diana Rigg was no less easy on the eye than Honor Blackman, one of the many weird things about *The Avengers* was how little it traded, in narrative terms at least, on the beauty of its stars. Indeed, according to Patrick Macnee, baffled network executives were pressing for Steed to get it together with his lovely assistant/s all through the series's run.[29] He never did.* And so, while viewers at home were free to fantasise about being tumbled around by Rigg, none of the men Emma Peel met in the course of her adventures ever remarked on her looks, never mind came on to her. To be sure, the RADA-trained and Royal Shakespeare Company-experienced Rigg has a way of making Emma so imperious, so haughtily unapproachable, that she's almost beyond sexiness.† Still, you'd think that someone would give this belle dame sans merci the up and down – if only because she spends so much of the time wearing next to nothing.

True, in one episode Emma shows off her judo skills while wearing a tweedy two-piece that, adjusted for fit, wouldn't look out of place on Margaret Rutherford's Miss Marple. Elsewhere, though, she wears the briefest of mini-skirts or skin-tight jumpsuits cut either from leather or (after the show abandoned monochrome for colour photography‡) from Crimplene. These last, incidentally, boast semicircular, cut-out side panels specially designed to show off the extravagant swell of hip over which so many villains are thrown. A few years after Rigg quit the show, the theatre critic John Simon vilified her for stripping off midway through a Broadway production of Ronald Millar's *Abelard and Heloise* and exposing to the world what he called a body 'built, alas, like a brick basilica with

---

* Although at the end of season five, when Emma's husband Peter showed up to take her off to her new life (after Rigg quit the show), he turned out to be a dead-ringer for John Steed. He was, of course, played by Macnee.

† Four years before joining *The Avengers* she had played Bianca in an RSC production of *The Taming of the Shrew*. Good though one imagines Vanessa Redgrave was in the title role, one can't help thinking the future Mrs Emma Peel would have given her a run for her money . . .

‡ Colour is more challenging to light and shoot, and the reflective surface of leather makes it more challenging still.

inadequate flying buttresses'.[30] Each to his own, though Rigg's doffing off as Heloise was hardly much of an exposure. Anyone who'd followed her antics in *The Avengers* had seen almost as much in every episode in which she appeared.

Indeed, 'The Girl From Auntie' opens with a shot of Emma leaning leggily on her Lotus Elan, dressed only in the scantiest of bikinis. From here on in though, Roger Marshall's script works to subvert every sexist stereotype the conventional thriller deals in. Moments later, we cut to a shot of a little old lady bicycling down a country lane – though she soon turns out to be a far cry from the beneficent icon hymned in Orwell's 'The Lion and the Unicorn'. After seeing her fall off her bike, Emma comes to the assistance of this putative sweetie – and for her favours is rewarded with an injection from the hypodermic needle the old lady has been concealing about her person. Our heroine, it transpires, is being kidnapped and held for auction to the highest bidder – though not for her beauty. As the auctioneer has it, Emma is 'A most desirable acquisition. I understand that she carries most of the dispositions of Western defence bases in her head, is a cypher expert of no mean ability, and would be a splendid addition to any intelligence system.' Some guys have all the luck.

Steed, meanwhile, has been away on holiday, and on his return finds an imposter in Mrs Peel's apartment. She turns out to be Georgie Price-Jones, a thespian hopeful the baddies have hired to impersonate Emma but who otherwise has no idea what she's got herself involved in. So far, so ordinary, because Georgie is played by Liz Fraser – an actress second only to Barbara Windsor in the sixties' big-bosomed dumb blonde stakes. But as Steed asks for her help in rescuing Mrs Peel, Georgie turns out to be a fast learner, hurling hoodlums through the air even as she reads how to do so from Mrs Peel's self-defence manual. (Emma, she says to herself, 'must have some very aggressive boyfriends'.) By the end of the episode, she is knocking villains out with a single blow while Steed makes to rescue Mrs Peel. Still wearing nothing but that bikini, Emma turns out to have been held prisoner in an oversized aviary. 'No cracks', she cautions Steed, 'about birds and gilded cages.'

Punning brainbox beauties, murderous old ladies, ditzy dolly birds capable of transforming themselves into fighting machines – given the existence of *The Avengers* you wonder how much Kate Millett and Germaine Greer had to do. (Hilariously, none of this proto-feminism obtained in the show's real, off-set world. One of the reasons so many of the episodes were dominated by the female of the Avenger species was that Patrick Macnee's contract allowed him rather more holidays than his co-stars. Macnee was paid rather more per episode than Rigg, too, though she was less troubled by this than by her discovery, part-way through her first series, that she was being paid £30 a week less than the cameraman.)[31]

Nor was the emphasis on girl power all that made the fourth season of *The Avengers* revolutionary. As we have seen, all through the Honor Blackman years, the intrigues our intrepid duo found themselves involved in remained those of the run-of-the-mill cop show – kidnappings, thefts, murders, etc. Not so once Mrs Peel arrived on the scene. Gone, now, were the nods to psychological realism (unlike her predecessor, Mrs Peel wasn't bent on any kind of vengeance: as far as she was concerned international espionage was no more than a joshing lark). Gone, too, the common-or-garden crooks and their down-to-earth plots.

In their place was, well, what? It is hard to say. Far from being just another humdrum spy series, the 1965 season of *The Avengers* was a lunatic delight – a Magritte-like cocktail of the bucolic and the psychedelic, of the scientific and the romantic, in which the pop-art-costumed Mrs Peel and the increasingly Edwardian-garbed Steed surreptitiously introduced the mass British audience to the spaced-out, hallucinatory delights of the burgeoning drug culture. At the end of one episode, the Robert Banks-Stewart scripted 'Quick-Quick Slow Death', Mrs Peel tells Steed that the police have 'just arrested a band leader for being drunk in charge of a pram containing a man in full evening dress with a plaster cast on his head, tattooed on his right wrist, clutching a dance diploma in one hand and a garlic sausage in the other'. People have come down from acid trips with less to report.

Greil Marcus once said that the fugitive timelessness of Bob Dylan's *Basement Tapes* served as a map to the communal imaginary of 'the old, weird America'.[32] From 1965 on, *The Avengers* offered viewers a way into the new, weird England. To be sure, the show served up the imagery of Orwell's 'England Your England' – the England of narrow country lanes, of farmyards and church spires, of cricket on the village green and pubs in which nobs mix with yobs and yet everyone knows their place. This is the England of Tory Party conferences, the England of Ealing comedy and Gainsborough melodrama (surely, you find yourself thinking throughout the series, these are the same sets in which James Mason and Margaret Lockwood had at each other in *The Man in Grey* and *The Wicked Lady*). 'The England', the writer and executive producer of *The Avengers* Brian Clemens once said, 'of "Is there honey still for tea?" that people imagine existed even if it didn't.'[33]

And, of course, it didn't – or hadn't, at least, since the Industrial Revolution, as the show slyly acknowledged. Witness the lengthy scene in 'The Grave Diggers' set inside a train carriage that is travelling past one pastoral idyll after another. Except that it isn't: the landscape imagery is painted on a cyclorama, to whose existence the camera keeps alerting us in a series of Brechtian backstage cuts. For the England of *The Avengers* is an England, too, of jarring events and inexplicable juxtapositions, an England in which the realist iconography of the conventional thriller is abandoned for a repertoire of altogether more disturbing imagery.

Take 'Town of No Return', the first show in the 1965 season. The paraphernalia of Brian Clemens's storyline, which is about murderous spies hiding out in submarines off the coast of England, can be traced back to the Edwardian derring-do cum realpolitik of John Buchan's *The Thirty-Nine Steps* and Erskine Childers's *The Riddle of the Sands*. But whereas Childers and Buchan's prose is forever out to convince you of the reality of the intrigues it depicts, 'Town of No Return' announces right from the off that it has nothing at all to do with the real world. In its opening shots we see a fisherman, all beard and peaked cap and chunky cable-knit sweater, at work on his nets. Then we watch with him as he sees what can best be described as a large black plastic bin-liner walking out of the sea. Once on shore, the creature doing the walking pierces the bin-liner from inside and peels it off to reveal . . . a city gent in country gear – all chequered trilby and felt waistcoat, with a brolly ready to use as a walking stick hanging from a button on his jacket. What on earth was going on?

It's not as if these scenes (which might be thought to echo the opening moments of *Goldfinger*, in which Sean Connery's James Bond made his entrance by climbing out of the sea dressed in scuba gear and with a plastic duck attached to his head) are being played for laughs. Rather, they are played with the insouciant straightness of one of those Magrittes in which we take it for granted that streets can be dark even as the sun beats down on them, that mirrors can reflect not just what is in front of them but what isn't, that men in suits and bowler hats can have apples for heads – or even faces that float free of their bodies. Indeed, there is a Magritte canvas, *The Man of the Sea*, 1927, which, with its wooden-headed, rubber-clad figure standing aggressively on a beach in front of an incongruously sited marble fireplace, might be a blueprint for 'Town of No Return's surreal opening.

The weirdness is compounded a few minutes later when, on a train bound for that seaside village, Steed offers Mrs Peel a cup of tea – and proceeds to produce a full tea set, complete with kettle and cake-stand, from his carpet bag. And it is compounded yet more by the fact that Mrs Peel doesn't so much as blink at this vision of absurdist whimsy. Then again, how could she? After all, she is wearing, in this fusty, tweedy, bowler-hatted world, a glossy, vinyl beret whose pop-art-style target design might have been borrowed from Gerald Laing's painting of *Brigitte Bardot* (1962). And we know from the previous scene that the door to her apartment is adorned with a foot-wide model of Salvador Dalí's *The Eye* (1945) – an eye that she can 'open' and peer through whenever anyone has rung the bell. (Not that Steed's apartment is any more of a home to the rational and logical. The end of the second episode in the series, 'The Murder Market', takes place in his lounge, wherein Mrs Peel is lying on the sofa oom-pah-pahing on a trombone while Steed himself is standing on the dining table sporting plus-fours and teeing-off golf balls. They might be auditioning for a new Dada show at the Cabaret Voltaire.)

At the start of this fourth season of *The Avengers* the Dadaist fancies were confined to the show's design, fashion and iconography. In 'The Gravediggers' we see statues being ministered to by robot surgeons – Lautreamont's operating table come to life. In 'A Surfeit of H$_2$O' we see Mrs Peel pour herself tea while sheltering under an umbrella – in a farmhouse kitchen. In 'Small Game for Big Hunters' Steed and Mrs Peel venture into a tropical jungle that inexplicably transpires to be tucked away in deepest Hertfordshire. In 'Too Many Christmas Trees' Steed finds himself being cackled at by a monstrous, masked Santa Claus. This last incident takes place amid a stylised forest of cardboard cut-out Christmas trees on a set that is an unashamed copy of those designed by Salvador Dalí for Alfred Hitchcock's *Spellbound* (1945).

But *The Avengers* only got more aggressively Dada as the series went on, and the writers and producers gained in confidence, and the stories themselves became increasingly weird. By the middle of the season the show had abandoned pretty much all pretence of being in the espionage thriller game. Instead, it was as close as popular television drama has ever got to acknowledging the lessons of modernism. For this series about international intrigue was actually engaged in a little subterfuge of its own – smuggling the subversive mechanisms and meanings of the avant-garde into the heart of a mainstream entertainment. It would be an exaggeration to say that without the arch modernity of *The Avengers* the Beatles would have been unlikely to conceive and record, say, *Sgt. Pepper's Lonely Hearts Club Band*. Still, there is no formal invention to be found on that album that is not prefigured in Steed and Mrs Peel's adventures of 1965.

Not that *The Avengers'* middle period boasted any formal inventions of its own. While the show's stories and imagery and overall aesthetic were revolutionary as far as the television was concerned, they would have looked very familiar to anyone who had kept up with the so-called *nouvelle vague* in recent European cinema. If the grainy montage of *The Avengers'* jump-cut credit sequence plainly owed a lot to the self-consciously abrasive editing Jean-Luc Godard had used in movies like *A bout de souffle*, so too did so much of the show's approach to character construction. Even *Alphaville*, which opened in May 1965 just as the scripts for the fourth series of *The Avengers* were being drafted, allowed its hero, Peter Cheyney's private eye Lemmy Caution, rather more by way of motivation than Steed and Emma were granted. In other words, *The Avengers* actually upped Godard's radical ante. Indeed, by yoking the alienated ennui of the *nouvelle vague* aesthetic to tales of putatively international intrigue the show subverted dramatic expectations far more than Godard could hope to, while also casting doubt on the idea that the Cold War (and by extension that in Vietnam) was being fought according to codes of chivalry. When even our top secret agents seem to float mockingly above the spying game, why should we in the audience take it any more seriously?

But there was another side to the *nouvelle vague* – one that was less interested in agitprop than it was in the art-for-art's sake aesthetic of self-reflexivity. Certainly the best way of understanding an episode as bafflingly story-free as, say, 'The Hour that Never Was' is to see it as a joshing take on the contemporaneous movies of Michelangelo Antonioni – *L'Avventura* meets *The Avengers*. For like Antonioni's Golden Globe-winner, 'The Hour that Never Was' is a film dominated by visions of emptied out landscapes through which people wander looking for they know not what. And as in *L'Avventura*, when, at the end of 'The Hour that Never Was', all is revealed, it turns out that nothing is being revealed at all.

The plot, if we can so label series of the narrative-free, motivation-free, non-dramatic episodes the show is made up of, has no ending because it has no real beginning and therefore explains nothing of the mysteries it engenders. Asked what happened to the girl who went missing at the start of *L'Avventura* (and who is never found), Antonioni replied, 'I don't know. Someone told me that she committed suicide, but I don't believe it.'[34] The mysteries of 'The Hour that Never Was' are solved no more convincingly. Beyond its symmetries of action, its aural and visual rhymes and rhythms, Roger Marshall's story makes no sense. It is what the theatre critic Kenneth Tynan would have called 'a dramatic vacuum'.[35]

The phrase comes from Tynan's review of Samuel Beckett's *Waiting for Godot*, another drama that bears a curious resemblance to 'The Hour that Never Was'. Like Beckett's play, this *Avengers* story is less linear than circular. Indeed, while Beckett's work has been described as a play in which 'nothing happens twice',[36] Roger Marshall's screenplay is actually structured around a repetition of the same series of non-events. Halfway through the episode, Steed is bumped on the head and when he comes round he does so back in the car that he crashed right back at the start of proceedings. Moreover, both these two near-identical acts begin in precisely the same place as Beckett's play, namely: 'A country road. A tree'.[37] It is true that Beckett's heroes, Vladimir and Estragon, are not driving down the country road, as Steed and Mrs Peel are as 'The Hour that Never Was' gets into what one hesitates to call its swing, much less that they plough said car into said tree, but otherwise the parallel holds and goes on holding.

Both dramas, for instance, centre on two people debating time and space – and in the process making all attempts at action seem futile, even laughable. When Steed and Mrs Peel do finally stumble across the villains, they do so in a room filled with laughing gas, reducing the show's supposedly dramatic denouement to a comic sideshow. (Reshoot the scene, with unknowns taking the parts of Steed and Emma, and it'd be a natural for the Turner Prize shortlist.) But most of the time there is a lot less action than that. Our two heroes drift around quite as aimlessly as Beckett's Vladimir and Estragon, with Mrs Peel more than once looking despondently at the vast, empty RAF station she and Steed are stumbling through and asking what Beckett describes as Estragon's 'despairing' question: 'You're sure it was here?' Nor, at any point during the show's second half, would it be out of place for Steed to begin quoting Vladimir's speech from Act Two of *Godot* in which he wonders 'Was I sleeping, while the others suffered? Am I sleeping now? Tomorrow, when I wake, or think I do, what shall I say of today?' As if to hammer home the parallels with Beckett, midway through the story a very *Godot*-like tramp is brought on in the shape of Roy Kinnear's Benedict Napoleon Hickey – a stoic scruff who, like Nell and Nagg in Beckett's follow-up to *Godot*, *Endgame*, lives in – or at least out of – dustbins.

The avant-garde theatre and cinema weren't the only influences at work on *The Avengers*. If anything the show was even more attuned to developments in the art world. Just as the Bond movies were busy mobilising the iconography of pop to tell you adventure stories, so *The Avengers* of 1965 and beyond drew on the language of minimalism and conceptualism to subvert viewers' expectations of the tidily structured narratives of the mystery thriller. At one point in 'The Hour that Never Was' Steed comes across an electric razor that has been left switched on, buzzing redundantly away in the drawer of a dressing table. What it's doing there we don't know, and nor do we ever find out. The idea of machines coming back to life after a power shut-down was, of course, a staple of science fiction.* But even assuming that this razor has come back to life after such a shut-down, it does so while tucked away in a drawer – so what would it be doing, powered up, in there? No realist reason suggests itself. Patently, it was just a nice visual and aural idea (and, fittingly, one that looks forward to Richard Hamilton's 1968 work *The Critic Laughs*: a set of false teeth attached to an electric tooth-brush that whir with purposeless abandon at their owner's desire).†

So too the appearance of a jumbled stack of milk crates on the air base's hitherto empty landing strip. In dramatic terms, this stack of crates serves no function. And yet O'Hara's camera returns to it again and again, in a variety of framings. Shot first from afar, then from close up, now from on high, now from low down, it is made to seem like a sculpture in a museum – Marcel Duchamp's *Bottle Rack* (1914), say, or, more contemporaneously, the 'specific objects'[38] of Donald Judd, Robert Morris and Walter de Maria. Like the rows of Plexiglas boxes Judd began exhibiting in 1965, the stack of milk crates in 'The Hour that Never Was' dismisses, in its radical meaninglessness, any suggestion that a work of art or a story ought to have any a priori *raison d'être*. Certainly nobody can have ever tuned in to *The Avengers* in 1965 in expectation of the conventional thrills and spills of espionage.

Even as the show was going out, the Italian semiotician (and subseqently best-selling novelist) Umberto Eco was postulating that what Ian Fleming's fans liked about his Bond novels was the very formulaic quality his more astringent critics were forever decrying

---

* See Robert Wise's *The Day the Earth Stood Still* (1951) or Wolf Rilla's movie version of John Wyndham's *Village of the Damned* (1960).
† Hamilton's 1963 art stunt, in which, dressed as a US fullback complete with rugby-style football, he climbs into a mocked-up spaceship was surely one of the key inspirations on the fourth and subsequent series of *The Avengers*.

him for. 'The reader's pleasure', argued Eco, 'consists of finding himself immersed in a game of which he knows the pieces and the rules – and perhaps the outcome – drawing pleasure simply from the minimal variations by which the victor realises his objective.'[39] All good and true in relation to Bond and sundry other spy action-ers, but emphatically not true of high-period *Avengers* – in which it is all but impossible to take sides against the baddies for lack of knowing just what it is they would like to achieve.

Nor, their glamour and style aside, does one really side with the Avengers themselves. After all, there was no longer even the trace of a pretence that they were avenging anything.* Steed and Mrs Peel seemed merely to be larking around. Thanks to the bracingly mocking presence of Sean Connery, the Bond movies had done much to tell the sixties audience that the spying game really was just a game. The 1965 series of *The Avengers* and its successors leavened things yet more by not even affecting to believe the game was worth playing, while the novels of John le Carré and Evelyn Waugh suggested it was a game no one would ever convincingly win. Out in the real world, the world of the Cold War and Vietnam, more and more people were coming to the same conclusion.

---

* According to Brian Clemens, not even Sidney Newman, the producer who invented the show, knew why its heroes were called *The Avengers*. 'I don't know what the hell it means,' he told Clemens, 'but it's a good title, so now go and write something to go with it.' See Winston Dixon Wheeler, 'The Man who Created *The Avengers*: An Interview with Brian Clemens', *Classic Images*, 287, May 1999, p.20.

9

NEVER SUCH INNOCENCE

In which the censors cannot hold

'We have now domesticated all the animals that usually dwell in our cities or houses; only man remains undomesticated.'

Edward Bond

'Censorship ends in logical completeness when nobody is allowed to read any books except the books that nobody can read.'

George Bernard Shaw

In September 1965 the writer and critic Pamela Hansford Johnson published *Cork Street, Next to the Hatter's*, 'a novel', its subtitle claimed, 'in bad taste'. It tells of one Tom Hariot, 'a remote and ineffectual don', who is so shocked at what is going on in the nation's theatres that he sets out to write a play so offensive it can't possibly be performed. 'The play shall not be described', Johnson writes, 'since it was meant to be unspeakable, it is right that it not be spoken of.' In the event, of course, Hariot's play, *A Potted Shrimp*, does find a home, in an avant-garde club theatre, and its shocked author finds himself begging his young, acne-ridden producer that he use a stuffed – rather than a live – goose for the play's sex scene because he (Hariot) is rather fond of animals. On opening night he interrupts the performance to condemn the play, but to no avail: the audience is hooked.

Back in the real world, something mighty similar was happening. Just a couple of months after the appearance of *Cork Street, Next to the Hatter's* the members of another private club gathered together to watch a baby being stoned to death in its pram. The club in question was the English Stage Society of London's Royal Court, hitherto – and subsequently – a theatre. Why the change in status? Because for more than 200 years, since 1737 in fact, plays had been subject to licence by the Lord Chamberlain, who had the right to veto their public production if he saw fit. In 1965 he saw fit to veto *Saved*, Edward Bond's first play, halfway through which the baby-stoning scene occurs.

To be fair to Bond, audiences didn't actually see the baby in its pram. Stranger still, though, they never heard it cry out as its tortures proceeded – from hair-pulling, through being used as a punchbag, through being urinated on, to having its face wiped in its own excrement, and on to its eventual stony death. Nor was the baby's silence merely a sop to tastefulness, an attempt at making a horrible scene slightly less unbearable. An audience at *Saved* knows that the baby can scream, because the baby has spent the whole of scene four (the scene in which the real crime is committed, according to the show's first director, William Gaskill[2]) doing just that, while its mother, Pam, and its grandparents ignore it in favour of watching the TV and getting ready to go out. So the baby's silence as it is being stoned to death is meant to suggest that it is already inured to a world in which its cries go unheard, is already as brutalised by its environment – the high-rise council estates of south London – as its murderers.

If murderers they are. One of the things Bond's gruesomely lengthy scene makes plain is that these louts and lowlifes don't set out to kill the baby. They don't set out to do anything. They wouldn't have the moral imagination for that. They'd have to believe that life was worth living in order to think it might be fun to end someone else's. They aren't even sure what fun is – they merely know that they aren't having any. Violence, even violence towards a defenceless child, means nothing to these alienated and affectless youths, because violence is all they have ever known. They are able to stone a baby because they have spent their lives being figuratively – and perhaps occasionally literally – stoned by everyone around them. Death, Wittgenstein once said, isn't an event in life. Bond's youths wouldn't agree: for them, life isn't an event in death – life is death, and death life. Hence, at the end of the scene, when Pam shows up to take the baby home, she is so uninterested in her offspring that she doesn't even notice it is dead. As Tony Selby, who made his acting debut in the play, once said, 'Saved is about ignoring young life. The baby is a sacrifice. In actual fact, the baby is saved. It's saved from a non-existent life.'[3]

So much can one extract from Saved after the fact. During performances of the play itself, however, the only thing one would like to extract is oneself from the auditorium. Watching Bond's debut is a (designedly) grimy, dispiriting experience. 'I meant the violence in Saved to shock because I wanted to make the loathsomeness of all violence unequivocal,'[4] Bond wrote a week after the show's opening – and who could say that he failed?

Quite a few people, actually. One critic said of the play that while 'it may not be the feeblest thing I have seen on any stage . . . it is certainly the nastiest, and contains perhaps the most horrid scene in the contemporary theatre'.[5] Another dismissed it not in 'horror at the presentation of wretched lives being lived in contemporary England' but because he thought it necessary to 'protest against the use of these lives as a subject for sensationalism, and the degradation of the theatre into a twentieth-century equivalent of bear-baiting or cock-fighting'.[6] You don't have to agree with such verdicts to feel some sympathy for those members of the original audience who, despite having made the effort to become members of a private club in order to watch the play, and therefore surely had some idea of what they were in for, nevertheless booed during what would become its most infamous scene.

But should audiences have been prevented from seeing the play in the first place? That, after all, is why they had been obliged to become members of the English Stage Society's private club. Though the Lord Chamberlain's chief examiner of plays, Charles Heriot, thought, 'reluctantly', that *Saved* ('a revolting amateur play ... the writing is vile and the conception worse'[7]) should be given a licence, the Lord Chamberlain himself, Lord Cobbold, was less sure. He insisted on no fewer than fifty-four changes or excisions to Bond's text, among them sundry 'arse's, 'bugger's 'crap's, 'shag's, 'piss off's and 'get stuffed's, as well as the entire scene that builds to the stoning of the baby. Nor was there to be 'any indecent business with the balloon'.

William Gaskill was incensed. The Lord Chamberlain was, he later wrote, 'limiting not just the scope of what could be shown on the stage, but the strength and vitality of the language'.[8] Nor was Bond happy to go along with the request for changes. While the Royal Court's recently retired – though far from retiring – artistic director, George Devine, counselled caution, telling Bond to 'Swallow [his] pride and reinvent, even one's own swear words and phrases. Rewrite scenes, if necessary, to retrain intrinsic rhythms rather than arguing over words and phrases he will never yield on,'[9] Bond refused. 'I would do almost anything to prevent my play being banned,' he confided to his notebook, 'except alter one comma at the request of the Lord Chamberlain.'[10] So it was that a public theatre became a members' club – 'the nearest approximation', Sir Laurence Olivier wrote, 'we in the theatre can make to the X certificate'.[11]

Lord Cobbold, though, was having none of it. He thought the Royal Court's decision to go ahead with the production without making his suggested changes was practically an act of civil disobedience, and that he had, therefore, no alternative but to take action. Not everyone agreed with him, of course. Cobbold had to threaten his resignation before the Attorney General and the Director of Public Prosecutions would agree to his demands that a prosecution be brought against the theatre. And so, in February 1966, Gaskill (by now the new artistic director of the Royal Court), Greville Poke (the theatre's honorary secretary) and Alfred Esdaile (its licensee), were found guilty of presenting an unlicensed play 'for hire'* and therefore breaching Section 15 of the 1843 Theatres Act and fined £50 expenses. Despite Olivier's contention that Chekhov would have approved of Bond's 'marvellously observed dialogue and first-rate dramatic form',[12] the play was taken off.

Reviewing *Saved* in the *Sunday Times*, the paper's arts and literary editor Jack Lambert said that it 'represent[ed] something of a crux in modern drama: a clear demonstration of what is permissible, what is not, and why'.[13] He believed that the baby was silent during the stoning sequence not for any aesthetic or dramatic reason, but for the purely practical purpose of making a sickening scene endurable for the audience the play was out to deprave. 'Was there ever', he wondered, 'a psychopathic exercise so lovingly dwelt on as this, spun out with such apparent relish and refinement of detail?'[14] Well, maybe a couple, starting with *Edward II* and *King*

---

* Over the years, Lords Chamberlain had been willing to turn a blind eye to one-off club or society performances of plays they disapproved of, because the uniqueness of the event was almost certain to guarantee that everyone who attended would be a bona fide member of the club in question. This was highly unlikely to be the case, Cobbold maintained, with a production that went on for several months.

Lear.* Indeed, none other than Pamela Hansford Johnson uncon-sciously conceded such artistic precedent when she wrote to *The Times* about another very violent play presently doing the rounds: '"What modern dramatist", demands your Special Correspondent today, reviewing *The Revenger's Tragedy* in Cambridge, "would dare show a man making love to a poisoned skeleton and being subse-quently trampled to death?" Oh, come now, pretty well any of them.'[15] Nice try, but if Tourneur had been portraying necrophilia on stage at the start of the seventeenth century, the modern drama-tists Miss Johnson had thought to satirise were hardly vanguard figures of some new beastliness.

Meanwhile, a very similar opinion was being delivered on a tel-evision drama broadcast on the same night that *Saved* had its opening. Ken Loach's BBC *Wednesday Play* version of Nell Dunn's novel *Up the Junction* shocked one viewer so much she thought it 'enough to make anyone pick up his or her pen and write to their MP'. The crucial scene, as far as she was concerned, was the one depicting 'a screaming girl undergoing an illegal abortion'. To be sure, she said, 'the sooner those terrible back-street abortionists are put out of business the better!' Nonetheless the real problem was that Loach (and Dunn) were dramatising what simply oughtn't to be seen. 'What about a play', Mary Whitehouse went on to ask, 'which would make it clear that any kind of abortion, legal or oth-erwise, has dangers to mental and bodily health far greater than natural childbirth? How about a programme which would demon-strate that clean living could cut out a great deal of this problem at the root?'[16] By the end of the month she had officially launched The National Viewers' and Listeners' Association (NVALA), an organisation that she hoped would represent the opinions of

---

* Not that the Lord Chamberlain could have censored Shakespeare even if he'd wanted to. He had no power over plays written before 1843, the year in which the Theatres Act had been passed.

normal, average people across the land and thereby encourage broadcasters to make such shows.*

She had her work cut out for her.

Earlier in the year, just as the Rolling Stones' inability to get any 'Satisfaction' had taken them to the top of the charts, Bob Guccione had launched the mainstream pornographic magazine *Penthouse*. This was a downmarket rival to Hugh Hefner's massively successful *Playboy* – which meant fewer contributions from esteemed writers like Kenneth Tynan (who had indeed written for Hefner's publication) and rather raunchier photographs than the competition had ever seen fit to muster. Whitehouse was outraged – though not as outraged as she was when, a few years later, the pornographer David Sullivan launched a porn magazine actually named after her.

Ken Tynan, meanwhile, was being no slouch in the controversy stakes. Back in June he had given over a large chunk of his *Observer* cinema column to a diatribe on the issue of censorship. Taking issue with the ban on the movie version of John Cleland's *Fanny Hill*, Tynan argued that bad though Albert Zugsmith's film was, 'erotic stimulation is a minor but perfectly legitimate function of art.'[17] And then, on 13 November 1965, on the live, late-night chat show *BBC3*, he became the first person to utter the word 'fuck' on television.† And though Tynan claimed in the sentence in which he used it that he doubted whether there were 'very many rational people in this world to whom the word "fuck" is

* The NVALA had been inaugurated a few months earlier, on 16 March 1965, and had in June presented its 'Clean Up TV' petition to Parliament. Signed by some 366,355 people, this last argued 'that the BBC be asked to make a radical change of policy and produce programmes which build character'.

† It is only fair to point out that Tynan's record-making status has been the subject of some debate. Almost a decade earlier, the poet and playwright Brendan Behan had apparently used the word repeatedly during a drunken interview for a 1956 edition of *Panorama*. There were, though, no complaints about this incident – although a lot of people did ring in to complain about the incomprehensibility of Behan's thick Dublin brogue.

particularly diabolical or revolting or totally forbidden', the BBC was obliged to apologise for the incident after four House of Commons motions were signed by 133 MPs. Mary Whitehouse, having delivered herself of the opinion that Tynan should have had his bottom smacked – little knowing how much that anally fixated sado-masochist would have enjoyed the act – wrote to the Queen about the incident.[18]

Terence Rattigan once said that when writing his plays he had in mind an imaginary viewer called Aunt Edna. She was, he said, 'a nice, respectable, middle-class, middle-aged, maiden lady, with time on her hands and money to help her pass it, who resides in a West Kensington hotel'.[19] Mary Whitehouse was married and lived in the Midlands, but otherwise she was Rattigan's fictional aunt to a T.*

It was while she was working as an art teacher, at Madeley School for Girls in Shropshire, with additional responsibilities for pastoral care and sex education, that Whitehouse first registered the major social changes of the sixties. She came to see what an effect the modern world – for which read television and the pill – had had on the ideas of chastity she had been raised to believe in (and which she was sure stemmed directly from the Christian religion and the binding laws of God). What worried her most was what she saw as the lack of moral norms that defined this newly permissive age. At school one day, a girl who had watched a television programme on

---

* She was also, of course, a shoo-in for Joe Orton's Edna Welthorpe, the writer of numerous irate letters to the papers about what she saw as dubious theatrical goings-on. In 1964, as Whitehouse was first making a name for herself, Edna wrote to the *Daily Telegraph* to complain about Orton's first major West End success, *Entertaining Mr Sloane*, saying that she was 'nauseated by this endless parade of mental and physical perversion. And to be told that such a disgusting piece of filth now passes for humour!' Warming to her theme she said, 'Today's young playwrights take it upon themselves to flaunt their contempt for ordinary decent people. I hope that the ordinary decent people of this country will shortly strike back!' In just such tones would Whitehouse and her acolytes launch that strike.

sex education told her that she now knew 'not [to] have intercourse until I am engaged', a line that might have been (and in this case almost certainly was) designed to goad a certain type of teacher. Certainly it goaded Mary Whitehouse into believing the children in her charge had, by means of 'a few brief words . . . been won over to a sub-Christian concept of living'.[20]

The key to Mary Whitehouse, who was born Constance Mary Hutcheson in 1910 in rural Warwickshire, is the affair she had as a 20-year-old teacher with a married man almost twice her age. Whitehouse was always at pains to insist that 'there was no misbehaving'[21] between them, and that she ended the affair when saw the man's wife looking disconsolate. 'I just knew', she said, 'that if I was the cause of so much unhappiness, our relationship could not be right.'[22] Perhaps without her ever quite knowing it, her public pronouncements were made not from the moral high ground of one immune to temptation, but from the rather more lowly reality where, even if they are not acted upon, desires exist. Tempted herself, she sought to camouflage the fact by very visibly wanting to save everyone else from temptation. Disgusted with herself, she projected her disgust onto everyone else.

The end of the affair coincided with the break-up of her parents' marriage. Doubly distraught, she sought consolation in the certainties of religion. She got involved with the Oxford Group, an evangelical Christian organisation founded by the American missionary Dr Frank Buchman and bent on what he called 'moral rearmament'. (Indeed, from 1938, a couple of years after Whitehouse signed up, the Oxford Group changed its name to Moral Re-Armament (MRA).) Having joined the MRA, where she met Ernest Raymond Whitehouse, the man who in 1940 would become her husband, she said that she 'asked God to take my life and use it'.[23]

Demanding from its members the biblically capitalised 'Absolute Honesty, Absolute Purity, Absolute Unselfishness and Absolute

Love', the MRA's core principles were that men and women are sinful, but that they can be put on the right track if they submit to God's will and follow the divine guidance he gives them. To assist them in this goal, the group held 'Sharing' and 'Guidance' sessions, the former not unlike AA meetings in which a member would confess his sins to a 'house party', the latter more private occasions in which confessors would sit quietly and wait for God's counsel to come. In essence, the whole of Mary Whitehouse's subsequent life and work can be seen as a reaction to her belief that television might have been invented in order to prevent God's voice getting through.

Still, for all its emphasis on godliness, the MRA's essential thrust was utterly worldly and pragmatically ideological. It was convinced, for instance, that British institutions were being infiltrated by communist agents. 'I thank heaven for a man like Hitler,' Buchman once said, because he 'built a front-line of defence against the anti-Christ of Communism.'[24] The Whitehouses themselves were fearful of that anti-Christ too. While Ernest Whitehouse once confessed that he couldn't 'from a Biblical point of view [see] how one can support socialism', he insisted that his and Mary's opposition to communism was grounded in its atheism.[25] And when she wrote an 'Open Letter to the Prime Minister'[26] to tell him that thanks to 'broadcasting, and television in particular ... Britain is in the process of taking on a character alien to herself' she sounded like nothing so much as the heroine of a fifties sci-fi movie – terrified that she and her family and community and country were about to be taken over by creatures from another planet whose ideology was patently of the Red Scare variety.*

But while Whitehouse herself always said she was interested not in right and left but in right and wrong, and was keen to play down

---

* See, from the top of my head, Don Siegel's *Invasion of the Body Snatchers* (1956) or Robert Aldrich's *Kiss Me Deadly* (1955).

any suggestion that the MRA was an influence on her campaigning, there is no getting away from the fact that politics made their way into her speeches. 'The enemies of the West', she said in 1965, 'saw that Britain was the kingpin of Western civilization; she had proved herself unbeatable on the field of battle because of her faith and character. If Britain was to be destroyed, those things must be undercut.'[27] The sixties' (often enough naive) faith in liberty was, she thought, little more than a 'front for Communism'.[28] For the communists were everywhere: 'They've infiltrated the trade unions,' she said. 'Why does anyone still believe they haven't infiltrated broadcasting?'[29] It followed that the BBC, as a proponent of the 'secular/humanist/Marxist philosophy', was at the heart of the new permissiveness.[30]

Certainly Ken Loach would happily endorse all those descriptions of his life and work. But wasn't there something a little permissive about Whitehouse, too? She had a licence to see filth everywhere. It was one thing to argue that the abortion scene in *Up the Junction* ought not have been broadcast. Even those people – indeed, precisely those people – who wanted abortion legalised,* would have blenched at Loach and his actors' terrifyingly realistic depiction of the dreaded amateur operation. It was quite another to take issue with, say, *Doctor Who* ('Teatime brutality for tots'[31]) or a BBC dramatisation of *The Three Musketeers* in which King Charles I was beheaded.[32] Note to Mrs Whitehouse: in 1649, Charles I did indeed lose his head on a scaffold in Whitehall.

But ignorance of the facts never stopped Mary Whitehouse. She once complained to the BBC, for instance, for playing the Rolling Stones' *Exile on Main Street* on Radio 1. 'This record', she moaned, 'uses four-letter words. Although they are somewhat blurred, there is no question about what they are meant to be.'[33] Alas, there are

---

* Among them the Church of England who had just published a report, 'Abortion: An Ethical Discussion', which argued in favour of reform.

quite a lot of questions, and Mrs Whitehouse's letter is sweet nonsense. The album *Exile on Main Street* contains precisely one swear word – a solitary 'shit' at the end of 'Sweet Virginia' – and even then the word is being used metaphorically, in reference to drug use. Moreover, Radio 1 had never played that track, as Lord Hill – then the chairman of BBC governors – made clear in his letter of reply. 'Could it be', he wondered, 'that, believing offending words to be there and zealous to discover them, you imagined that you heard what you did not hear?'[34] Certainly the theatre director and producer of *Play for Today* Richard Eyre thought Whitehouse could take offence where none was intended. Replying to her letter bemoaning the language in Trevor Griffiths's television play *Comedians*, Eyre told her that while he took 'note of your objections ... It seems that even your typewriter is infected by your prurience and your vision of universal corruption for "brothel" should, of course, read "brother".'[35]

Nothing daunted, Whitehouse went on being distraught at almost anything that passed in front of her gaze or by her ears. She took issue with the BBC for airing the Beatles' *Magical Mystery Tour* because the song 'I Am the Walrus' contained a line about a naughty girl having dropped her drawers – a lyric with whose cautionary, chastening sentiment she might have been expected to agree. Subsequently, she decried everything from Elvis's 'It's Now or Never' (adapted, of course, from the Neapolitan standard ''O Sole Mio'), with its insistence that 'my love won't wait', to Chuck Berry's cover of 'My Ding-a-Ling' with its, well, its what? As Charles Curran, the BBC's director general at the time Berry's record went to number 1 in the charts, noted, the song 'begins with such a clear account of the contraption in question including bells, that although the possibility of a double entendre was recognised, we decided that it could be broadcast at the discretion of the producers according to the context and character of their programmes'. And though he acknowledged that quite a few people had written to him with similar complaints, Curran also pointed out that he had received 'more than twice as many ... expressing strong disagreement with your attitude'. Many of these writers, he said, had wondered 'whether the record* would have remained in a high position in the charts for such a long time without the publicity attendant upon the publication of your comments'.[36]

Nor were her complaints always about the content of artworks. Gradually, she developed an interest in the more formal aspects of expression, too. In 1968 she lamented not only the presence of 'Jimmy [sic] Hendrix' ('the most obscene thing I, at any rate, have ever seen on television') in Tony Palmer's BBC *Omnibus* documentary about pop and politics *All My Loving*, but also the show's 'use of psychedelic and hypnotic techniques which build up frenzy and eroticism'.[37] And perhaps they do, though only a few years later she was to be found complaining about similar techniques in a BBC *Election Special*, whose 'montages of rapidly changing images' were surely migraine-inducing.[38] It was this scattergun approach that helped many people to the belief that the National Viewers' and Listeners' Association shot nothing but blanks. Whitehouse's inverse-pantheism, her ability to see the devil's work wherever she cast her gaze, not only made her message tedious. It made it otiose. If evil could be detected in everything the world threw at you, then maybe it wasn't evil. Maybe it was the way of the world.

More bafflingly still, Whitehouse picked fights with shows that to any sane viewer looked very much like they were on her side. True, Alf Garnett, who was introduced to British television screens in July 1965, just as the NVALA was finding its feet, had what sensitive souls might consider a foul mouth.† But otherwise he could have

---

* By some measure, Chuck's worst.
† In fact, the Garnetts did not become the Garnetts until the show was commissioned for its first full series in 1966. For the 1965 *Comedy Playhouse* special, Alf and his family were the Ramseys. Their name was changed so as to avoid confusion with – and possibly offence to – the then England football manager.

been a fully paid-up member of the NVALA. Like Whitehouse and her acolytes, he was a monarchy worshipping, do-gooder despising, knee-jerk reactionary convinced that the country was going to the dogs. Yet not even the sight of Alf, fresh from a visit to the 'karsy', clutching a copy of Whitehouse's book *Cleaning-Up TV* (complete with a bog-paper bookmark) and saying he 'agree[s] with every bloody word of it', could get her on his side. She was forever writing to the BBC to complain about the show. Alf's habitual use of the word 'bloody' – as in 'Mary bloody Whitehouse' – was, she said, anti-Christian, 'but you can pick a bunch of them any Monday, family viewing time ... and stand a good chance of having a "bitch" or "dirty devil" thrown in for good measure'.[39] To say, fifty years later, that such language reads as unutterably tame is not to make Whitehouse's point. It is not the case that *Till Death Us Do Part* brutalised its audience into accepting a deeper and deeper degradation of the national language. Alf's language wasn't the language of the gutter, as Whitehouse would have had people believe, but the language of the world as it was.

Not that Whitehouse and the NVALA could be said to have misunderstood the show. 'Our intention', its producer, Dennis Main Wilson, said, 'was to hold a mirror up to the world. Let it see itself – warts and all. Garnett was to be put in the pillory of public shame. With his loud-mouthed bigotries he was to be the anti-hero. He was to be laughed *at* – not *with*. It didn't really work out that way. A few people sensed what we were up to. The majority just enjoyed the show and missed the point.'[40] And yet, and yet ... Mary Whitehouse might not have enjoyed *Till Death Us Do Part* but that didn't mean she missed its point. 'He [Johnny Speight] portrays Alf as he does', she once told the BBC chairman Sir Michael Swann, 'in the hope that the public, in rejecting Alf, will reject also these things which he holds dear.'[41] What things were these? An NVALA briefing paper quoted the BBC's director general, Sir Hugh Greene, to explain:

'The amusing thing about Alf [Greene told *Time* magazine] is the intense fury aroused among those who share his prejudices. The programme offends a great many people – but those one is glad to offend.' [...]

To see exactly what prejudices Sir Hugh finds so funny, turn to the *Radio Times* of June 2nd, 1966 where Sir Hugh Greene's own paper tells us: 'Alf Garnett. He is working class, skilled at his trade, three generations behind the times and is well endowed with most natural human failings ... He is also a Tory and a Monarchist, but he has never forgiven Edward Heath for trying to get us into the Common Market. It need hardly be said, therefore, that Harold Wilson and the Labour Party are utterly wrong as far as he is concerned. The same goes for General de Gaulle, the Russians, the Chinese [...]'.

Sir Hugh has certainly declared himself with a vengeance, Working class, skilled at his trade, Tory and a Monarchist, against the Common Market, against Harold Wilson and the Labour party, the Russians, the Chinese ... one does not need to be an expert on aversion therapy to understand the game.[42]

In other words, Whitehouse wrote in her autobiography, 'the man we were supposed to hate [was] a loyal patriot who believed in God and was devoted to the Queen. If we could be made to hate his offensiveness and prejudice, then we would perhaps also turn against his loyalties.'[43]

But logic wasn't always Whitehouse's strong point.* She argued, for instance, that television failed to reflect the fact that 'the vast majority [of people] in this country adhere to the Judaeo-Christian

---

* Nor the NVALA's generally. Her colleague David Sturdy, for instance, once argued that a sex education programme called *Living and Growing* would both put people off having babies (by showing how traumatic birth is) *and* encourage sexual experimentation. See Michael Tracey and David Morrison, *Whitehouse* (Macmillan, 1979), p.125.

faith',[44] without pausing to wonder whether that might mean TV wasn't as all-powerful and hegemonic as she liked to believe. When Robert Kennedy was assassinated in 1968, she wrote an editorial for the *Viewer and Listener* headlined 'Violent world of TV makes murder climate' which claimed that 'violence on television is bound to play its part and a very vital part in the creation of an increasingly violent society ... And it is now being increasingly recognized that the amount of violence shown on American TV screens could have played a significant part in creating the climate of behaviour in which the tragic events of last month were played out.'[45] Could have played? Or had played? And if television violence had influenced Kennedy's assassin, how to account for the assassination of Kennedy's brother, Jack, five years earlier? Of the assassinations of William McKinley, of James A. Garfield, of Abraham Lincoln – to name only those US presidents who were murdered before the advent of television?

It was this perhaps wilful blindness to debates around nature and nurture that most undid Whitehouse's claims to any serious attention. On the one hand, her calls for censorship were premised on a Lockean belief that birth bequeathed us nothing but a blank slate upon which the world of experience would write our very being. On the other, her faith in existential freedom and responsibility meant she believed that people could choose to live moral lives.

Taking issue with a Radio 3 series called *Young Marriage*, she complained that the programmes were 'devoted almost wholly to the biological and psychological aspects of sex. Very much the flat humanist approach. Apparently one's future behaviour totally conditioned by one's early relationships, particularly with the mother. No suggestion of the possibility of rising above environment and experience.'[46] But if one is capable of 'rising above' one's background and history, then surely one can watch TV, no matter how pernicious and malevolent what is being broadcast, while having risen above the horrors on display. And if that is the case, what is the point of an organisation devoted to exposing television's malicious influences? No such influences can exist. As Whitehouse's colleague David Sturdy self-defeatingly argued (apropos of *Living and Growing*, a series of sex-education programmes aimed at ten- to thirteen-year-olds): 'The justification for this series is based on the theory that illegitimacy and VD are caused by ignorance. Yet most unmarried pregnant women who come to a doctor's surgery are usually by no means ignorant. Their pregnancy is more often due to an irresponsible attitude to life.'[47] In which case, such a show's influence is neither here nor there.

One labours the nature vs nurture debate because it came to headline prominence in October 1965, with the arrest of a young Manchester stock clerk. Police had been summoned to a house in the city's Gorton area, where, wrapped in a carpet, they found the body of a 17-year-old apprentice engineer, Edward Evans. He had been beaten to death with an axe. The man accused of wielding the axe, Ian Brady, and his colleague and girlfriend, Myra Hindley, were subsequently found guilty of killing at least four other people, all of them children, all of them subjected to horrific sexual assault, all of them subsequently buried by the Hitler-loving, Marquis de Sade-worshipping Brady on Saddleworth Moor. Questions about Brady's evil, questions about whether he had been born wicked or had had wickedness thrust upon him by an increasingly prurient media, have never gone away.

How could they? Brady and Hindley were modern Britain's first encounter with what has come to be called the serial killer. The Moors Murders (as the papers named them) were the biggest shock to the country since the truth about the Nazi Holocaust had emerged. The arresting officer in the case, Superintendent Bob Talbot, spoke for the nation when he said that he had to 'keep reminding myself that this isn't a tale – that it's been happenin'', as you might say, *in our midst*. Even as a hardened copper, you just rub your eyes.'[48]

Violent death always shakes people, of course, but in most cases the murder eventually turns out to be explicable in recognisable human terms. Not so this time. True, there are some grounds for believing Hindley, who died in prison in 2002, thirty-six years into her life sentence, was the classic victim of a *folie à deux*: had she not met the wrong man at the wrong time – and had what she would later call her father's tyrannical violence not predisposed her to be sympathetic towards other violent men – she might well have lived a blameless suburban life. For Brady, though, who is still alive, locked up in Merseyside's Ashworth Hospital, where he is said to have more than once asked to be allowed to die, no such exculpatory narratives have ever quite convinced.

He was born Ian Stewart in January 1938, the illegitimate progeny of a brief liaison between a Glasgow tea room waitress known as Maggie and – probably – a reporter on one of the city's newspapers. (The man is said to have died three months before his son's birth.) A few months later, the baby was put up for adoption – and taken in (though not actually adopted) by a Gorbals couple, John and Mary Sloan, who had four children of their own already. But those children (two boys, two girls) were all a good few years older than little Ian, and though the Sloan household was decent and decorous, the new arrival was never really taken to the heart of the family. Perhaps things would have worked out better if Maggie, trying to put matters behind her by calling herself Peggy, hadn't insisted on coming to see the little boy every evening. Then again, there are lots of illegitimate, unadopted children who grow up into stable adults . . .

When he was nine years old, a family birthday took Ian on his first trip out of the Gorbals. The Sloans made up a picnic, jumped on a bus, and took themselves off to Loch Lomond. There, Ian became entranced by the mountains. He set off to climb one, reaching a height of 1,500 feet, and spent an hour and more up there, gazing at the view, oblivious to the shouts from the Sloans that it was time to go home. In the end, he had to be coaxed begrudgingly down. What had he seen? More mountains, of course, and the loch beneath him, looking like a dark, dappled, steely mirror, and the world – or a bigger section of it than he had ever been able to glimpse before – laid out flat, like a pattern, and the people on it, lazing in the sun, blind to the Promethean liberties of ascendancy. 'He who climbs upon the highest mountains laughs at all tragedies, real or imaginary,'[49] wrote Nietzsche, and we know that Ian Brady treated tragedy as lightly as anyone ever has. We know, too, that he adored Orson Welles's Harry Lime in *The Third Man* – a man whose big speech, made from the top of the big wheel in Vienna, asks whether his friend would 'really feel any pity if one of those dots [down below] stopped moving forever? If I offered you £20,000 for every dot that stopped, would you really, old man, tell me to keep my money? Or would you calculate how many dots you could afford to spare?' Brady's own efforts lack Lime's (or Graham Greene's) portentous rhythms, but they clearly owe them a debt: 'People are like maggots,' he wrote in his journal, 'small, blind worthless fish bait.'[50] Then again, there are lots of people who climb mountains and revere nature and pity their fellow man for not having the moral wisdom to be up on the heights with them – and who would not harm a fly . . .

That same year he started a collection, as so many boys before and since have done. Still, his field of interest wasn't your run of the mill cigarette cards or footballers' autographs. He was interested in the Nazis, hoarding old photographs, medals, bits of uniform, helmets and, of course, weaponry. When one of his schoolmates let it be known that he had an elder brother in the forces and stationed in Germany, Ian's pestering to meet him became non-stop. He was, a psychiatric report would later say, 'exhilarated by [the Nazis'] loss of feeling . . . it appeared as a liberation or a freedom'.[51] Later in life he would encourage Hindley to dye her naturally brown hair into a blonde shock in homage to Hitler's faith in the Aryan supremacy. Then again, it is not a sin to be interested in figures from history, no matter how malign their actions; and lots of people have entertained themselves with dictatorial fantasies ...

In his teens, not long after he discovered he had been born a bastard, he took to petty crime. There is, it seems, no truth in the stories about his having tied a schoolmate to a pole and set fire to him. (At least the boy in question doesn't recall it as anything other than some fun with rope and matches during a harmless game of cops and robbers.[52]) But he did capture a cat and inter it in one of Glasgow's bombed-out graveyards for several days and nights. Then he started housebreaking. More than once, he was caught by the police and arraigned in the juvenile court. One arrest, he said, was the result of a putative partner in crime turning snitch. That boy, he was fond of telling Hindley and his other workplace colleagues, was to be found buried in one of the Gorbals' many bombsites – dead at his hand. Given what we know happened subsequently, there may be some truth to the claim. Then again, the world is full of decent, hard-working men who were once boastful young tearaways in trouble with the police ...

In late 1954, not long before Ian was about to turn seventeen (and thereby become eligible to serve time in prison), he was told by a judge who was due to give him his third probationary sentence that he could avoid prison if he were willing to go and live with his mother, who had moved to Manchester. Brady (and after his move to Manchester that was the name, the name of his mother's new husband, that he took) acceded, but was quickly discontented with his new life. The Sloans had been only too happy to see the back of him, but the feeling hadn't been mutual. Certainly the people who had been with him through childhood and adolescence meant more to Brady than the birth mother who had abandoned him ever could. Then again, the world is full of people who have adjusted to new lives, new surroundings, even to new parents, and not felt the need to avenge themselves on life by making others as unhappy as they are themselves . . .

For a while it looked as if Brady had adjusted. Shortly after his arrival in Manchester, just before Christmas, he got a job portering at Smithfield Market. He held it down for more than a year, until, in early 1956, just after his eighteenth birthday, he was arrested for stealing lead seals from boxes at the market. He got two years in Borstal, in Hatfield, Yorkshire, where work and training and the team-spirit were encouraged, and where he did little but concoct himself a drink made up of lemon juice and surgical spirit. In his cups he is said to have boasted of the money he had made working as a rent boy. It is an odd bit of showing-off for such a forbiddingly homophobic environment – unless, of course, he was doing it to suggest that the same services were available to his fellow inmates. But there is little room for doubting that Brady was a troubled homosexual. Certainly there was a homoerotic impulse underlying his murderous spree of a few years hence. Edward Evans was known to Brady as a practising homosexual, and the forensic examiner found hairs from Hindley's dog on the *inside* of his trousers, suggesting they had been removed before he was murdered. And Hindley's brother-in-law, David Smith, who eventually reported the murder, has remembered how, as Brady brought the axe down on Evans's head he was calling him a 'dirty bastard'.* In classic, self-loathing style,

---

* Over the past few months Brady had been indoctrinating Smith in the ways of violence and perversion, lending him his books on the Nazis and on de Sade. He had even staged Evans's murder for Smith's delectation, though things didn't quite work out that way. While Smith did help Brady and Hindley clean up what Brady called 'the messiest yet', he then went home and vomited before working up the courage to call the police. Asked during the trial why he made the call, he said simply that had he not 'I could never have lived with myself.' So much for the influence of the tide of filth Brady had ensured he push his eyes through.

Brady was killing his repressed self, the self he could not abide. Then again, the world is full of homosexuals ashamed of their proclivities, whose guilt manifests itself in nothing worse than neurosis and depression . . .

All of which is a way of saying that Brady was a one-off. It may be that the events of his unhappy life fashioned him into a killer. It may be that he was born a killer. It may be that his malignity was motiveless, or it may be that it had been made by the circumstances of his upbringing. But short of locking him up from the moment of his first wayward act and keeping him under observation twenty-four hours a day, would there have been any way of preventing it?[*] At which point re-enter Pamela Hansford Johnson saying, Yes, there most certainly would. Despatched to Chester by the *Sunday Telegraph* to report on the trial of Brady and Hindley, she became convinced that their choice of reading spoke volumes not just about their horrific crimes but about the souring of the culture whence they sprang.

The victims of the Moors Murders had been killed, she argued, by people who were victims in their turn. Brady and Hindley had been made monsters by what she called the 'all-permissive . . . "swinging" society' beneath whose 'Big Top, the whole garish circus of the new freedom to revel, through all kinds of mass media, in violence, in pornography, in sado-masochism'[53] plied its wicked trade. Though keen to distance herself from any suspicion that she might be 'speaking for any organized body, for Moral Rearmament . . . [or any] . . . "clean-up campaigns", which always wreck their own hopes by bringing their sledge-hammers to crush ants',[54] she shared a Whitehouse-like certainty that we were 'in danger of

---

[*] One journalist has argued pretty much that. He believes that since psychiatrists had worked out that the 17-year-old Brady was a psychopath, he should have been kept 'in captivity, where society could have studied Brady carefully'. See Fred Harrison, *Brady & Hindley: Genesis of the Moors Murders* (Grafton, 1987) pp.25–6.

creating an affectless society, in which nobody cares for anyone but himself, or for anything but instant self-gratification'.[55] The swinging society circus was headed for the moral chaos Dostoyevsky had foreseen in *The Brothers Karamazov*: 'If God is dead, then everything is permitted.'

Certainly Brady was a fan of Dostoyevsky. A copy of *Crime and Punishment* was among the books police found at the house he shared with Hindley. Also on the shelf were Hitler's *Mein Kampf*, *History of Torture Through the Ages*, *Orgies of Torture*, *Sexual Anomalies*, *The Cradle of Erotica* and Geoffrey Gorer's *The Life and Ideas of the Marquis de Sade*. And we know that Brady had read de Sade's *Justine*, a book in which it is decreed that children be murdered, and that his own notebooks were studded with aperçus gleaned from his studies of the Divine Marquis. The prosecutor at the trial read out several, among them Sade's suggestion that murder is 'necessary, never criminal', 'a hobby and a supreme pleasure', and that 'Rape is not a crime, it is a state of mind'.

But thousands of people have read *Justine* (which, like Sade's letters, was first published in English in 1965) and *The Cradle of Erotica*[*] and not become child killers. Nor had every concentration camp guard worked his way through *Mein Kampf*. Perhaps if these books had been banned Ian Brady wouldn't have murdered those children. But as Jack Lambert – the same Jack Lambert who had thought *Saved* a 'grubby maelstrom of spiritual under-nourishment'[56] – remarked of Miss Johnson's book, 'the appetites of people like Brady are formed long before any books can have influenced them. Their appetites will lead them to literature, not vice versa.'[57] Indeed, he detected in the whole debate about permissiveness what he called a 'disguised authoritarianism,

[*] Not what you might be thinking: the book's subtitle is 'A study of Afro-Asian Sexual Expression and an Analysis of Erotic Freedom in Social Relationships', which doesn't sound much fun.

no longer acceptable in societies which have moved beyond the primitive'.*[58] And since, for all its silliness, Britain's burgeoning counterculture was not known for its love of violence even as it was known to love de Sade (one of the few writers the hippies didn't dismiss merely for the fact of being dead), Lambert would seem to have had the last word.

What the censorship debate in sixties Britain really came down to, of course, was snobbery. It wasn't that the would-be censors believed there were things they shouldn't know. It was that they believed there were things *other people* shouldn't know. The would-be banners of books and plays and television shows never seem to have asked themselves why, during their investigations into the art they thought offensive and reprehensible and corrupting, they themselves hadn't been corrupted. Had they paused to wonder – or been pressed on the point by an independent observer – they would have eventually been obliged to acknowledge that they thought there was one rule for us and one rule for them. They would have had to admit that, in essence, they thought many people unfit to read de Sade or watch *Till Death Us Do Part* or *Saved*. Certainly Irving Wardle, who gave *Saved* a hostile notice in *The Times* and later acknowledged that it had been 'the biggest mistake of my reviewing career', came to see that he had viewed

---

* One of the most disturbing aspects of the Moors Murders was Brady's love of – and use of – new technologies. The members of the (deliberately all male) jury at Chester Crown Court had to look at photographs Brady and Hindley had taken to record the internment of their victims. They had to listen to a sixteen-minute tape recording of little Lesley Ann Downey pleading for mercy and help. And they had to look at photographs of her in the moments before her death. Crime reporters of many years standing told Miss Johnson that no trial they had ever attended could have prepared them for hearing that tape recording. So the trial of Brady and Hindley offered a hint that the consumer revolution in gadgets and gizmos might not be all for the good. Whatever else they were responsible for, Brady and Hindley brought about (along with mass car ownership) one of the biggest cultural changes in Britain of the past fifty years – the fact that children are pretty much kept at home and not allowed to play outside without (heavily vetted) adult supervision.

the play through class-tinged spectacles. What had disturbed him about Bond's drama, he realised, wasn't its violence but the fact that its characters 'spoke like urban cavemen ... what reconciled me to the enactment of atrocities [in other violent plays] was a nice turn of phrase such as you find in Pinter and Joe Orton.' Added to that, said Wardle, he had never lived near 'people like Bond's stunted characters', a fact that assisted him in his leap 'to the conclusion that they didn't exist at all outside the playwright's sordid imagination'.[59]

The weird thing is that Edward Bond saw himself as singing from a similar hymn sheet to his moralistic critics. Just as Mary Whitehouse believed she was standing up for the provincial and the uneducated against what she saw as the Oxbridge elites who dominated broadcasting and government,* so Bond claimed in the Preface to *Saved* that his was a play about the bewilderment ordinary people feel in a rationalist, scientistic culture that nonetheless derives what morality it clings to from religion. 'If we are to improve people's behaviour', he wrote, 'we must first increase their moral understanding, and this means teaching morality to children in a way that they find convincing. Although I suppose that most English people do not consciously disbelieve in the existence of God, not more than a few hundred of them fully believe in his existence. Yet almost all the morality taught to our children is grounded in religion. This in itself makes children morally bewildered. Religion has nothing to do with their parents' personal lives, or our economic, industrial and political life, and is contrary to the science and rationalism they are taught at other times.'[60]

Bond was – and is – a Marxist, of course, and was arguing that under an economic system predicated on making human labour as

---

* Her son Richard saw things rather differently. 'She was', he said, 'a bit of a snob. She'd grown up in a house with live-in servants and she had this rather Victorian attitude towards people.' *Daily Mail*, 28 May 2008.

cheap as possible, it is no wonder that people come to think of other people as cheap. Weirdly, again, Mary Whitehouse, for all her loathing of the 'enemies of the West', came to mighty similar conclusions. Her objection to pornography was that it dehumanised all its participants, an argument that is premised on just the kind of claims about capitalist reification that any good Marxist would recognise.*

On 8 November 1965, just a month after the arrest of Ian Brady and Myra Hindley, the House of Commons voted to abolish the death penalty for murder. Writing at the end of the Moors Murders case, Elwyn Jones declared that, 'If a trial is a drama, then that at Chester has lacked climax and catharsis.'[61] The people of Manchester agreed. After the trial and verdicts, 30,000 people signed a petition asking that the government 'bring back the noose'.[62] But a trial isn't a drama, and though one knows what Jones means about a cathartic shortfall, there is no denying that aestheticising death is precisely what Brady – and Hitler and de Sade – had indulged in.

Edward Bond, on the other hand, was emphatically not aestheticising death. Nobody could call *Saved* a pleasant experience, but it is a purgative and purifying one. It is a play that offers not a mirror to the nature of the conventional middle-class playgoer but what Sir Laurence Olivier called 'the sacramental catharsis of a very chastening look at the sort of ground we have prepared for the next

---

* Mrs Whitehouse, predictably enough, had been against the publication in 1960 of the unexpurgated edition of *Lady Chatterley's Lover*, yet there are times when she can sound positively Lawrentian: 'The greatest danger of pornography, it has always seemed to me, lies in its impersonality. If sex does not have to do with communications between people, then it is a travesty. To be stimulated by the exposed genitals of some two-dimensional female is to be impoverished indeed. No talk, no process of discovery of mind and body, no mystery, no tenderness, no shared passion – pornography is such a *travesty* of sex.' (Quoted in Tracey and Morrison, op. cit., p.183) There speaks someone whom the more thoughtful members of the counterculture might have enjoyed listening to.

lot'.[63] And fittingly enough, the play had its own catharsis, in that it was mightily instrumental in the abolition of stage censorship that the British government surreptitiously embarked upon in November 1965.

When Lord Cobbold told the new Home Secretary, Roy Jenkins, that he would consider the government to be undermining his position as theatre censor unless it agreed to the prosecution of those involved in the production of *Saved*, Jenkins acquiesced. But he did so only because he believed that the case would rebound on the prosecutors and make them look absurd. And then, a couple of days after Gaskill, Poke and Esdaile's arraignment, he had his friend Lord Annan initiate a House of Lords debate on the very existence of theatre censorship. Annan proposed that a joint committee from the Lords and the Commons be appointed 'to review the law and practice relating to the censorship of stage plays'.[64]

Annan was if anything more opposed to the Lord Chamberlain than Jenkins. Lord Cobbold was, he later recalled, 'advised by a staff of retired Guards officers' who thought it 'pretty daring when a character [in a play] spoke of something going arse over tip'.[65] And though 'it was terribly difficult to praise the Lord Chamberlain [because] Cobbold was really an awfully stupid man',[66] still Annan ensured that the Lords debate didn't ridicule the Lord Chamberlain for fear of undermining his case. When the committee published its report, in the autumn of 1967, its recommendation that theatrical pre-censorship should end was unanimously agreed upon. Even then, though, Jenkins had a job of it ensuring his measures went through. It wasn't until July 1968 (by which time Jenkins had been moved to the Exchequer and James Callaghan had been made Home Secretary) that the Theatres Act became law.

Cobbold, meanwhile, insisted until the end that playwrights ought not to be allowed to represent real living people in their plays, a sentiment that understandably carried weight with the highest in the land. Certainly neither Buckingham Palace nor the Prime Minister were very keen on the idea of abolishing theatre censorship – largely because both feared impersonation and ridicule. They were right to do so, because once Jenkins had got the bill through Parliament (having had to threaten Wilson with his resignation, it should be said), both were indeed the subject of more or less vicarious dramas. The Prime Minister was, he said, made 'out to be a complete mugwump'[67] in Richard Ingrams's and John Wells's 'affectionate lampoon' *Mrs Wilson's Diary* (an adaptation of their long-running *Private Eye* skit), which debuted at the Criterion Theatre in October 1967.

As for the Queen, while for the moment she herself escaped parody, her great-great-grandmother Queen Victoria was one of the lead characters in *Early Morning* – Edward Bond's 1967 follow-up to *Saved*. In the play, Victoria is not only found in the arms of one of her prime ministers, but is also revealed to be involved in a lesbian love affair with Florence Nightingale.[68] *Early Morning*, which parodies a gangster thriller and shows the royal family plotting to do away with Disraeli and Gladstone, ends in heaven – with the characters abandoning internecine squabbling for out and out cannibalism.* The play was refused a licence, and after its first very short run, audiences had to wait until 1969 to see it in a run of full and free public performances. That same year the Royal Court also put on a new production of *Saved* – this time to far more understanding and positive reviews.

Ken Loach's *Up the Junction*, meanwhile, played its part in what would become the Abortion Act of 1967 – the Act that legalised abortion by registered practitioners and made their practices available through the National Health Service. On 30 November, four weeks after Loach's play went out on TV, Lord Stonham told a House of Lords debate on the abortion bill that 'No one who saw

---

* As did Jean-Luc Godard's *Weekend*, released the same year.

the television film *Up the Junction* can have any illusions about the nature of the evil we are discussing' and that it was time to stop 'living in a world in which many thousands* of teenage girls and young women ... conceive in ignorance and abort in terror'.[69] In the House of Commons, meanwhile, Jenkins argued that an 'uncertain, archaic and harsh' law that ensured many otherwise law-abiding citizens were branded criminals was a bad law – and bad laws could undermine the whole fabric of the state. Moreover, just as with censorship, the question of class clung to the abortion issue, too. Everyone knew that the law was forever being flouted by those who could afford to pay for the services of expensive illegal practitioners, meaning that the law 'blatantly favoured the rich against the poor'.[70] Not any more it didn't.

Perhaps the censors were right after all, then, in their claim that plays and movies had the capacity to change minds. For while it is hard to prove that works of art have any kind of influence – malign or otherwise – on individual consciousness, there can be no denying that they have their effects on the body politic. Certainly Loach's television drama and Bond's stage play had helped change the rules. So too the Moors Murders: Ian Brady was such a radically monstrous figure that to attempt to explain his crimes away as the product of over-permissiveness was to insult not only the memory of his victims but the intelligence of the general public. And so while over the succeeding half century our culture has fallen prey to sporadic outbursts of censoriousness, the people of Britain have shown no interest in undoing the good, liberating work of 1965. They know there is no going back to that mythical vision of a world before the fall. And they know that anyone who imagines he can take them back there needs watching very carefully.

---

* As many as 100,000 a year, according to Lord Silkin in the same debate.

10

THE NEW ARISTOCRACY

In which the new great and good
are set before the nation

*'This is an English habit, to categorise: that if you read
Shakespeare you can't read comics, that if you read science
fiction you can't be serious.'*

Brian Aldiss, *Encounter*, March 1965

O n the evening of 8 December 1965 an Oxford scholarship
undergraduate told the viewers of BBC television that he had
trouble coping with the fact that his father was a miner. Come
vacation time, when he went home to the pit village he had been
raised in, his father and his friends made it plain that they thought
his six-week-long breaks were a decadence no real man could
entertain. Turning to the camera and addressing the viewer directly,
this ambitious young man said that for all the joys of Oxford, and
for all the advantages that his place there would bring him, he felt
estranged from his own life.

Not that he had been all that secure before. For all the comforts
of the family home, he never looked, well, at home there. In

historical footage we see him as a child struggling to fit into a community in which to dream of other worlds, never mind find ways of accessing them, is automatically to exclude yourself from a comfortable residency. Hence, as his teacher bluntly addresses the camera, 'clever children from common homes like his have to be, shall I say, separated from their – ah – backgrounds. I say nothing controversial.'[1]

Nor did she, of course, though separation from one's background turned out to be no more easy for this young man than it had for Dorothy in *The Wizard of Oz*. Certainly he stands at distinct unease in his Oxford gown and mortar board while telling us that he 'fought his way through clouds of coal dust to get here'.[2] The net result of his endeavours has been to leave him restless and rootless in a country he has a less firm grasp on than he did before he started excavating himself from it. Travelling 'between two utterly different worlds' he 'sometimes feel[s] that I need a passport'.[3]

The young man in question was called Nigel Barton, and he was actually the fictional creation of the writer Dennis Potter. Not all that fictional though. Potter's own background was very similar to Nigel's. Like Nigel's, Potter's father had been a miner (though in the Forest of Dean on the England–Wales border rather than in the South Nottinghamshire coalfields in which *Stand Up, Nigel Barton* was filmed). Like Nigel, Potter had made it 'up' to Oxford to read PPE thanks to 'the grace of God and the eleven plus'.[*4] And for all his intellectual brio and aggression, Potter, like Nigel – 'whippet-fancying and bitter by descent' – couldn't help but feel baulked when he finally found himself 'set down among the dreaming spires'.[5] The television producer Lewis Rudd, who met Potter at university, has mockingly

* 'One says "up" at Oxford,' Nigel is obliged to correct his father early on in the play. 'You come "down" when you finish there.'

remembered him as 'The Only Person With a Humble Background at Oxford'.[6]

Autobiographical hero that he was, Nigel Barton was also representative of the kind of alienated aspirant delineated so precisely in Richard Hoggart's book about working class culture, *The Uses of Literacy*. Like Potter and Nigel, Hoggart had been born into the proletariat (in a back-to-back house in Leeds), and then uprooted anxiously from it as his intellect took him off to university. Such a man, Hoggart wrote, feels 'cut off by his parents as much as by his talent which urges him to break away from his group'.[7]

But having broken away, Hoggart argued, these scholarship boys often enough find themselves working in jobs in advertising, publishing and television – jobs that thanks to the ideological underpinnings of mass language might be designed to ensure that their class compatriots are kept firmly in their place. At the same time, the mass culture that results from such endeavours – film, TV, rock and roll – succeeds only in divorcing what is left of the proletariat from its own real, authentic way of life. Designed to breed dissatisfaction, pop was just so much unconsciously politicised pap, and there was an end of it.

Potter was having none of this. Returning home to Berry Hills to make a TV documentary he reported that in the Working Men's Club he found 'nothing to suggest a lumpen, apathetic . . . society' that was being manipulated by the mass media.[8] Far from it – so far from it in fact that Potter took a diametrically opposed view on the power of popular culture. Rather than divide people, he said, the radio and TV and popular song brought them together. Television, he would recall many years later, offered 'at least the possibility of a common culture'. Why? Because it told stories largely in visual rather than verbal form, thereby 'jumping over' what Potter called 'the hierarchies of the printed word'.[9] And because pretty much everyone had access to a TV – and in the days of only two channels to which Potter was referring pretty much had to watch the same shows at the same time as everyone else* – it wasn't, as Hoggart and his acolytes believed, an atomising medium that divorced people from their friends and neighbours and common culture. It was a unifying medium that pulled everyone together. 'All sorts of human beings could share the same experiences,' said Potter, indeed they '*do* share the same experiences'.[10]

Hence Potter was adamant that he wanted to write plays for television rather than for the stage. He saw television as the medium best suited to breaking down the class barriers that he and Hoggart (and Nigel Barton) had had to negotiate a way around. Unlike the theatre, which was popular largely with the middle classes, and the cinema, which was far more the art form of the working class, television was watched by everyone. In the West End theatre, Potter argued, the audience for *Stand Up, Nigel Barton* 'would have been largely on only one side of this particular fence. If it [the play] had worked at all in the cinema, the sort of tensions which any play creates in an audience might have compromised the effectiveness of the story, which attempted to use the specially English embarrassment about Class in a deliberately embarrassing series of confrontations. But with television, I knew that, in small groupings, both coalminers and Oxford dons would probably see this play.'[11]

As well as its ubiquity, television had the virtue of serendipity. More than a few people turned the box on not in the expectation of something in particular but in the expectation of anything in general. At the theatre or the cinema you know in advance – or at least have an idea – what it is that you've bought tickets to see. Not necessarily so with the television, which is far more open to

---

* As late as 1977, the *Morecambe and Wise Christmas Show* had an audience of almost 28 million people – at that time more than half the population of the UK.

random access, because either people simply switch it on to see what's being broadcast, or find themselves watching something they didn't intend to watch because it is being broadcast before or after something they do want to see. Hence Potter's faith in television not only as a kind of pictorial pulpit, but as a kind of accidental, fortuitous pulpit, too. From it you could preach not only to the converted and the unconverted, but to those who had no idea there might be a preaching – and, who knows, a possible conversion – in the offing.

Potter's radicalism in his choice of medium was matched by the formal radicalism of his screenplay. Both *Stand Up, Nigel Barton* and its successor *Vote Vote Vote for Nigel Barton* make use of Brecht's theories of epic theatre and distanciation – theories that at the time one could have been forgiven for thinking ineluctably undermined by the fact of television's intimacy. But Potter had no time for the callow realism that was and is the dominant mode of expression in British television (and cinema). He liked his artistry upfront. He might not have wanted to write for the theatre, but he had learned an awful lot from it.

At Oxford, he had played Azdak in a production of *The Caucasian Chalk Circle*, and throughout his subsequent career he would lean heavily on Brecht's idea that drama should be an arena for estranging its audience from any notion that they might be doing anything other than watching a play. The last thing epic theatre should do, said Brecht, was engender illusion. Rather, it was the purpose of drama to point up its own constructed nature, the better for the audience to grasp the constructed nature of what they too often took for reality outside the theatre. When Nigel (or his teacher) turns to the camera and comments directly to the audience on the action it has just witnessed, he is reminding you that you are watching a carefully constructed dramatic conceit, and forcing you to ask yourself where you stand on the issues it is structured around. He is, in other words, playing the Brechtian game for all it is worth.

Not that the televisual powers thought it was worth all that much. 'It was a time when people tended to say "Oh, you can't do that",' Potter's director, Gareth Davies, has remembered. Nigel's 'address to the audience ... wasn't normally done in [television] plays. Of course, it's done all the time in the theatre, which was my background. So I had no problem with it. We talked about how to distort it. Dennis was always very receptive to technical notions. We decided to ease in with the turret camera on a wide, 35-degree* lens to distort the face gradually. Dennis never wanted realism.'[12] Except, of course, that he did. The issues underlying *Stand Up, Nigel Barton* were absolutely rooted in the real world. Distrusted at home for his Oxbridge ways and disdained at college for his working-class origins, Nigel was a powerful metaphor for those people struggling to keep up with the socio-political change 1965 had helped usher in.

But not everyone found it a struggle. Even as Nigel was airing his confusions about class on TV, the photographer David Bailey was unveiling his *Box of Pin-Ups* – an unbound collection of thirty-six monochrome portraits of what the journalist and soon-to-be Tory MP Jonathan Aitken called 'a Debrett of the new aristocracy'.[13]

Everyone from Terence Stamp to Mick Jagger, from Jean Shrimpton to Michael Caine, from David Hockney to Vidal Sassoon found themselves inside Bailey's LP-sleeve-sized box. A motley-seeming crew – though not, in fact, all that disconnected. Because outside the confines of *Box of Pin-Ups*, so many of its subjects were, like Bailey himself (and like his fellow East End snappers Brian Duffy and Terry Donovan), all working-class kids on the make and on the rise. The rockers and popsters aside, none of Bailey's subjects could have come to fame in the previous decade. (And had Jagger or Lennon been born ten years earlier,

---

* There is no such thing. I assume he means a 35mm lens – a fairly wide-angle lens, that would indeed distort facial features without rendering them globular and unreadable.

they could not have made it to the top as rebellious rockers: pop stars of the fifties were clean-cut kids who never did anything bad – indeed, who never did anything unless their manager and/or backer told them to.)

Nowhere was this class mobility more apparent than in the most (in)famous picture in Bailey's box – its portrait of the three Kray brothers. For the Krays – the twins Ronnie and Reggie and their older brother Charlie – were post-war Britain's most notorious criminals. By 1965 these putatively gentleman villains – of whom it was said that they looked after their own while ensuring the innocent never got hurt – had been running the organised crime in their home patch of London's East End for the best part of a decade. At the same time, they were to be seen hobnobbing with actors and showbiz types, prominent politicians (Ronnie Kray, a homosexual, was said to have had affairs with MPs from both the Tory and Labour parties), even members of the aristocracy proper.

And so, while there was no denying that the Krays were murderous butchers, nor was there any getting away from the fact that they were also emblems of sixties Britain's crumbling class structure. On 19 April 1965, when Reggie married Frances Elsie Shea at St James-the-Less Church, Bethnal Green, he had the event photographed by none other than the country's most famous snapper, David Bailey, who arrived at the church in a blue velvet suit with matching blue Rolls-Royce, for all the world like Cecil Beaton recording the Queen's Coronation of twelve years earlier.

There was, it should be said, something of the butchery about Bailey's work too. The bulk of the portraits in the *Box of Pin-Ups* were composed with one or more brutal crops. Michael Caine had the top of his head lopped off, the pop singer P. J. Proby, who was posed as for a crucifixion, was missing both hands, and now that he wasn't standing for a formal wedding portrait even Reggie

Kray had lost an arm to Bailey's blade-like eye. His lighting was harsh, too – sharply snooted and angled from on high at his models' faces, and with a very strong lamp on the pure white background that ensured his subjects were absolutely isolated in space. The result was what Bailey would later call his 'hard-edged'* style – portraits that might have been tin cut-outs were it not for the astonishing gradation of detail (on skin tones and shirt collars, for example) that he ensured remained in his other-wise stark bank of images. The effect was to decontextualise these people, to suggest that they had somehow sprung, fully formed, into the new meritocratic republic that was being born all around them.

For all that, there was a moralising tone to much of the criticism of the *Box of Pin-Ups*. More than one pundit delivered himself of the opinion that Bailey's collocation of images was both fatuous and dangerous. It wasn't thought quite right that some of the highest and mightiest in the land should be seen keeping company with some of the lowest forms of human life. Malcolm Muggeridge, who believed the camera to be 'the most characteristic and sinis-ter invention of our time' because it had 'ushered in – perhaps, better, crystallised – a religion of narcissism, of which photogra-phers such as Mr Bailey are high priests', said he couldn't find anything to admire in Bailey's choice of subjects, much less enjoy.[14] And perhaps he couldn't, though four years later, when Bailey invited him to sit for a subsequent collection of portraits, he was only too happy to oblige.†

---

* The term was minted for the op art movement we have discussed elsewhere. And indeed, more than one of the images in *Box of Pin-Ups* puts you in mind of Bridget Riley's geometric style.

† Muggeridge being Muggeridge this wasn't much of a volte-face. He changed his mind on everything, though each change was remarkably similar to the last. He was forever admonishing others for indulging in the practices he himself had hitherto enjoyed more than most. While he went through the sixties haranguing the young for their sexual laxity,

But to moralise about the *Box of Pin-Ups* was to miss its point. Bailey's subjects weren't really people at all: they were shapes and lines out of which he could make images. In other words, Bailey was using his camera as the modernist painters had used their canvas and brushes – not to record the world but to make one. All that tight cropping, all those excisions of arms or tops of heads, had the effect of emphasising composition rather than subject: these are pictures about pictures far more than they are pictures about celebrity or notoriety.

By rendering the real world abstract, Bailey was subverting the ur-purpose of his medium – the realistic recording of the illuminated world on light-sensitive film. For almost a century, painters had believed their role as visual transcribers of external phenomena had been usurped (or, depending on your point of view, rendered blessedly null and void) by the invention of the camera. Bailey's portraits of the mid-sixties complicated that story, turning the visual recording medium par excellence into a vehicle for the mechanical production of art-for-art's-sake imagery. The photographer, long the poor relation of that image-maker proper the painter, was becoming a creator himself.

Not that everyone was convinced. Even as Bailey's pin-ups were being boxed, the Italian film director Michelangelo Antonioni was in London (accompanying his then lover, Monica Vitti, during the closing stages of the shoot for Joseph Losey's *Modesty Blaise*[*] [1966]) – and pondering blowing the gaff on Swinging London's idea of the snapper as the latest line of creative genius. The result was

he had spent his own younger life bedding anything that moved. Once, drunk with the novelist Kingsley Amis – of whom more in a little while – he had insisted that they take George Orwell's equally drunken widow Sonia home and have their way with her, turn and turnabout. See Amis's characteristically hilarious chapter on Muggeridge in his *Memoirs* (Hutchinson, 1991), pp.231–2, for this and many other wonderful stories.

[*] Perhaps the ultimate pop-art movie, large chunks of which take place in sets built out of cod Bridget Riley canvases.

Blow-Up (released in 1966), an intellectual thriller in which the very David Bailey-like photographer Thomas (David Hemmings) is made to doubt the underlying reality of the pictures he makes his living by taking.

The story is simplicity itself. After a day snapping illicit shots of a kissing couple in a park, Thomas (a fashion photographer by trade) takes to his darkroom. He is interrupted in developing his pictures, however, by the intrusion of Jane (Vanessa Redgrave), one half of the couple he has just been spying on. She pleads for and then demands the negatives, saying that he had no right to take the pictures. Thomas manages to fob her off with another roll of film, convinced that her desperate need to have the pictures means there's more in them than has yet met his eye. And so he takes to blowing the frames up, bigger and bigger, until he has what looks awfully like the storyboard sketches for the outline of a movie pinned up on the wall of his studio. Then he gets his magnifying glass out and after much poring and probing and re-photograph-ing and enlarging decides that a tiny cluster of high-lit grains in a distant bush in the background of the shot is light reflecting off the barrel of a gun. Unwittingly, he believes, he has – like Abraham Zapruder before him – photographed a murder.

But has he? Or is he just seeing what he wants to see, subcon-sciously nudging his own flattened-out existence in the direction of drama? Thomas has form, after all, as a *maker* (rather than just a taker) of images. Shooting catwalk models in his studio with a suc-cession of ever-lengthening lenses, he isn't above grinding them to near orgasm in order to get just the picture he needs. Were he a more thoughtful man, that is, he might be able to grasp that it is not only not true that the camera never lies – but that it lies all the time. All photographs, including the gritty, grainy monochrome ones he takes of London's dossers and down-and-outs in an attempt to salve his artistic conscience, are fictions – tricks the mind works on our so readily seduced eyes. How else but by trickery could film – which is no more than the speedy projection of still images – convince us that the movies move? 'To see or not to see,' as Antonioni once sagely ribbed Alberto Moravia, 'that is the question.'[15] And if seeing is the answer, then photography will be of no help to you. Photography, *Blow-Up* suggests, doesn't dig down deep, as real art has always claimed to do, but merely serves up tonalised reflections of the surface of the world.[16]

And yet, and yet. If you want to know what London looked like in 1965 – just before the city started its heavily commercialised, sensationalised swing – *Blow-Up* should be among your first ports of call. Whatever else the movie offers, it grants you as pointed and precise a vision of the mid-sixties city as anything discussed in this book. Antonioni's modernism never veered too far into full-on abstraction, partly because he was making a kind of thriller, but mostly because the action of that thriller took place in the streets and parks and snickets of a London that, for all the pockets of pink and purple Carlo Di Palma's camera tracks down, was still, two decades after the end of the war, grimy and grungy and generally ground down. Drab and down-at-heel – such was the landscape in which the sixties revolution of dayglo and tie-dye took root.[*]

But if Thomas's (and Bailey's) photography wasn't quite an art, was Antonioni's cinema? Arguments had raged for decades about the status of film. Was it populist tosh in the business of serving up agitprop fodder to the masses, as many a literary-minded aesthete had declaimed down the years? Or was it a seventh art to add to the six Hegel had isolated in his *Lectures on Aesthetics* in the early nineteenth century?[*] How could a form that required a collective of talents – writers, actors, wardrobe people, lighting technicians –

---

[*] The other movie that best captures the magical weirdness of London as it got set to swing was, of course, the Beatles' *Help!*

[*] Reg Maudling would have known them already, but for the record: architecture, sculpture, painting, dance, music and poetry.

ever make work that was, as all art surely had to be, the expression of a single soul coming to terms with the world?

To take *Blow-Up* – still by some measure one of the most wilfully artistic conceits the cinema has given us – as an example: the film had its origins in a short story by the Spanish writer Julio Cortázar; its script was by the English playwright Edward Bond (on whose *Saved* we have already touched); it starred David Hemmings, a fine actor, to be sure, but (like the Bailey on whom he was modelled) undeniably a pretty boy, too; one of his co-stars was Vanessa Redgrave, a leggy beauty, and scion of a distinguished acting family; one of its scenes consisted of Thomas watching the Yardbirds perform one of their hit songs. (The even more famous The Who had been due to sing but couldn't make the shoot.) All these attractions or distractions meant that there was a far greater number of reasons for going (or not going) to see *Blow-Up* than there were for reading a novel by any author you care to name. It followed, said the critical elites, that film wasn't an art but – a very different thing – mass entertainment.

Not so, said a thirty-something Home Counties English teacher. In September 1965, Robin Wood published a small monograph with the title *Hitchcock's Films*. That possessive was quite deliberate. The book's thesis was that one could – and should – as readily talk of a film directed by Alfred Hitchcock as of, say, a symphony by Wolfgang Amadeus Mozart or a play by William Shakespeare. Those high-culture references were deliberate, too. For Wood, Hitchcock (and several other mainstream moviemakers: Howard Hawks, Orson Welles, Arthur Penn, to name a few) wasn't just a masterly filmmaker. He made films that were as intensely expressive and finely wrought as *Hamlet* and *King Lear* and *The Magic Flute*. And he did so, even if he didn't know he was doing it. For Wood, Hitchcock was far more than the *soi-disant* light entertainer the man himself had bodied forth in a thousand interviews and press releases. Wood's Hitchcock was a moralist, an artist who could see deep into the workings of the human heart, and whose chief concern throughout his career had been less with the thrills of suspense and more with the relations between men and women.

North by Northwest, perhaps Hitchcock's most perfectly realised light thriller, turned out, in Wood's account, to be a condemnatory analysis of moral irresponsibility (both individual and social) and the stunted lives that result when people refuse to put away childish things. *Psycho*, far from being the cheapie shocker even Hitchcock himself had derided it as, was 'one of the key works of our age',[17] a depth-charged examination of the machinations of the evil and the desolate horrors of the human condition. But it was in *Vertigo*, a film that people had laughed at upon its initial release in 1958, that Wood really saw the possibilities for cinematic art. *Vertigo* wasn't a gimcrack thriller in which Hitchcock mistakenly gave the game away halfway through. Looked at objectively and without preconceptions, said Wood, the picture was 'Hitchcock's masterpiece',[18] one of the most profound investigations of romantic love in the whole of Western art, and a film that could 'be taken to represent the cinema's claims to be treated with the respect accorded to the longer established art forms'.[19]

To those critics who (rather like Hitchcock himself) said, but they're only movies, you can't take them seriously, Wood retorted that Shakespeare had been the leading popular dramatist of his day and that Mozart had written music that was intended to be talked over and through. High art, that is, hasn't always been seen as high art. Today's elite cultural artefact was yesterday's pop cultural experience. Snobbery about film was just that – snobbery, premised on the notion that certain forms of entertainment are intended for the lower classes and certain other forms aimed at those higher up the cultural food chain. While a student at Cambridge, Wood tells us in the preface to one of the book's many revised editions he was to be found 'sneaking off (when my intellectual friends, to whom I stood in awe, weren't looking)' to see movies at the local cinema.[20]

At base Wood's argument was that Hitchcock was the author of his films. Hence the name of the theory from which his book essentially derived – the auteur theory. Auteur, because talk of the director's importance in filmmaking hadn't started in Britain. It was a French idea, elaborated in the mid to late fifties by a group of writers and thinkers – Jean-Luc Godard, Claude Chabrol, Jacques Rivette, Eric Rohmer and others – who were bent on auteuring films themselves. Auteurs weren't, of course, like authors proper, in sole creative charge of the stories they told. Nonetheless, a great auteur was possessed of such a unified vision of the world and everything in it that he or she was able, through force of personality and artistic focus, to be in sole creative charge of the set of sub-creators – actors, lighting crews, set designers and the like – working for him or her. That meant that the work of a great auteur could, like the work of a great novelist or painter, become the expression of a single spirit. Alfred Hitchcock might appear to have been working within the confines of the dominant Hollywood genres (thrillers, romances, horror, international intrigues). But the potency of his imaginative reactions to those forms (as well as to the forms that life itself offered him) meant that despite working in a collective field he was in fact the 'onlie begetter' of the movies that bore his name.

In the half century since its first publication, *Hitchcock's Films* has rarely been out of print. The book invented the idea of serious film criticism in Britain, and has a large claim to being the foundation stone of what in schools and universities around the world are now called film studies. But its power went further than the origination of a new academic discipline. Wood's core argument, that a film director had the potential to be an artist, accounts for the fact that today even the least cine-literate people can be heard talking of the new Guy Ritchie film or the latest pictures from the Coen brothers. Things were not always so. Prior to the publication of Wood's book, people tended to discuss movies in terms of their stars. Now everyone knows who the directors worth talking about are.

Fifty years on, it is difficult to grasp what a sea change this was in terms of what we would now call film aesthetics. *Hitchcock's Films* engendered a whole new field of study. Over the next few years shelves began to strain under the weight of books that were published on one or other hack movie director who turned out to have been an artist all along. Not even the best efforts of as formidable a thinker as Pauline Kael – whose first book, *I Lost it at the Movies*, was published in 1965, and in which she took issue with what she called the 'rigid formula' of auteurism – were enough to stop the tide of director worship.[21] The desire to dignify mass culture, to find significance where previously there had only been seen silliness and sentimentality, was too great to be done away with.

Not even that ever-sceptical novelist and poet Kingsley Amis, who had become famous over the past decade for saying what others thought unsayable, was immune. Ever since the publication of his first novel in 1954, one of Amis's main concerns had been what he saw as the declining standards in British education. Anyone who thinks that worries about educational dumbing down began in the eighties or nineties should read *Lucky Jim*. Fully thirty years earlier, Amis's hero, Jim Dixon, himself a beneficiary of the post-war opening up of university life to the working and lower-middle classes, was to be found railing against the expanding numbers of substandard students who have to be given degrees regardless of their abilities (because if they aren't then the local authorities who subsidise them are going to come asking why their money is being squandered).[22]

Not that Amis – or Jim – was any kind of snob. A scholarship boy himself, Amis was a meritocrat who believed that talent should be encouraged wherever it was found. And in 1965 he made it known that he found a great deal of evidence for it in the works of the recently deceased thriller writer Ian Fleming. *The James Bond Dossier*, the book Amis published on Fleming's oeuvre within a few weeks of the appearance of *Hitchcock's Films*, made no pretence to academic status. Scholarly though its take on the Ian Fleming phenomenon was – Amis found in Bond a hero of Byronic romanticism, and among those people the book references or mentions in passing are Aristotle, the Brontës, Shakespeare and Matthew Arnold – it was also a sly dig at a culture industry unwilling to take seriously anything liked by lots of people. Amis had recently given up his job as an English don at Cambridge, and after a decade and more of talking to frequently refractory and recalcitrant readers, was, he said, 'drawn to any form of writing which (like science fiction) reaches no part of its audience through compulsion'.[23]

But just because the Bond novels were popular didn't mean that they were mere escapist nonsense, said Amis. Or rather, if Fleming was pandering to the escapist impulse then this is hardly shocking. All art, up to and including *Hamlet*, is inescapably escapist. This is so not simply because we turn to art to console ourselves against the depredations of the world, but because art's essential impulse and meaning, 'that life is coherent and meaningful', is as escapist a fantasy as there is.[24]

Perhaps unsurprisingly, then, unsurprising even though he had made his name as a social realist moralist with a sharp eye for the quotidian and the mundane, Amis was also a fan of science fiction. Indeed, in 1959, when he was lecturer and resident fellow in what he called 'Creadive Wriding' at Princeton University, he had chosen to give the prestigious Gauss Seminars on the subject.[25] And now, a few weeks after the publication of *The James Bond Dossier*, he was to be found contributing to Brian Aldiss and Harry Harrison's *SF Horizons* – a new scholarly journal, and the first given over to what can only be called science-fiction criticism.

But the serious treatment of what had hitherto been thought mere lower class frippery was suddenly everywhere in 1965. As we have seen, back at the start of the year, mere days after the death of

T. S. Eliot, the *Observer* – by some measure the newspaper with the highest brow in Britain – had appointed George Melly as its first 'critic of pop culture'. His task was to alert a readership already in the know about the lies of Degas and Donizetti that the likes of Dylan and *Doctor Who* were worth a look, too. During the course of his first year in the job, Melly took in blues gigs, rock concerts, *Top of the Pops* and *Ready Steady Go!*, the semiotics of Acker Bilk's bowler hat and the self-pitying memoirs of Sammy Davis Jr. His seventh column of the year took for its subject what he called 'the British version of Rhythm and Blues' which has 'elbowed the Liverpool beat groups, always excepting the Beatles, out of the charts'. Always excepting indeed. For the Beatles, who have woven their way through so much of this book, weren't just forever in the charts in 1965. They were everywhere.

One of the places they were was Buckingham Palace – there to pick up the MBEs they had been awarded in the Queen's Birthday Honours List. This was, it should be said, an astonishing moment. These days we take it for granted that rock and royalty belong together on the same show-business bill. Not so in 1965. Back then, pop stars were regarded by pretty much anyone older than their young fan base as minor league reprobates at best. (As late as the 1980s, when pop wasn't merely the country's main cultural export but one of its major commercial exports, Margaret Thatcher could deliver herself of the opinion that this rock music stuff was so much moral detritus sapping the will of youth.*)

But it was precisely pop's appeal to youth that explained why Buckingham Palace was so keen to have the Beatles on board, argued Tony Benn. By demonstrating that they were down with the kids, the royals were thinking to strengthen their own position

---

* Asked once if she liked any pop music she declared a fondness for the Tornados 'Telstar', a shabby Joe Meek cash-in from 1962 on the then new satellite. What she liked about the record, she said, was that it was about technology.

in an increasingly egalitarian and meritocratic society. So too, of course, was the Prime Minister, though Benn wasn't entirely convinced by the plan. 'I think that Harold Wilson makes the most appalling mistake if he thinks that in this way he can buy popularity,' he noted in his diary, 'for he is ultimately bolstering a force that is an enemy of his political stand.'[26]

Nor were the papers over-impressed. 'It seems', noted a *Sun* editorial, 'that the road from rebellion to respectability is much shorter than it used to be.'[27] Not that the Beatles laboured overmuch to pretend to respectability. McCartney's 'I think it's marvellous. What does that make my Dad?'[28] was as obsequious as the Fabs got about their elevation to high society. After the ceremony they made it known that they had enjoyed a calming joint in one of Buck House's loos. Suitably relaxed, they were soon wisecracking about their gongs. 'I'll keep it to dust when I'm old,' Ringo said.[29] 'I didn't think you got that sort of thing just for playing rock and roll,' said George Harrison.[30] His sceptical tones were echoed by John Lennon, who told the post-ceremony press conference that he thought the Beatles had been singled out for their awards because 'We've paid the government quite a bit in tax.'[31] Later on the scepticism turned to cynicism. 'I thought you had to drive tanks and win wars to get the MBE,' he told a reporter.[32]

He wasn't alone. Quite a few tank-driving types agreed with him. For weeks after the awarding of the Beatles' MBEs, Buckingham Palace received one letter after another from irate honorees. George Read, a coastguard decorated for bravery, was 'so disgusted with the Beatles being given this award that I am considering sending mine back'.[33] Colonel George Wagg needed no time for such niceties. He returned twelve of his medals to the palace – and resigned his membership of the Labour Party (which had put the Beatles up for the award) to boot.[34] Paul Pearson, a former RAF squadron leader, sent his MBE back too. 'I feel', he told *The Times*, 'that when people like the Beatles are given the MBE the whole thing becomes debased and cheapened. I am making this gesture in the hope that the Queen's position in this situation can be reinforced so that she can resist and control her Ministers.'[*][35] (Four years later, in November 1969, Lennon would return his own MBE to Buckingham Palace as a protest against Britain's involvement in various wars around the world.)

As rock royalty, of course, Lennon and McCartney were among those photographed for Bailey's *Box of Pin-Ups*. Dressed in black,[†] and shot with Paul crouching and John kneeling behind and above him, Lennon's wrists resting on McCartney's upper arms, they made for one of the *Box*'s most abstract compositions. Bailey's high-contrast printing turns the twosome into a series of interlaced strokes and lines that evokes rather more potently than Lennon and McCartney themselves ever did outside the musical arena how dependent on each other's strengths their own talents were.

Certainly the Beatles' two main songwriters were barely writing together by 1965. Georges Braque once said that when they were creating cubism he and Picasso had been 'roped together like mountaineers'. So too Lennon and McCartney, though by 1965, after eight long years of working together, the rope had begun to work its way around their necks. (Intriguingly, the Beatles final album, *Abbey Road*, was originally to have been called *Everest*.) McCartney's musical bonhomie became an increasing affront to Lennon. Lennon's increasingly modernist aesthetic seemed to McCartney like an insult to music lovers proper.

Still and all, while hordes of screaming schoolgirls attested to

---

[*] Three hundred and twenty years or so earlier, of course, the English people had fought another war to prevent the monarch doing just that.

[†] Not strictly true – contact prints of the shot evidence an impressively large tonal range – but Bailey so burned in the dark parts of the image that his subjects might as well have been wearing nothing but black.

the fact that John and Paul harmonised beautifully, there is no denying that their real genius was for counterpoint. Macca's sweetness was forever being soured by Lennon's fury, Lennon's romantic heat always being tempered by McCartney's classical cool. McCartney would never let Lennon get away with the tuneless ranting Yoko Ono would later license, and Lennon would never let McCartney write the twee ditties that have littered so much of his post-Beatles career. For though they rubbed each other up the wrong way, Lennon and McCartney never rubbed each other out. Harmony made them famous, but it was disharmony that made them great. Great artists are always in two minds, and with McCartney as the ego to Lennon's id the resultant musical personality wasn't so much split as perfectly balanced: two bits of grit, two glorious pearls.

Nonetheless, by the time of the release of the Beatles' fifth album, *Help!* (in August 1965), and its successor *Rubber Soul* (released in December 1965) both Lennon's and McCartney's (and George Harrison's and Ringo Starr's) creative partner of choice was marijuana. So reliant on the drug were they that Lennon later said he and his fellow Beatles were smoking it for breakfast during the making of Richard Lester's film *Help!* (released in July 1965).[*]

It was on *Rubber Soul*, though, that the Beatles' love affair with dope was really made manifest. You can hear it in Lennon's deliberately pronounced – and heavily miked up – intake of breath after he sings the chorus line on 'Girl'. ('Oh, girl, phfffffffft'). You can see it on the album's sleeve art. For one thing, Robert Freeman's portrait shows that by the autumn of 1965 the boys were all growing their hair longer than their fans' parents might approve of. For another, the picture, like that on the front of Dylan's *Bringing It All Back Home*, had a whacked-out, ever so slightly spacey feel.

---

[*] One could fill a whole page of this book with similar sets of parentheses about the Fabs' achievements during 1965.

In Dylan's case this had been achieved by fogging and blurring everything but the central image (an effect arrived at with no more than the judicious application of a little Vaseline to the outer rim of the photographer's lens). For *Rubber Soul*, though, the startling visuals were the product of an accident. When Freeman was showing the band the slides he'd taken, the screen on which he was projecting them tilted away from the vertical, with the result that the image itself tilted away into the distance too. (To picture the effect, think of the title credits in *Star Wars*, in which the type drifts off into space at an angle to the screen while shrinking towards a Renaissance-style vanishing point.) The result was that the Fabs' faces were somehow stretched and flattened out on the album sleeve – or on another plane altogether, to use a phrase that was about to start buzzing, as if hovering in that mysterious fourth-dimension of space intersected by time that is familiar to all tokers.

Inside that sleeve, the record itself was no less artful. Each of the Beatles' four previous LPs had been some kind of improvement on its predecessor, but with *Rubber Soul* the band began to move into areas hitherto unexplored by mere pop groups. Robert Freeman has said that he wanted his cover shot to have 'an entirely different tonality'[36] from those that had gone before it. It was an ambition shared by the record itself. For a pop album, *Rubber Soul* is marked by a tonal ambiguity that owes as much to Richard Wagner as it does to rock and roll. 'Think For Yourself' hovers between the major and minor variants of G, 'Michelle' plays the same trick in the key of F, while 'Girl' modulates constantly between C minor and its relative major of E flat. 'If I Needed Someone' meanwhile (written by George Harrison under the influence of his new interest in Indian music) ventures from A major to B minor, a thrillingly rare manoeuvre that could so easily be distractingly self-obsessed but sounds here almost like musical second nature.

Nobody knows how the Beatles arrived at such harmonic

sophistication, at such dauntingly inventive musical architecture.* It is true that thanks to his father's love of music hall and show tune standards, Paul McCartney grew up listening to more than just foursquare, meat and potatoes rock and roll on the radio. Nonetheless, rock and roll had dominated his life, just as it had dominated Lennon's and Harrison's (and Ringo Starr's) – and rock and roll, which consisted largely of songs written around the I, IV and V chords (i.e. the major chords) of a scale, had so few lessons to teach songwriters as inventive as the Beatles.

Certainly once they had mastered the form, they quickly sought to widen it. McCartney's love of tin-pan alley songs might have irked Lennon, but he felt sufficiently threatened by his partner's pushing the envelope that he was soon pushing at his own. Harrison, meanwhile, was moved to shake things up in his own songwriting by his burgeoning interest in all things Indian. *Rubber Soul* was the first of many sixties pop records to feature the droning twang of the sitar.

And then there was the Beatles producer, George Martin (still the man most overlooked in terms of the Beatles' astonishing musical development), a classically trained pianist and a musician whose work with the likes of the Goons and Peter Sellers in the fifties had seen him experiment relentlessly with the possibilities of the recording studio. This last was the side of his talents that mattered most to the Beatles. They were the first rock and roll band to break out of the form's aesthetic straitjacket of guitar, drums and bass.†
Martin's virtuosity wasn't, it should be said, always for the best.

---

* Years after the Beatles had gone their separate ways McCartney was offered lessons in music theory at a top academy. After only a couple of sessions the teacher told him there was no point going on – not because he was a hopeless student, but because there was nothing he hadn't worked out for himself long ago.
† Forty odd years later Ian McEwan would have a character in one of his novels wonder why rock and roll bands required a drummer: the beat was so plain and straightforward that the piano and guitar were more than capable of doing the work. (See *On Chesil Beach*, Jonathan Cape, 2007)

Rubber Soul's perfection is marred by the presence of an insipid, clever-clever keyboard solo he wrote for the end of 'In My Life'. Still, the Beatles' increasingly varied choice of instrumentation serves to remind us that only ten years into its life, rock and roll was running short on endogenous inspiration and looking to the music it had thought to overthrow for ideas.

Rubber Soul was an idea in itself. The title is both a sly bit of word-play (rubber-soled shoes are still available) and a comment on the inauthenticity putatively inherent in pop itself. McCartney had overheard a conversation between black musicians in which Mick Jagger's singing was deemed to be 'plastic soul' – i.e. not the real thing. Nobody could say the same of *Rubber Soul*, a work of authentic artistry and the first long-playing pop record to really merit the term 'album'. Unlike earlier Beatles LPs, and emphatically unlike those LPs being made by other bands, it was recorded in a set and fixed period of time (astonishingly, a mere four weeks* rather than just thrown together as and when the Fabs had time to spend in the studio between gigs and radio appearances and television interviews. As such, it was far and away the most coherent and unified work of art the Beatles had yet created. It was also the album that proved that rock and roll could be suitable for adult audiences.

Which isn't to say it was any less vital than its predecessors. One of the great joys of the Beatles is that they never quite put away childish things. What marks *Rubber Soul* out in their canon is that it is on this album that they began to ask themselves questions about what those childish things meant. Having spent the past few years stirring and spicing the salty lusts of adolescence (rock and roll's essential theme), the Beatles changed the recipe for an even headier mix. The idyllic boy–girl romance that had figured so heavily

---

* A year or so later the Beatles went into the studio to start work on *Sgt. Pepper's Lonely Hearts Club Band*, an album that would take some 129 days to record.

on all the Beatles' previous records was here complicated by the admission that things weren't often always that ideal. Harrison's 'If I Needed Someone', by some measure the best song he had yet written, was a declamation of his own state of emotional independence. McCartney's 'Drive My Car' (on which we touched in chapter 4), 'You Won't See Me' and 'I'm Looking Through You' all exhibit a for him uncharacteristically brooding and abrasive quality. The inspiration for 'You Won't See Me', for instance, was the fact that McCartney's girlfriend, the actress Jane Asher, had left him alone in London while she was playing the title role in Frank Marcus's *Cleo* at Bristol's Little Theatre. (Feminism might have been on the rise in 1965, but it plainly hadn't got anywhere near the toppermost of the poppermost.) Indeed, the only song on the album on which he sounds like the mooning, love-struck Macca of old is 'Michelle' – a delightful number, but one which in pastiching a thousand French folk songs plays up to the very inauthenticity McCartney had thought to call time on: plastique soul.

Unsurprisingly, Macca's putative partner's contributions to the album were even more brutal in their candour. Lennon, after all, had a history of violence towards women (once, at a college dance, he punched his wife-to-be Cynthia in the face 'so hard that her head struck a heating pipe on the wall' before 'walk[ing] off without a word'[37]), though only those close to him would have known so at the time. Now, though, it is plain as day that 'Girl', with its gripes about 'the kind of girl who puts you down when friends are there', the kind of girl who believes that 'pain would lead to pleasure', is an anti-feminist rant. That 'Run for Your Life' is unreconstructed macho nonsense. And that while 'Norwegian Wood (This Bird Has Flown)' was the first demonstration of Lennon's capacity for writing melodies as coilingly beautiful as those of McCartney, the comic story of misogyny it tells is only a notch away from Les Dawson.

On the other hand, there is no denying that it was on *Rubber*

Soul that Lennon found a way towards a new sensitivity in his work. True, the sensitivity was reserved almost entirely for songs that took as their subject Lennon himself, but there is no point pretending that this wasn't some kind of aesthetic development. Take 'Nowhere Man': its vision of ennui and alienation may verge on the self-indulgent, but it also takes the album to within striking distance of the existential terrain that Bob Dylan had spent the past year or so staking out. The song's closing refrain, meanwhile, which asks whether the Nowhere Man mightn't be 'a bit like you and me', is far more directly challenging than the neurotic aggression of the Dylan songs Lennon was clearly out to best.

The odd bit of sexual coding aside, the Beatles always wrote in the kind of plain words that Ernest Gowers would have approved of. Both McCartney and – especially – Lennon loved wordplay, but the Beatles could never have cooked up the numinous, nonsensical stews that Dylan dined out on in the mid-sixties. Even the songs of their high psychedelic period – which begins with *Rubber Soul*'s 'The Word' – are so easy to get a handle on that they seem positively homely. Magritte made the suburban surreal, but the Beatles made the surreal suburban. The charm of a song like 'Lucy in the Sky with Diamonds', with its 'marmalade skies', 'tangerine trees' and 'cellophane flowers', lies in the down-at-heel domesticity of its subversions. Even as the counterculture he helped inspire danced crazily around him, McCartney was to be found composing a cosy ditty wishing 'Everybody everywhere [a] Good Night'. And when, a year after the release of 1968's 'The White Album', Charles Manson claimed he had been inspired to kill by the track 'Helter Skelter', a prickly Macca ridiculed the claim, arguing that it was about a fairground ride. For all the song's violence, its wrenching cacophonous whorls, there is no reason to think its writer disingenuous.

For the innocence of childhood – both Lennon and McCartney had lost their mothers while young – was one of the Beatles great themes. Despite all the revolutionary impetus of their work from *Rubber Soul* on, the Beatles' music was suffused with nostalgia for a world gone by. Come the Summer of Love they weren't to be found wearing beads and kaftans but military uniforms borrowed from the Edwardian era of their grandparents. That is why the Beatles, like the countercultural movement they drove, never talked about the promise of a better tomorrow, never even pretended to know how things could be ordered better in the here and now. Earlier generations of rebels had premised their insurrection on the idea of how things would be once they were in charge. The Beatles generation had no such fantasies. They didn't want to be in charge. They didn't want the responsibility.

Not that this made them anti-revolutionaries – any more than the Rolling Stones in-your-face stroke and strut was necessarily insurrectionary. Unconscious and ill thought out as it was, the Beatles' worship of childhood innocence linked them to the sixties only truly radical fantasy – the non-repressive-, pleasure-principle-based society dreamed of in the philosophy of Herbert Marcuse and the anti-psychiatry of R. D. Laing we have discussed elsewhere.

More important, at least in artistic terms, is that the Beatles' worship of childish innocence ensured that their eyes were open to new experiences far more than even their most experimental competitors. As apprentice musicians in Hamburg at the start of the sixties, they met and befriended people who had a very un-English openness to both modernist aesthetics and the free-spirited take on life they believed they had found in French existentialism. A fan of Camus and Sartre and even the Marquis de Sade, Astrid Kirchherr, girlfriend of the Beatles' original bassist, Stuart Sutcliffe, and the photographer who took the first iconic pictures of the band, called herself an 'Exi', a nomenclature the Fabs themselves were happy to steal.

How much of Sartre's *Being and Nothingness* or Camus's *The Rebel* the Beatles actually read need detain us as little as one suspects the books themselves detained them. What matters is that after being exposed on no matter how lowly a plane to new ideas and concepts they were determined to do the same for their audience. The avant-garde tics and tricks the band increasingly used as the sixties wore on had their roots in the self-consciously arty subculture of Hamburg's philosophically questioning youth. Without such influences we would likely not have tracks like Lennon's 'Revolution 9' or 'A Day in the Life' – tracks whose arrant meaninglessness couldn't have existed without a largely unschooled middle-class boy from the English suburbs having some kind of grounding in the often impenetrable angst of post-war European thought. Even McCartney, that devotee of the sweetening melody, was bitten by the existential bug. What is the titular character of 'Eleanor Rigby', who 'Waits at the window, wearing the face that she keeps in a jar by the door', but an emblem of the alienated, non-authentic life Sartre and co. were forever holding up to the light?

By broadening the range of its subject matter, and by widening the field of sounds that it could be made from, the Beatles reinvigorated the pop tradition. More, they reminded pop fans that what they loved really was part of a tradition – that even if it wanted to, rock and roll, no matter how innovative, could never negate what had gone before. It was part of what had gone before. There was room for argument when critics began talking of 'Lennon and McCartney as the greatest songwriters since Schubert'[38] – better than Richard Strauss, better than Rodgers and Hart, better than Bacharach and David? – but only someone as brilliantly confused as Glenn Gould could have sought to deny that they were part of the same tradition.[39] For what the Beatles served – and serve – to remind us is that in art there is only one tradition. Ever since the Industrial Revolution, Western culture had been split on what were essentially class lines. There was high art and there was popular culture, and it was as impossible to appreciate both as it was to hide your origins in declaring to which you gave your allegiance. The

Beatles' achievement was to lay waste to this tragic bifurcation, and to remind us that the only split that counts is the one that separates good from bad.

This is not to deny that the mass literacy the Industrial Revolution gave birth to did not in its turn give birth to acres of trash. Nor is it to suggest that the modernist experiment that grew out of a horror of what that revolution had engendered at the social level was absolutely misguided. But it is to say that the Beatles – like all the other painters and writers and moviemakers we have discussed throughout this book – had worked out a navigable route through that cultural Scylla and Charybdis, had found a way of unifying the shallow certainties of mass culture with the dread doubts of modernism. Despite Duke Ellington's contemporaneous suggestion that most people 'still take it for granted that European-based music – classical music, if you will – is the only really respectable kind',* the Beatles (like Dennis Potter, like Kingsley Amis, like George Melly, like Robin Wood) had shown not that popular culture could be art but that it already *was* art.

---

* The remark was made in response to the news that the Pulitzer committee had turned down Ellington's nomination for its 1965 Music Prize. Resignations followed, and no prize was awarded that year. 'Fate', Ellington quipped, 'is being kind to me. Fate doesn't want me to be famous too young.' At the time, he was 66.

EPILOGUE

In which today comes into view

The Beatles might have been made MBEs in 1965, but the footballer Stanley Matthews was knighted – the first player to be so honoured, and the only one to have been so while still actually playing. But there was another, more culturally vital footballing first that year. Among the players lining up for Leeds United against Liverpool at Wembley stadium on 1 May 1965 was a left-winger called Albert Johanneson. He was the first black man to play in an FA Cup Final.

Johanneson had been a prodigy since his early teenage days in South Africa's industrial heartland. A Johannesburg cobbler, he had developed his skills playing for Germiston Callies and the even less well-known Hume Zebras. He was a big fish in a small pond. Then, in 1961, one of the small fish, Barney Gaffney, put a call through to the big pond and suggested they might want to come take a look. A scout for Leeds United flew over, and Johanneson, then only nineteen, was immediately signed up to play alongside the likes of Billy Bremner and Johnny Giles in Don Revie's Second Division team.

He spent the rest of the sixties with Leeds, moving to York City for the early part of the next decade. He was, a later Leeds manager, Howard Wilkinson, once said, 'our first glimpse of that kind of silky soccer player'. In the first three years after his signing he scored thirteen League goals, and Leeds were promoted to the First Division. Then things moved up another gear for them. In 1965 they were runners-up to Manchester United in the League, and they lost to Liverpool in that Cup Final.

Truth be told, Johanneson's performance that day was one of his least impressive. But it was a history-making appearance, all the same. There had been professional black soccer players in Britain since the Edwardian era – Walter Tull played for Tottenham Hotspur – and amateurs since the Victorian, but to play in the Wembley Stadium was a whole new ball game. Four years earlier, within minutes of Johanneson's arrival at London airport, he had heard a passer-by call him a 'nigger', and while Johanneson was adamant that he'd 'found no colour prejudice in England', there is no denying that when Leeds played at Anfield in the mid-sixties, fans at the Kop would chant 'Coco-pop, Coco-pop' at him. Which means that his appearance at Wembley was a milestone of a kind in the history of race relations in Britain.

There was an even bigger one to come. On 8 December 1965, the government's new Race Relations Act came into force. This forbade discrimination on the 'grounds of colour, race, or ethnic or national origins' in public places. Thanks to amendments forced by the opposition, the new law did not actually outlaw racial discrimination but made it merely a civil offence. Nonetheless, the Act was the first of the Labour government's many reforms designed to usher in what their chief architect had earlier called 'the civilized society'.

The architect in question was Roy Jenkins, at the time the Wilson government's Minister of Aviation, and the author of a Penguin Special entitled *The Labour Case* which devoted a whole chapter to answering the question 'Is Britain Civilized?' On the whole, Jenkins thought, the answer was no. A radical reformer (his radicalism was what commended him to Wilson who was chary of being seen to run a merely competent government), he thought the country repressed and repressive, intolerant and old-fashioned, and in need of a good shake-up on the personal liberty front.

Theatre censorship, on which we have already touched, was out of touch and out of date; capital punishment was a 'useless' and 'barbaric' penalty; the prohibition of (male) homosexuality was an unreasonable and illegitimate hangover from the days of Victorian brutality; the laws on abortion were 'harsh and archaic'; the divorce laws led to both 'unnecessary suffering and a great number of attempts (many of them successful) to deceive the courts'. The laws of Sunday observance, which prohibited the use of buildings and rooms for public entertainment or debate on the Sabbath day, were 'ridiculous and (fortunately) largely unenforceable'.

Two days before Christmas 1965, Jenkins was sworn in as Home Secretary and began putting his plans for a newly civilised country into action. Over the next couple of years he legitimised and concretised so much of what the pioneers of our year had been fighting for. After setting up the Race Relations Board he quickly set about bolstering and building on the Race Relations Act, a modified and strengthened version of which appeared in 1968. Soon he began work on liberalising the laws on divorce, homosexuality and abortion and ensuring that the temporary stay in the death penalty was made permanent. He had flogging removed from the penal code and eventually from the prison discipline code.

Friends and foes alike are agreed that Jenkins remains the most influential Home Secretary of the twentieth century and the chief political architect of the Britain we live in today. (Margaret Thatcher vies with Jenkins for ideological import, but she could not have risen as far as she did without the benefit of the reforms he introduced.) Charged, by the likes of Thatcher and Norman Tebbit, with having inaugurated what they called 'the permissive society' Jenkins said that he thought of it as 'the civilized society', adding that if they thought his legislation so poor they should surely amend or repeal it.

But even if it sincerely believed that it would do the country good to once more outlaw, say, homosexuality, what government could even dream of reversing Jenkins's reform? What government could imagine that making abortion illegal again would win them votes, that toughening up the laws on divorce would make it more popular, that kowtowing to racists or censors would beef up its support? Jenkins once called his stint at the Home Office 'the liberal hour'. It has turned into a liberal half-century, and there is no prospect of our turning the clock back on his reforms.

Nor can there be any turning the clock back on the cultural revolution of 1965. It was fifty years ago today, as the Beatles almost sang, but it is also only yesterday (as the Beatles really did sing in another, rather different song). The year really is that recent, because we are still living through the aftershocks of its impact. By breaking down cultural and political barriers, by erecting new social barriers, by closing the gap between putatively high and low cultures, by rendering the popular modernist and the modernist popular, the Britain of 1965 gave us the Britain we all of us live in. It was the year that gave us a new tomorrow – the tomorrow that is our today.

ACKNOWLEDGEMENTS

Writers write when they are alone, but to be alone when not writing is not good for one's sanity. So for help, ideas, memories, jokes, digs, walks, drinks, I'd like to thank a few back-stage helpers.

My agent, Ben Mason, was a patient but properly taxing task-master when it came to fleshing out the briefest of pub-chat ideas into a coherent structure.

Sharon Kemp, to whom the book is dedicated, was patient, too, refusing to get annoyed or angry when I suggested I might have to spend another evening watching Diana Rigg in *The Avengers*.

My good friend Sinclair McKay, a fellow writer and *Avengers aficionado*, helped out with tapes and DVDs, books and ideas, not to mention mocking irony. There was more, a lot more, of the last from Tim Roberts. Paul Fisher was always on hand to discuss the finer points of just about everything.

The staffs at the London Library, the British Film Institute and more than one newspaper cuttings room have all assisted me in my research.

Leon Wieseltier, Lucas Wittman, Lisa O'Kelly, Will Skidelsky, Lorien Kite, Katy Guest, Caroline Jowett, Andrew Davies, Kate Mossman, Jude Rogers and Will Eaves are among the arts and books editors who have asked me to write on subjects that related in one way or another to this rather bigger project.

For the production of the book I have to thank Colin Midson, who commissioned it, and Mike Jones and Abigail Bergstrom who took it over – and wielded wondrously blue pencils on my wickedly purple prose – when Colin moved on. Anneka Sandher designed a wonderful dust jacket. Martin Bryant's probing edit of the finished manuscript was a revelation, for which many thanks. Needless to say, all errors and omissions are my own.

I wasn't quite three years old when the events with which this book begins were taking place, not quite four at the time of the book's close. A far from fully sentient being, in other words, although I am told that one of my earliest utterances was that Winston Churchill was 'dead and dying'. I came to full consciousness in the 1970s, and one of the first things I was conscious of was the feeling that I had just missed out on the greatest party ever. Somehow or other, from half-heard conversations among older cousins at family weddings, from a friend's obsession with reruns of *The Prisoner*, from my older brother's obsession with Bob Dylan, from my own obsession with Sean Connery, I came to believe that there had been a lot more fun to be had in the sixties than looked like ever being on offer to adolescents of my age. Johnny Rotten and Elvis Costello and Robert De Niro soon came along to disprove this theory, but that doesn't mean that the decade that I missed out on stopped haunting my reveries. I hope this book shows that it still does.

SELECT BIBLIOGRAPHY

Ackroyd, Peter, *T. S. Eliot*, Hamish Hamilton, 1984

Adams, Hugh, *Art of the Sixties*, Phaidon, 1978

Addison, Paul, *Churchill: The Unexpected Hero*, Oxford University Press, 2005

Adonis, Andrew and Pollard, Stephen, *A Class Act: the Myth of Britain's Classless Society*, Hamish Hamilton, 1997

Aird, Alisdair, *The Automotive Nightmare*, Hutchinson, 1972

Aitken, Jonathan, *The Young Meteors*, Secker & Warburg, 1967

Aldgate, Anthony, Chapman, James, Marwick, Arthur (eds), *Windows on the Sixties: Exploring Key Texts of Media and Culture*, I. B. Tauris, 2000

Alvarez, A., *The Savage God: A Study of Suicide*, Weidenfeld & Nicolson, 1971

Amis, Kingsley, *The James Bond Dossier*, Jonathan Cape, 1965

Annan, Noel, *Our Age: Portrait of a Generation*, Weidenfeld & Nicolson, 1990

Armes, Roy, *A Critical History of the British Cinema*, Secker & Warburg, 1978

Barnes, Mary and Berke, Joe, *Mary Barnes: Two Accounts of a Journey through Madness*, Free Association, 1991

Berke, Joseph (ed.), *Counterculture*, Peter Owen, 1969

Bernstein, George L., *The Myth of Decline: The Rise of Britain Since 1945*, Pimlico, 2004

Beveridge, Allan, *Portrait of the Psychiatrist as a Young Man: The Early Writing and Work of R. D. Laing, 1927–1960*, Oxford University Press, 2011

Bond, Edward, *Saved*, Methuen, 1966

Bond, Edward, *Notebooks*, vol. I, Methuen, 2000

Booker, Christopher, *The Neophiliacs: A Study of the Revolution in English Life in the Fifties and Sixties*, Collins, 1969

Buono, Oreste Del, and Eco, Umberto (eds), *The Bond Affair*, translated by R. A. Downie, Macdonald, 1966

Burston, Daniel, *The Wing of Madness: The Life and Work of R. D. Laing*, Harvard University Press, 1996

Calvocoressi, Peter, *The British Experience 1945–75*, The Bodley Head, 1978

Campbell, Christopher, *Mini: An Intimate Biography*, Virgin, 2009

Campbell, John, *Roy Jenkins: A Biography*, Weidenfeld & Nicolson, 1983

Campbell, John, *Edward Heath: A Biography*, Jonathan Cape, 1993

Carey, John, *The Intellectuals and the Masses: Pride and Prejudice Among the Literary Intelligentsia, 1880–1939*, Faber & Faber, 1992

Caulfield, Max, *Mary Whitehouse*, Mowbrays, 1975

Chapman, James, *Saints and Avengers: British Adventure Series of the 1960s*, I. B. Tauris, 2002

Clarke, Nick, *The Shadow of a Nation: The Changing Face of Britain*, Weidenfeld & Nicolson, 2003

Clarke, Peter, *Hope and Glory: Britain 1900–1990*, Allen Lane, 1996

Clay, John, *R. D. Laing: A Divided Self*, Hodder & Stoughton, 1996

Connolly, Cyril, *The Selected Works – Volume One: The Modern Movement*, Picador, 2002

Connolly, Ray (ed.), *In the Sixties*, Pavilion, 1995

Cook, William (ed.), *Tragically I was an Only Twin: The Complete Peter Cook*, Century, 2002

Cott, Jonathan (ed.), *Bob Dylan: The Essential Interviews*, Wenner, 2006

Crosland, Susan, *Tony Crosland*, Jonathan Cape, 1982

Crossman, Richard, *The Diaries of a Cabinet Minister* (3 volumes), Jonathan Cape, 1975, 1976, 1977

De Jongh, Nicholas, *Politics, Prudery and Perversions*, Methuen, 2000

Dickstein, Morris, *Gates of Eden: American Culture in the Sixties*, Harvard University Press, 1997 (revised edition)

Diski, Jenny, *The Sixties*, Profile, 2009

Eliot, T. S., *For Lancelot Andrewes: Essays on Style and Order*, Faber & Gwyer, 1928

Eliot, T. S., *Thoughts After Lambeth*, Faber & Faber, 1931

Eliot, T. S., *Notes Towards the Definition of Culture*, Faber & Faber, 1948

Eliot, T. S., *Selected Essays*, Faber & Faber, 1951

Fack, Dietmar, *Automobil, Verkehr un Erziehung: Motorisierung und Sozialisation zwishcen Beschleunigung und Anpassung, 1885–1945*, Leske & Budrichnn, 2000

Foot, Paul, *The Politics of Harold Wilson*, Penguin, 1968

Fuller, John, Mitchell, Julian, McLaren, Robin, Donaldson, William (eds), *Light Blue, Dark Blue: An Anthology of Recent Writing from Oxford and Cambridge Universities*, Macdonald, 1960

Gilbert, W. Stephen, *Fight and Kick and Bite: The Life and Work of Dennis Potter*, Hodder & Stoughton, 1995

Goodman, Jonathan, *The Moors Murderers: The Trial of Myra Hindley and Ian Brady*, David & Charles, 1973

Green, Jonathon, *All Dressed Up: The Sixties and the Counterculture*, Jonathan Cape, 1998

Harrison, Fred, *Brady & Hindley: Genesis of the Moors Murders*, Grafton, 1987

Harrison, Paul, *The Black Flash: The Albert Johanneson Story*, Vertical Editions, 2012

Hattersley, Roy, *Fifty Years On*, Little Brown, 1997

Hayman, Ronald, *The Death and Life of Sylvia Plath*, Heinemann, 1991

Henshaw, David, *The Great Railway Conspiracy*, Leading Edge, 1991

Heylin, Clinton, *Revolution in the Air: The Songs of Bob Dylan 1957–1973*, Constable, 2009

Heylin, Clinton, *Behind the Shades*, Faber & Faber, 2011

Hobsbawm, Eric, *Age of Extremes: The Short Twentieth Century 1914–1991*, Michael Joseph, 1994

Hobsbawm, Eric, *Interesting Times: A Twentieth Century Life*, Allen Lane, 2002

Hughes, Robert, *The Shock of the New*, BBC, 1980

Jenkins, Peter, *Mrs Thatcher's Revolution: The Ending of the Socialist Era*, Jonathan Cape, 1987

Johnson, Pamela Hansford, *Cork Street, Next to the Hatter's: A Novel in Bad Taste*, Macmillan, 1965

Johnson, Pamela Hansford, *On Iniquity: Some Personal Reflections Arising out of the Moors Murder Trial*, Macmillan, 1967

Judt, Tony, *Postwar*, Heinemann, 2005

Judt, Tony, and Snyder, Timothy, *Thinking the Twentieth Century*, Heinemann, 2012

Kudielka, Robert (ed), *Bridget Riley: Dialogues on Art*, Zwemmer, 1995

Ladd, Brian, *Autophobia: Love and Hate in the Automotive Age*, University of Chicago Press, 2008

Laing, Adrian, *R. D. Laing: A biography*, Peter Owen, 1994

Laing, R. D., *The Divided Self*, Tavistock, 1960

Laing, R. D., *The Self and Others: Further Studies in Sanity and Madness*, Tavistock, 1961

Laing, R. D., *Reason and Violence: A Decade of Sartre's Philosophy, 1950–1960*, Tavistock, 1964

Laing, R. D., *Knots*, Tavistock, 1970

Laing, R. D., *The Politics of the Family and Other Essays*, Tavistock, 1971

Laing, R. D., *The Facts of Life*, Allen Lane, 1976

Laing, R. D., *The Voice of Experience*, Allen Lane 1982

Laing, R. D., *Wisdom, Madness and Folly: The Making of a Psychiatrist, 1927–1957*, Macmillan, 1985

Le Carré, John, *The Spy Who Came in from the Cold*, Gollancz, 1963

Le Carré, John, *The Looking Glass War*, Heinemann, 1965

Levin, Bernard, *The Pendulum Years: Britain and the Sixties*, Jonathan Cape, 1970

Levy, Shawn, *Ready, Steady, Go!: Swinging London and the Invention of Cool*, Fourth Estate, 2002

Lucie-Smith, Edward, *Movements in Art Since 1945*, Thames & Hudson, 1969

MacDonald, Ian, *Revolution In the Head: the Beatles records and the Sixties*, revised edition, Fourth Estate, 1997

Malcolm, Janet, *The Silent Woman: Sylvia Plath and Ted Hughes*, Vintage, 1995

Marqusee, Mike, *Chimes of Freedom: The Politics of Bob Dylan's Art*, New Press, 2003

Marwick, Arthur, *The Sixties*, Oxford University Press, 1998

Masters, Brian, *The Swinging Sixties*, Constable, 1985

McKie, David and Cook, Chris (eds), *The Decade of Disillusion*, Macmillan, 1972

Melly, George, *Revolt Into Style: The Pop Arts in the 50s and 60s* (revised edition), Oxford University Press, 1989

Miller, Toby, *The Avengers*, BFI, 1997

Mullan, Bob, *Mad to Be Normal: Conversations with R. D. Laing*, Free Association Books, 1995

Mullan, Bob (ed.), *R. D. Laing: Creative Destroyer*, Sage, 1997

Mullan, Bob, *R. D. Laing: A Personal View*, Duckworth, 1999

Murphy, Robert, *Sixties British Cinema*, BFI, 1992

Nadeau, Maurice, *The History of Surrealism*, Jonathan Cape, 1968

Nader, Ralph, *Unsafe at Any Speed*, Grossman, 1965

Nuttall, Jeff, *Bomb Culture*, MacGibbon & Kee, 1968

O'Brien, Geoffrey, *Dream Time: Chapters from the Sixties*, Viking, 1998

Plath, Sylvia, *Ariel*, Faber & Faber, 1965

Plath, Sylvia, *Letters Home*, Faber & Faber, 1992

Plath, Sylvia, *Journals: 1950–1962*, Faber & Faber, 2000

Plowden, William, *The Motor Car and Politics: 1896–1970*, Bodley Head, 1971

Potter, Dennis, *The Nigel Barton Plays*, Penguin, 1967

Riley, Bridget, *Paintings and Drawings, 1961–2004*, Ridinghouse, 2004

Rose, Jacqueline, *The Haunting of Sylvia Plath*, Virago, 1991

Roszak, Theodore, *The Making of a Counter Culture: Reflections on the Technocratic Society and its Youthful Opposition*, Faber & Faber, 1970

Russell, John and Gablik, Suzi (eds), *Pop Art Redefined*, Thames & Hudson, 1969

Sedgwick, Peter, *Psycho Politics*, Pluto, 1982

Sked, Alan and Cook, Chris, *Post-War Britain: a Political History, 1945–1992*, Penguin, 1993

Sked, Alan, *An Intelligent Person's Guide to Postwar Britain*, Duckworth, 1997

Stevenson, Anne, *Bitter Fame: A Life of Sylvia Plath*, Viking, 1989

Taylor, A. J. P., et al, *Churchill: Four Faces and the Man*, Penguin, 1969

Thompson, Ben (ed.), *Ban This Filth!: Letters from the Mary Whitehouse Archive*, Faber & Faber, 2012

Tiratsoo, Nick (ed.), *From Blitz to Blair: A New History of Britain Since 1939*, Weidenfeld & Nicolson, 1997

Tracey, Michael and Morrison, David, *Whitehouse*, Macmillan, 1979

Wagner-Martin, Linda, *Sylvia Plath: A Literary Life*, Macmillan, 1998

Walker, Alexander, *Hollywood UK: the British Film Industry in the Sixties*, Stein and Day, 1974

Wheen, Francis, *The Sixties: A Fresh Look at the Decade of Change*, Century, 1982

Whitehouse, Mary, *Cleaning-Up TV: From Protest to Participation*, Blandford Press, 1967

Whitehouse, Mary, *Who Does She Think She Is?*, New English Library, 1971

Williams, Emlyn, *Beyond Belief: A Chronicle of Murder and its Detection*, Hamish Hamilton, 1967

Wolmar, Christian, *Broken Rails: How Privatisation Wrecked Britain's Railways*, Aurum, 2001

Wood, Robin, *Hitchcock's Films Revisited* (revised edition), Columbia University Press, 2002

Young, Michael, *The Rise of the Meritocracy, 1870–2033: An Essay on Education and Equality*, Penguin, 1961

Ziegler, Philip, *Wilson: The Authorised Life*, Weidenfeld & Nicolson, 1995

Ziegler, Philip, *Edward Heath: The Authorised Biography*, Harper Press, 2010

NOTES

Introduction

1 See Jann Wenner's interview with Lennon, *Rolling Stone*, 4 February 1971.

2 Quoted in Shawn Levy, *Ready, Steady, Go!: Swinging London and the Invention of Cool* (Fourth Estate, 2002), p.353.

3 Dominic Sandbrook, *White Heat: A History of Britain in the Swinging Sixties* (Little Brown, 2006), p.798.

4 Robert Hughes, 'On Lucian Freud', *New York Review of Books*, 13 August 1987.

5 Margaret Thatcher, speech to Conservative Central Council, Harrogate, 27 March 1982. The full text is available online at www.margaretthatcher.org/document/104905

1. Goodbye to All That

1 *Sunday Times*, 31 November 1944, quoted in T. S. Eliot, *Notes Towards the Definition of Culture* (Faber & Faber, 1948), p.17.

2 And 'always surrounded by crooks' too. See *Evelyn Waugh: The Letters of Evelyn Waugh*, edited by Mark Amory (Weidenfeld & Nicolson, 1980), p.630.

3 Evelyn Waugh, *Brideshead Revisited: The Sacred and Profane Memories of Captain Charles Ryder*, revised edition (Penguin, 1962), p.177.

4 Quoted in Mary Soames, *Clementine Churchill: The Biography of a Marriage* (Cassell, 1979), p.488.

5 Quoted in Anthony Montague Brown, *Long Sunset* (Phoenix, 1996), p.171.

6 From Munnings' speech to the Royal Academy, 1949.

7 *The Times*, Monday, 25 January 1965, p.12.

8 Quoted in Anthony Storr, 'The Man' in *Churchill: Four Faces and the Man*, A. J. P. Taylor et al (Penguin, 1969), p.230.

9 Quoted in John Wheeler-Bennett, *Action This Day: Working with Churchill* (Macmillan, 1968), p.236.

10   *Guardian*, 21 April 1963.

11   Quoted in Robert L. Sullivan, *Macaulay: The Tragedy of Power* (Harvard, 2010), p.132.

12   Quoted in David Stafford, *Churchill & Secret Service* (Thistle, 2013), p.1.

13   Winston Churchill, *My Early Life: 1874–1904* (Thornton Butterworth, 1930), p.44.

14   'Election Intelligence', *The Times*, 6 July 1899.

15   Winston Churchill, *My Early Life: 1874–1904* (Thornton Butterworth, 1930), p.44.

16   Winston Churchill, *The Second World War* – abridged one volume edition (Pimlico, 2002), p.220.

17   T. S. Eliot, 'Wells as Journalist', *New English Weekly*, 8 February 1940.

18   Roy Jenkins, *Churchill* (Macmillan, 2001), p.95.

19   Elsewhere in the same piece Grigg called the end of the Second World War 'a delusive victory for Britain'. Since during the 2010 election campaign the leader of the Liberal Democrats, Nick Clegg, was denounced by the press for saying much the same thing, one could be forgiven for thinking Grigg's confidence misplaced. 'Churchill and after', *Guardian*, 25 January 1965.

20   The Queen's message of sympathy to Lady Churchill. Quoted in *The Times*, 25 January 1965, p.12.

21   John Ramsden, *Man of the Century: Winston Churchill and his Legend since 1945* (HarperCollins, 2002), p.3.

22   Richard Lamb, *The Macmillan Years 1957–1963: The Emerging Truth* (John Murray, 1995), pp.164–5.

23   Alphonse de Lamartine, *Méditations* (Cambridge University Press, 1920), p.9.

24   A. L. Rowse, 'Churchill's place in history', in Charles Eade (ed.), *Churchill by His Contemporaries* (Hutchinson, 1953), p.507.

25   Isaiah Berlin, 'Mr Churchill', *Atlantic*, September 1949.

26   Quoted in Ramsden, op. cit., p.14.

27   Richard Crossman, *The Diaries of a Cabinet Minister: volume 1, 1964–66* (Jonathan Cape, 1975), p.145.

28   Quoted in Peter Boyle, 'The "Special Relationship" with Washington', in John W. Young (ed.), *The Foreign Policy of Churchill's Peacetime Administration, 1951–1955*, Leicester University Press, 1988.

29   From Lloyd George's diary entry, 17 January 1920, quoted in Paul Addison, *Churchill: The Unexpected Hero* (Oxford University Press, 2005), p.93.

30   Sarah Churchill, *A Thread in the Tapestry* (Andre Deutsch, 1967), p.17.

31   John Fowles, *The Magus* (Jonathan Cape, 1966), p.3.

32   Grigg, op. cit.

33   The editor in question was Anne Ridler. See Peter Ackroyd, *T. S. Eliot* (Hamish Hamilton, 1984), p.255.

34   *The Times*, Friday, 8 January 1965, p.11.

35 Cyril Connolly, *The Selected Works – Volume One: The Modern Movement* (Picador, 2002), p.227. The piece originally appeared in the *Sunday Times* in 1965.

36 *Paris Review,* Issue 21, 1959. Reprinted in the *Paris Review* Interviews: 1 (Picador USA, 2006), p.79.

37 T. S. Eliot, *Selected Essays* (Faber & Faber, 1951, third edition), p.289.

38 See Eliot's 'London Letter' in *The Dial*, October 1921, vol. LXXI, no.4.

39 Ibid.

40 See Stephen Spender, *Eliot* (Fontana, 1975), p.129.

41 T. S. Eliot, *Thoughts After Lambeth* (Faber & Faber, 1931), p.10.

42 *Paris Review*, Issue 21, 1959. Reprinted in the *Paris Review* Interviews: 1 (Picador USA, 2006), p.70.

43 *New Yorker*, 16 January 1965, p.25.

44 T. S. Eliot, *For Lancelot Andrewes: Essays on Style and Order* (Faber & Gwyer, 1928), p.ix.

45 Lionel Trilling, *Prefaces to the Experience of Literature* (Oxford University Press, 1981), p.277.

46 Lawrence Alloway, 'The Long Front of Culture', *Cambridge Opinion* 17 (1959), reprinted in John Russell and Suzi Gablik (eds), *Pop Art Redefined* (Thames & Hudson, 1969), p.41.

47 The basic argument of John Carey, *The Intellectuals and the Masses: Pride and Prejudice Among the Literary Intelligentsia, 1880–1939* (Faber & Faber, 1992).

48 Ackroyd, op. cit., p.239.

2. Far Out, Man!

1 John Lennon, *In His Own Write* and *A Spaniard in the Works* (joint edition, Pimlico, 1997), p.62.

2 Quoted in Elizabeth Thomson and David Gutman (eds), *The Lennon Companion* (Macmillan, 1987), pp.47–8.

3 See 'On the Teaching of Modern Literature' in Lionel Trilling, *The Moral Obligation to be Intelligent*, Leon Wieseltier (ed.) (Northeastern University Press, 2008), p.400.

4 Quoted in Philip Norman, *John Lennon: The Life* (HarperCollins, 2008), p.400.

5 Cook talking on *Person to Person*, BBC TV, 1979.

6 Jacques Vaché, 'Lettres de Guerre', quoted in Maurice Nadeau, *The History of Surrealism* (Jonathan Cape, 1968), p.25.

7 See 'Good Behaviour', John Bird, in Lin Cook, (ed.), *Something Like Fire: Peter Cook Remembered* (Methuen, 1996), pp.28–9.

8 Quoted in Harry Thompson, *Peter Cook: A Biography* (Hodder & Stoughton, 1997), p.81.

9 *Evening Standard*, 9 May 1968.

10 Quoted in John Lahr's *New Yorker* obituary cum tribute to Cook, reprinted in *Light Fantastic: Adventures in Theatre* (Bloomsbury, 1996), pp.110–11.

11   Quoted in Maurice Nadeau, *The History of Surrealism* (Jonathan Cape, 1968), p.25.

12   Thompson, op. cit., pp.180–1.

13   'Thoughts and Afterhoughts', Alan Bennett, in Lin Cook (ed), *Something Like Fire: Peter Cook Remembered* (Methuen, 1996), p.32.

14   Lahr, op. cit., p.108.

15   The script for the sketch, 'On Music', can be found in Peter Cook and Dudley Moore, *Dud and Pete: The Dagenham Dialogues* (Methuen, 1971), pp.27-38.

16   *Four Calling Birds*, BBC2, 1990. Reprinted in William Cook (ed), *Tragically I Was an Only Twin: the Complete Peter Cook* (Century, 2002), p.316.

17   'First Manifesto of Surrealism', Andre Breton (1924), reprinted in Charles Harrison and Paul Wood (eds), *Art in Theory: 1900–1990 – An Anthology of Changing Ideas* (Blackwell, 1992), p.438.

18   Roman Polanski, *Roman Polanski* (Heinemann, 1984), p.1.

19   See 'The importance of being Polanski', Lee Langley, *Guardian*, 10 May 1965.

20   Quoted in John Berger, *About Looking* (Bloomsbury reprint, 2009), p.163.

21   Roman Polanski, quoted in 'Surréalisme et Cinéma', *Etudes Cinémotagraphique* 41/42, 1965, p.171.

22   Quoted in Hans Richter, *Dada: Art and Anti-Art* (Thames & Hudson, 1965), p.72.

23   Quoted in Dawn Ades, *Dada and Surrealism Reviewed* (Arts Council of Great Britain, 1978), p.260.

24   John Lennon, op. cit., p.15.

25   Quoted in Thompson, op. cit., p.361

3. 'You're Going to Lose that Girl'

1   Riley in conversation with Andrew Graham-Dixon on Radio 3, 10 December 1992. Reprinted in Robert Kudielka (ed), *Bridget Riley: Dialogues on Art* (Zwemmer, 1995), p.69.

2   Quoted in Lynne Cooke, 'Encore', in *Bridget Riley: Paintings and Drawings, 1961–2004* (Ridinghouse, 2004), p.103.

3   Ibid., p.89.

4   Ibid., p.332.

5   'Perception is the medium', reprinted in Robert Kudielka (ed.), *The Eye's Mind: Bridget Riley – Collected Writings 1965–2009* (Thames & Hudson, 2009), p.90.

6   Bridget Riley, 'The Pleasures of Sight', 1984, reprinted in Robert Kudielka (ed.), *The Eye's Mind: Bridget Riley – Collected Writings 1965–2009* (Thames & Hudson, 2009), p.34.

7   Jonathan Aitken, *The Young Meteors* (Secker & Warburg, 1967), p.196.

8   Riley in conversation with Jenny Harper, 'The Spirit of Enquiry', reprinted

in Robert Kudielka (ed.), *The Eye's Mind: Bridget Riley – Collected Writings 1965–2009* (Thames & Hudson, 2009), p.176.

9   Riley in conversation with Michael Bracewell, 'A Plea for Painting', *Guardian*, 15 March 1997.

10   Ibid.

11   William Seitz, *The Responsive Eye* (MOMA, 1965), p.31.

12   Riley in conversation with Mel Gooding, 1988, 'The Experience of Painting', reprinted in Robert Kudielka (ed.), *The Eye's Mind: Bridget Riley – Collected Writings 1965–2009* (Thames & Hudson, 2009), p.147.

13   Michael Kimmelman, 'Modern Op', *New York Times*, 27 August 2000.

14   Bridget Riley, 'The Hermaphrodite' (1973), reprinted in Robert Kudielka (ed.), *The Eye's Mind: Bridget Riley – Collected Writings 1965–2009* (Thames & Hudson, 2009), p.41.

15   Ibid.

16   Ibid.

17   Ann Jellicoe, *The Knack* (Faber & Faber, 1962), p.11.

18   Ibid., p.69.

19   Ibid., p.16.

20   I am indebted to Neil Sinyard's monograph *Richard Lester* (Croom Helm, 1985) for this insight.

21   'Lady Lazarus', Sylvia Plath, *Ariel* (Faber & Faber, 1965), p.9.

22   See Alvarez, *The Savage God* (Weidenfeld & Nicolson, 1971), p.53.

23   Anthony Thwaite (ed.), *Selected Letters of Philip Larkin, 1940–1985* (Faber & Faber, 1992), p.660.

24   Philip Larkin, *Required Writing: Miscellaneous Pieces 1955–1982* (Faber & Faber, 1983), p.281.

25   'Daddy', Sylvia Plath, *Ariel* (Faber & Faber, 1965), p.48.

26   Sylvia Plath, *Journals: 1950–1962* (Bantam, 2000), p.221.

27   Quoted in Ronald Hayman, *The Death and Life of Sylvia Plath* (Heinemann, 1991), p.90.

28   Sylvia Plath, *Journals: 1950–1962* (Bantam, 2000), p.212.

29   Ibid.

30   Quoted in Anne Stevenson, *Bitter Fame* (Viking, 1989), p.76.

31   Ibid. (and p.77).

32   See Dido Merwin's Appendix to Stevenson, p.334.

33   See Janet Malcolm, *The Silent Woman: Sylvia Plath and Ted Hughes* (Vintage 1995), p.143, for the relevant letter.

34   See Nancy Hunter Steiner, *A Closer Look at 'Ariel'* (Faber & Faber, 1974), p.51 for the discussion of what Steiner calls Plath's 'periodic[. . .] symbolic salvations'.

35   Hughes' foreword to *The Journals of Sylvia Plath* (Bantam, 2000), p.xi.

36   See Hughes' introduction to Sylvia Plath, *Collected Poems* (Faber & Faber, 1981).

37 Hughes talking to the *Paris Review*, Spring 1995.
38 See the confused and confusing preface to Wagner-Martin's *Sylvia Plath: A Biography* (Chatto & Windus, 1988), pp.11–12 for more of this tautologous nonsense.
39 Quoted in Marjorie Perloff, 'Sylvia Plath's Collected Poems', *Resources for American Literary Study*, Autumn 1981.
40 Quoted in Janet Malcolm, *The Silent Woman: Sylvia Plath and Ted Hughes* (Vintage, 1995), p.36.
41 Sylvia Plath, *Letters Home* (Faber & Faber, 1992), p.233.
42 Malcolm, *The Silent Woman: Sylvia Plath and Ted Hughes* (Vintage, 1995), p.38.
43 Ibid.
44 Sylvia Plath, 'Daddy', *Ariel* (Faber & Faber, 1965), p.49.
45 This delightful phrase is Diane Middlebrook's, *Times Literary Supplement*, 27 October 1989.
46 See the Preface to John Fowles, *The Aristos* (Jonathan Cape, 1964), p.10.
47 Ibid.
48 John Fowles, *The French Lieutenant's Woman* (Jonathan Cape, 1969), p.69.
49 John Fowles, *The Collector* (Jonathan Cape, 1963), p.171.
50 I am indebted to Simon Loveday's *The Romances of John Fowles* (Macmillan, 1985) for this point. See p.13.
51 John Fowles, *The Magus* (Jonathan Cape, 1966), p.29.
52 Revised edition, p.264.
53 John Fowles, *The Collector* (Jonathan Cape, 1963), p.111.
54 *New Statesman*, 6 May 1966.
55 See 'An Interview with Julie Christie' in *Very Heaven: Looking Back at the 1960s*, Sara Maitland (ed.) (Virago, 1988), p.171.
56 *Daily Mail*, 14 September 1965.
57 Elizabeth Lane, *Hear the Other Side* (Butterworths, 1985), p.141.
58 From 0.3 per cent of married couples in 1965 to 0.5 per cent in 1970 and to a full 1 per cent by 1975.
59 Cate Haste, *Rules of Desire: Sex in Britain, World War I to the Present* (Chatto & Windus, 1992), p.293.

4. The Freedom Trap

1 Marshall McLuhan, *Understanding Media: the Extensions of Man* (Routledge, 1964), p.236.
2 See *Drive* magazine, http://www.jgballard.ca/deep_ends/drive_mag_article.html
3 E. J. Mishan, *The Costs of Economic Growth* (Praeger, 1967), p.94.
4 Department for Transport, *Transport Statistics Great Britain 2008* (HMSO, 2008), p.138.

5   G. M. Mackay, 'Automobile Design and Pedestrian Safety', *International Road Safety and Traffic Review*, XIII (3), 1965, pp.29–32.

6   Quoted in Alisdair Aird, *The Automotive Nightmare* (Hutchinson, 1972), p.188.

7   Ralph Nader, *Unsafe at Any Speed* (Grossman, 1965).

8   Geoffrey Moorhouse, 'Mr Nader holds his fire on Britain', *Guardian*, 15 June 1966.

9   Quoted in David Henshaw, *The Great Railway Conspiracy* (Leading Edge, 1991), pp.120–1.

10   William Plowden, *The Motor Car and Politics: 1869–1970* (Bodley Head, 1971), p.368.

11   *British Medical Journal*, 11 September 1965.

12   Hansard (Lords), 24 June 1965,

13   Hansard (Commons), 1 December 1965.

14   *Restoring the Quality of our Environment*, Environmental Pollution Panel of the President's Science Advisory Committee (1965).

15   Colin Buchanan, *Traffic in Towns* (Penguin, 1963).

16   Michel Ragon, *Paris, hier, aujourd'hui, demain* (Hachette, 1965), p.67.

17   'Road on stilts crash is their nightmare', *Sunday Citizen*, 28 March 1965.

18   Quoted in Plowden, op. cit., p.386

19   Loretta Lees, Tom Slater and Elvyn Wyly, *Gentrification* (Routledge, 2007), p.12.

20   See Richard Crossman's Diaries for more – a lot more – on the woman he called 'the Dame'. Crossman, it should be said, was no more charitable to what he called the 'middle-class ... snob appeal ... of rat infested slums', though throughout his Diaries he is more than once pleased to tell readers how much he adores Prescote, his Oxfordshire manor house surrounded by 500 acres ...

21   Quoted in Pieter Zwart, *Islington: A History and Guide* (Sidgwick & Jackson, 1973), p.121.

22   'Spaghetti Junction', *Birmingham Evening Mail*, 1 June 1965.

23   Barbara Castle, *The Castle Diaries 1964–70* (Weidenfeld & Nicolson, 1984), p.152.

24   *Birmingham Post*, 29 May 1999.

25   Henshaw, op. cit., p.147. I have relied extensively on this fine book for this section.

26   Ibid.

27   Ibid.

28   Hansard (Lords), 17 July 1969.

29   British Railways Board, *The Reshaping of British Railways*, part 1 (1963), p.57.

30   Quoted in Howard Hampton, *Public Power: The Fight for Publicly Owned Electricity* (Insomniac Press, 2003), p.171.

31   Quoted in Ian Jack, 'Asking business to reshape public services is not always mistaken', *Guardian*, 23 February 2013.

32   See Henshaw, op. cit., p.174.

33 See Tony Judt, 'Bring back the rails!', *New York Review of Books*, 13 January 2011.

34 See 'Transport and the Environment', Traffic Engineering and Control, May 1970.

35 Randall Jarrell, *Kipling, Auden & Co: Essays and Reviews 1935–1964* (Farrar, Straus & Giroux, 1980), p.277.

5. Something Is Happening Here

1 Hussey's letter to Bernstein, quoted in Humphrey Burton, *Leonard Bernstein* (Faber & Faber, 1994), p.347.

2 *Sunday Times*, 8 August 1965.

3 Bernstein writing to Hussey, quoted in Burton, op. cit., p.348.

4 Bernstein talking to Peter Rosen in the CBS film *Leonard Bernstein: Reflections: An Exploration of the Conductor's Career Over Three Decades* (1978).

5 James Baldwin, 'Stranger in the Village', originally published in 'Notes of a Native Son', in his *Collected Essays* (Library of America, 1998), p.121.

6 Frances Taylor, 'Dylan Disowns His Protest Songs', *Long Island Press*, 17 October 1965.

7 Joseph Haas, 'Bob Dylan talking', *Chicago Daily News*, 27 November 1965.

8 In December 1965. Quoted in Robert Shelton, *No Direction Home: The Life and Music of Bob Dylan* (revised edition, Omnibus, 2011), p.199.

9 The press conference can be seen at http://www.youtube.com/watch?v=Dc PoZZVm3Dk.

10 See Don Pennebaker's *Don't Look Back* (1967).

11 See Nat Hentoff, 'The *Playboy* Interview', reprinted in Craig McGregor (ed.), *Bob Dylan: A Retrospective* (Angus & Robertson, 1973), p.56.

12 *Time* magazine's Horace Judland in *Don't Look Back*.

13 Ibid.

14 See Derrida's *Of Grammatology* (Johns Hopkins University Press, 1976) for more on the Western habit of privileging spoken over written speech.

15 See Theodor Adorno, *The Culture Industry: Selected Essays on Mass Culture* (Routledge, 2001), p.37.

16 Quoted in Clinton Heylin, *Behind the Shades* (Faber & Faber, 2011), p.148.

17 Quoted in Anthony Scaduto, *Bob Dylan* (Abacus, 1972), p.175.

18 Quoted in Dorian Lynskey, *33 Revolutions Per Minute: a History of Protest Songs* (Faber & Faber, 2011), p.163.

19 Quoted in Shelton, op. cit., p.218.

20 Hentoff, op. cit., p.58.

21 Hentoff, op. cit., p.59.

22 Quoted in Shelton, op. cit., p.203.

23 Dylan to *Disc Weekly*'s Laurie Henshaw, quoted in Shelton, op. cit., p.204.

24 See http://www.phfilms.com/index.php/phf/film/dont_look_back/

25 Quoted in Cameron Crowe's liner notes to the *Biograph* box set.

26   Quoted in Heylin, op. cit., p.126.

27   Quoted in Peter Dreier, 'The political Bob Dylan', *Dissent*, May 2011.

28   Heylin, op. cit., p.17.

29   Quoted in Shelton, op. cit., p.201.

30   Quoted in Heylin, op. cit., p.461.

31   The quote is taken from Johns's Sketchbook A (1963–4), in Kirk Varnedoe and Christel Hollovoet (eds), *Jasper Johns: Writings, Sketchbook Notes, Interviews* (Harry N. Abrams, 1996), p.31.

32   See Dylan interviewed by Nora Ephron and Susan Edmiston, August 1965, collected in Jonathan Cott (ed.), *Bob Dylan: The Essential Interviews* (Wenner, 2006), p.50.

33   See, for instance, Fred Orton, *Figuring Jasper Johns* (Reaktion, 1994), p.98.

34   McGregor, op. cit., p.59.

35   Quoted in Heylin, op. cit., p.196.

36   See Charles Shaar Murray, *Crosstown Traffic: Jimi Hendrix and Post War Pop* (Faber & Faber, 2001), p.79.

37   Mike Marqusee, *Chimes of Freedom: The Politics of Bob Dylan's Art* (New Press, 2003), p.154.

38   Dylan interviewed by Ron Rosenbaum, *Playboy*, March 1978, reprinted in Jonathan Cott (ed.), *Bob Dylan: The Essential Interviews* (Wenner, 2006), p.222.

39   Hentoff, op. cit., p.56.

40   Ibid.

41   Quoted in Greil Marcus, *Like a Rolling Stone* (Faber & Faber, 2005), p.155.

42   Heylin, op. cit., p.212.

43   Quoted in Bob Spitz, *Dylan* (Viking, 1989), p.312.

44   Heylin, op. cit., p.228.

45   Shelton, op. cit., p.197.

46   Dylan interviewed by Nora Ephron and Susan Edmiston, August 1965, reprinted in Jonathan Cott (ed.), *Bob Dylan: the Essential Interviews* (Wenner, 2006), p.48.

47   See 'Bob Dylan's "Mr Jones" dies', *NME*, 28 November 2007.

48   Quoted in Clinton Heylin, *Revolution in the Air: The Songs of Bob Dylan*, vol. 1: 1957–73 (Constable, 2009), p.249.

49   See Nat Hentoff, op. cit., p.63.

50   Dylan interviewed by Ron Rosenbaum for *Playboy*, March 1978, reprinted in Jonathan Cott (ed.), *Bob Dylan: The Essential Interviews* (Wenner, 2006), p.207.

6. Class Acts

1   Quoted in John Ramsden, *The Making of Conservative Party Policy: The Conservative Research Department since 1929* (Longman, 1980), p.225.

2   Iain Macleod, 'The Tory Leadership', *Spectator*, 17 January 1964.

3   Philip Ziegler, *Harold Wilson* (Weidenfeld & Nicolson, 1993), p.150.

4 Richard Crossman, *The Crossman Diaries* (Hamish Hamilton, Jonathan Cape, 1981), p.1005.

5 Peter Jenkins, 'Edwardian or jet age?', *Guardian*, 20 January 1964.

6 Ibid.

7 *Observer*, 16 September 1962.

8 Ben Pimlott, *Harold Wilson* (Harper Collins, 1992), p.59.

9 The phrase comes from Heath's close party friend Sara Morrison, who was appalled at the snobbery the bulk of the Tories exhibited towards him. See Philip Ziegler, *Edward Heath: The Authorized Biography* (Harper Press, 2010), p.180.

10 *Panorama*, 26 July 1965.

11 Pimlott, op. cit., p.512.

12 Susan Crosland, *Tony Crosland* (Jonathan Cape, 1982), p.148.

13 See I. G. K. Fenwick, *The Comprehensive School, 1944–1970: The Politics of Secondary Education* (Methuen, 1976), p.129.

14 Giles Radice, *Friends and Rivals: Crosland, Jenkins and Healey* (Abacus, 2003), p.347.

15 Melissa Benn, *School Wars: The Battle for Britain's Education* (Verso, 2011), p.52.

16 Quoted in Adrian Wooldridge, *Measuring the Mind: Education and Psychology in England, c.1860–1990* (Cambridge University Press, 1994), p.332.

17 Anthony Crosland, *The Future of Socialism* (Jonathan Cape, 1956), p.261.

18 Quoted in Andrew Adonis and Stephen Pollard, *A Class Act: The Myth of Britain's Classless Society* (Hamish Hamilton, 1997), p.60.

19 Robin Pedley, *The Comprehensive School* (Penguin, 1963), pp.199–200.

7. Taking Over the Asylum

1 The phrase is Laing's own. See his memoir *Wisdom, Madness and Folly* (Macmillan, 1985), p.ix.

2 See R. D. Laing, 'Metanoia' (paper given to the Sorbonne University, Paris, 21 October 1967, published in Hendrik Ruitenbeek (ed.), *Going Crazy: The Radical Therapy of R. D. Laing and Others* (Bantam, 1972), p.141.

3 Quoted in Bob Mullan, *Mad to Be Normal: Conversations with R. D. Laing*, (Free Association Books, 1995), p.200.

4 Quoted in Mullan, op. cit., p.192.

5 Quoted in Mullan, op. cit., pp.180 and 181.

6 R. D. Laing, *The Divided Self* (Pelican, 1965), p.9. The book was first published in hardback in 1960, though it sold few copies. It was with the paperback edition of 1965 that sales – and Laing's reputation – really began to soar.

7 R. D. Laing, *The Divided Self* (Pelican, 1965), p.100.

8 R. D. Laing, *The Politics of Experience* (Penguin, 1967), p.110.

9 Quoted in Allan Beveridge (ed.), *Portrait of the Psychiatrist as a Young Man: The Early Writing and Work of R. D. Laing* (Oxford University Press, 2011), p.316.

10 T. S. Eliot, *Notes Towards the Definition of Culture* (Faber & Faber, 1948), p.43.

11 Reprinted in R. D. Laing, *The Politics of Experience* (Penguin, 1967), p.50.

12 Ibid., p.68.

13 Ibid., p.65.

14 Ibid., p.87

15 Victoria Brittain, 'An End to Fashionable Madness', *Times*, 9 October 1972.

16 'Heirs to a Name', *Sunday Times*, 24 November 1974.

17 Quoted in John Clay, *R. D. Laing: A Divided Self* (Hodder & Stoughton, 1996), p.178.

18 Ibid.

19 Quoted in Daniel Burston, *The Wing of Madness: The Life and Work of R. D. Laing* (Harvard University Press, 1996), p.122.

20 David Cohen, 'Laing, the Divided Prophet', *New Society*, 5 May 1977.

21 Clay, op. cit., unnumbered page.

22 Clay, op. cit., p.7.

23 Quoted in Bob Mullan, *Mad to Be Normal: Conversations with R. D. Laing*, (Free Association Books, 1995), p.50.

24 See Bob Mullan, *R. D. Laing: A Personal View* (Duckworth, 1999), p.186.

25 Ibid., p.110.

26 Antonin Artaud, 'Van Gogh: The Man Suicided by Society', *Horizon*, January 1948.

27 Ibid.

28 R. D. Laing, *Wisdom, Madness and Folly: The Making of a Psychiatrist 1927–1957* (Macmillan, 1985), p.95.

29 Ibid., p.96.

30 Ibid.

31 Ibid.

32 See Vincent's essay in Bob Mullan (ed.), *R. D. Laing: Creative Destroyer* (Sage, 1997), p.84.

33 Anthony Clare, *In the Psychiatrist's Chair* (Heinemann, 1992), p.209.

34 Laing (1985), p.98.

35 Quoted in Clay, op. cit., pp.48–9.

36 Mary Barnes and Joe Berke, *Mary Barnes: Two Accounts of a Journey through Madness* (Free Association, 1991), p.14.

37 See James S. Gordon, 'Who is Mad? Who is Sane? R. D. Laing: In Search of a New Psychiatry', *Atlantic Monthly*, January 1971.

38 See Thomas S. Szasz, 'Anti-Psychiatry: The Paradigm of the Plundered Mind', *New Review*, August 1976.

39 Elaine Showalter, *The Female Malady: Women, Madness and English Culture* (Pantheon, 1985), p.230.

40 Quoted in Beveridge, op. cit., p.67.

41 From a draft version of Laing's essay 'Philosophy and Medicine', *Surgo*, June 1949. The passage is omitted from the final edit.

42   Laing (1965) op. cit., p.12.

43   Ibid.

44   Joseph Berke, 'R. D. Laing', *British Journal of Psychotherapy*, Volume 7, issue 2, p.177.

45   R. D. Laing, 'Health and happiness' (unpublished essay).

46   Ibid.

47   John Clay, *R. D. Laing: A Divided Self* (Hodder & Stoughton, 1996), p.136.

48   As embodied in Roy Griffiths's 1988 report *Community Care: Agenda for Action*.

49   Quoted in Bob Mullan, *Mad to Be Normal: Conversations with R. D. Laing*, (Free Association Books, 1995), p.190.

50   Joseph Berke (ed.), *Counterculture* (Peter Owen, 1969), p.410.

51   Bowie was talking on the BBC documentary *Cracked Actor*, originally broadcast on 26 January 1975.

52   Quoted in Rob Chapman, *Syd Barrett: A Very Irregular Head* (Faber, 2010), p.203. Other members of Pink Floyd are less convinced Barrett ever made the effort to meet Laing, it should be said.

53   Quoted in Laura Bergquist, 'Curious story behind the new Cary Grant', *Look*, 1 September 1959.

54   Cynthia Lennon, *John* (Hodder, 2006), p.242.

55   Pattie Boyd with Penny Junor, *Wonderful Today* (Headline, 2007), pp.101–2.

56   Quoted in Clinton Heylin, *The Act You've Known for All These Years* (Canongate, 2007), p.6.

57   See David Ingleby's 'The View from the North Sea' in *Cultures of Psychiatry*, Marijke Gijswijt-Hofstra and Roy Porter (eds), (Editions Rodopi, 1998), p.311.

58   M. Sigler, H. Osmond, H. Mann, 'Laing's Models of Madness', *British Journal of Psychiatry*, vol 115, p.947.

59   Quoted in *Syd Barrett and Pink Floyd: Dark Globe*, Julian Palacios (Plexus, 2010), p.87.

60   Ibid.

61   See Adrian C. Laing, *R. D. Laing: A Biography* (Peter Owen, 1994), p.215.

62   Rosemary Dinnage, 'The rise and fall of a half-genius', *New York Review of Books*, 14 November 1996.

63   Quoted in Elaine Showalter, *The Female Malady: Women, Madness and English culture* (Pantheon, 1985), p.243.

64   R. D. Laing, *Facts of Life* (Allen Lane, 1976), pp.76–7.

65   David Ingleby 'Precocious and Alone', *TLS*, 11 October 1985.

66   Ibid., p.201.

67   Anthony Clare, 'Anthony Clare' in Bob Mullan (ed.), *R. D. Laing: Creative Destroyer* (Cassell, 1997), p.3.

8. Conduct Unbecoming

1   Harold Wilson, *The Labour Government 1964–70* (Weidenfeld & Nicolson, 1971), p.80.

2   Wilson quoted in *Liverpool Daily Post*, 3 May 1954.

3   Wilson quoted in *Daily Telegraph*, 3 May 1954.

4   See Rhiannon Vickers, 'Harold Wilson, the British Labour Party and the War in Vietnam', *Journal of War Studies*, vol. 10, no. 2 (Spring 2008), p.47.

5   See Michael Stewart, *Life and Labour* (Sidgwick & Jackson, 1980), p.153.

6   Quoted in Rhiannon Vickers, 'Foreign policy beyond Europe' in Peter Dorey, *The Labour Governments 1964-1970* (Routledge, 2006), p133.

7   Richard Crossman, *The Crossman Diaries: Selections from the Diaries of a Cabinet Minister, 1964–70* (ed. Anthony Howard), (Hamish Hamilton, 1979), p.456.

8   Geoffrey Goodman, *The Awkward Warrior: Frank Cousins, His Life and Times* (Davis-Poynter, 1979), pp.492–3.

9   Ungrateful as ever, Waugh has Guy find Churchill's wartime speeches 'painfully boastful'.

10   See Michael Davie (ed.), *The Diaries of Evelyn Waugh* (Penguin, 1979), p.451.

11   Mark Amory (ed.), *The Letters of Evelyn Waugh* (Weidenfeld & Nicolson, 1980), p.142.

12   Selina Hastings, *Evelyn Waugh: A Biography* (Sinclair Stevenson, 1994), p.424.

13   Ibid.

14   Amory, op. cit., p.141.

15   Evelyn Waugh, *The Sword of Honour Trilogy* (Penguin, 1984), p.396.

16   Ian Fleming, The Man with the Golden Gun (Jonathan Cape, 1965), p. 21.

17   See David Lewin's interview with Connery, *Playboy*, November 1965.

18   John le Carré, *The Spy Who Came in from the Cold* (Sceptre, 1999), p.220.

19   Ibid., p.21.

20   *Time*, 29 May 1964.

21   John le Carré, *The Looking Glass War* (Sceptre, 1999), p.166.

22   Ibid., pp.60–1.

23   Gertrude Stein, *Picasso* (Batsford, 1938), p.11.

24   Ibid., p.60.

25   Avengers writer Brian Clemens interviewed on *Night Waves*, Radio 3, 20 April 2011.

26   See www.honorblackman.co.uk

27   Stanley Reynolds on TV, *Guardian*, 16 January 1967.

28   *Avenging The Avengers*, Channel 4, 1992.

29   See, for instance, Thomas Andrae, 'Television's First Feminist: The Avengers and female spectatorship', *Discourse: Theoretical Studies in Media and Culture*, Spring 1996. Or listen to Bea Campbell and Sarah Dunant in conversation on *Front Row*'s *Avengers* special, Radio 3, 20 April 2011.

30   See Patrick Macnee and Marie Cameron, *Blind in One Ear: The Avengers Returns* (Mercury House, 1989), p.224.

31 John Simon, 'Abelard's Loss – and Ibsen's too', *New York Magazine*, 29 March 1971.
32 See Patricia Macnee and Marie Cameron, *Blind in One Ear* (Virgin, 1988), p.245.
33 See Greil Marcus, *Invisible Republic: Bob Dylan's Basement Tapes* (Picador, 1997), reissued as *The Old, Weird America* in 2011.
34 *Avenging The Avengers*, Channel 4, 1992.
35 Quoted in Ian Cameron and Robin Wood, *Antonioni* (Studio Vista, 1968), p.9.
36 From Tynan's *Observer* review of the show at the London Arts Theatre, 7 August 1955, reprinted in Kenneth Tynan, *Curtains* (Longmans, 1961), p.101.
37 Vivian Mercier, 'The Uneventful Event', *Irish Times*, 18 February 1956.
38 Samuel Beckett, *Waiting for Godot* (Faber & Faber, 1965), p.7
39 'Specific Objects' was the title of an essay Judd published in *Arts Yearbook 8*, 1965. The essay is reprinted in Thomas Kellein (ed.), *Donald Judd: Early Work, 1955–1968* (D.A.P., 2002).
40 See Eco's essay 'The Narrative Structure in Fleming' in Oreste Del Buono and Umberto Eco (eds), *The Bond Affair*, translated by R. A. Downie (Macdonald, 1966), p.58.

9. Never Such Innocence

1 Edward Bond, *Notebooks*, vol I (Methuen, 2000), 2 August 1965, p.91.
2 William Gaskill, *A Sense of Direction* (Faber & Faber, 1988), p.67.
3 Selby played Fred in the original production. See Maddy Costa, 'We didn't set out to shock', *Guardian*, 10 October 2011.
4 In a letter to the editor of the *Guardian*, 12 November 1965.
5 J. C. Trewin, *Illustrated London News*, 13 November 1965.
6 J. W. Lambert, 'Past the limits of brutality', *Sunday Times*, 14 November 1965.
7 Quoted in Nicholas de Jongh, *Politics, Prudery and Perversions* (Methuen, 2000), p.215.
8 William Gaskill, *A Sense of Direction* (Faber & Faber, 1988), p.68.
9 Quoted in Philip Roberts, *The Royal Court Theatre and the Modern Stage* (Oxford University Press, 1986), p.162.
10 Edward Bond, *Selections from the Notebooks*, vol. 1, (Methuen, 2000), p.87.
11 Laurence Olivier, 'Violence and the censor', letter to the *Observer*, 21 November 1965.
12 Ibid.
13 Lambert, op. cit.
14 Ibid.
15 *The Times*, 25 November 1965
16 Mary Whitehouse, *Cleaning-Up TV: From Protest to Participation* (Blandford, 1967), pp.167–8.

17 'Fanny Hill and the censors', *Observer*, 27 June 1965.
18 See Kathleen Tynan, *The Life of Kenneth Tynan* (Weidenfeld & Nicolson, 1987), p.237.
19 Terence Rattigan, *The Collected Plays*, vol. I (Hamish Hamilton, 1953), p.xi.
20 Mary Whitehouse, *Cleaning-Up TV: From Protest to Participation* (Blandford, 1967), p.16.
21 *Daily Telegraph* obituary, 24 November 2001.
22 Ibid.
23 Mary Whitehouse, *Who Does She Think She Is?* (New English Library, 1971), p.22.
24 *New York World-Telegram*, 26 August 1936.
25 See Michael Tracey and David Morrison, *Whitehouse* (Macmillan, 1979), p.64.
26 Published in the *National Viewers and Listeners Association News*, No 2 (November 1967).
27 Quoted in *Daily Telegraph* obituary, 24 November 2001.
28 Quoted in Max Caulfield, *Mary Whitehouse* (Mowbray's, 1975), p.140.
29 Ibid.
30 Mary Whitehouse, *Whatever Happened to Sex* (Wayland, 1977), p.72.
31 See Ben Thompson (ed.), *Ban this Filth!: Letters from the Mary Whitehouse Archive* (Faber & Faber, 2012), p.12.
32 Ibid., p.51.
33 Ibid., p.1.
34 Ibid., p.2.
35 Ibid., p.156.
36 Ibid., pp.103–4.
37 Ibid., p.93.
38 Ibid., p.247.
39 Mary Whitehouse, *Cleaning-Up TV: From Protest to Participation* (Blandford, 1967), p.128.
40 Quoted in Tracey and Morrison, op. cit., p.108.
41 Thompson, op. cit., p.160.
42 Thompson, op. cit., p.159.
43 Mary Whitehouse, *Who Does She Think She Is?* (New English Library, 1971), p.69.
44 Quoted in Tracey and Morrison, op. cit., p.81.
45 Quoted in Tracey and Morrison, op. cit., pp.83–4.
46 Quoted in Tracey and Morrison, op. cit., p.123. The shows were broadcast in October 1967.
47 Quoted in Tracey and Morrison, op. cit., pp.125–6.
48 Emlyn Williams, *Beyond Belief: A Chronicle of Murder and its Detection* (Hamish Hamilton, 1967), p.viii.

49   Friedrich Nietzsche, *Thus Spoke Zarathustra*, translated by R. J. Hollingdale (Penguin, 1961), p.68.

50   *Daily Telegraph*, 30 December 2005.

51   See Fred Harrison, *Brady & Hindley: Genesis of the Moors Murders* (Grafton, 1987), p.26.

52   Williams, op. cit., p.55.

53   Pamela Hansford Johnson, *On Iniquity* (Macmillan, 1967), p.17.

54   Ibid., p.54.

55   Ibid, p.18.

56   Lambert, op. cit.

57   Quoted in Ernest van den Haag, 'Is pornography a cause of crime?' (*Encounter*, December 1967), p.52.

58   J. W. Lambert, 'Pornography & censors' (*Encounter*, March 1968), p.55.

59   Wardle's remarks come from an unpublished lecture he gave to Banff in the summer of 1966, selections of which are quoted in Nicholas de Jongh, *Politics, Prudery & Perversions: The Censoring of the English Stage 1901–1968* (Methuen, 2000), pp.222–3.

60   Edward Bond, *Saved* (Methuen, 1966), p.7.

61   *Sunday Telegraph*, 8 May 1966. Jones is best known for his work on the BBC cop shows *Z-Cars* and its successor, *Softly, Softly*.

62   Williams, op. cit., p.357. Pamela Hansford Johnson couldn't go that far, but she did think that 'something violent should have happened to put an end to violence'. Pamela Hansford Johnson, *On Iniquity*, op. cit., p.89.

63   Olivier, *Guardian*, 12 November 1965.

64   http://hansard.millbanksystems.com/lords/1966/feb/17/theatre-censorship

65   Noel Annan, *Our Age: Portrait of a Generation* (Weidenfeld & Nicolson, 1990), p.133.

66   Quoted in de Jongh, op. cit., p.230.

67   Quoted by Andrew Adonis in his 'Roy Jenkins as transformational minister', Mr Speaker's lectures on great 20th century parliamentarians, 25 October 2011. Available at http://www.instituteforgovernment.org.uk/sites/default/files/Roy_Jenkins_as_transformational_minister_FINAL.pdf

68   Florence Nightingale was played in the eventual production by Marianne Faithfull. Queen Victoria, it was rumoured during the early stages of rehearsal, was to be played by a man. See Terry Coleman, 'High kinks with Queen Victoria', *Guardian*, 4 August 1967.

69   http://hansard.millbanksystems.com/lords/1965/nov/30/abortion-bill-hl

70   See 'Home Secretary's reform plea', *The Times*, 23 July 1966.

10. The New Aristocracy

1   Dennis Potter, *The Nigel Barton Plays* (Penguin, 1967), pp.31–2.

2   Ibid., p.40.

3 Ibid., p.72.

4 Ibid., pp.28 and 31.

5 See Potter's essay in John Fuller, Julian Mitchell, Robin McLaren and William Donaldson (eds), *Light Blue, Dark Blue: An Anthology of Recent Writing from Oxford and Cambridge Universities* (Macdonald, 1960), p.88.

6 Quoted in W. Stephen Gilbert, *Fight and Kick and Bite: The Life and Work of Dennis Potter* (Hodder & Stoughton, 1995), p.69.

7 Richard Hoggart, *The Uses of Literacy: Aspects of Working-Class Life with Special Reference to Publications and Entertainments* (Chatto & Windus, 1957, Pelican edition), p.294.

8 *Between Two Rivers*, BBC, originally transmitted on 3 June 1960.

9 Potter talking to Alan Yentob on *Arena*, BBC2, 30 January 1987.

10 Ibid.

11 Dennis Potter, 'Cue Teleciné – Put on the Kettle', *New Society*, 22 September 1966.

12 Quoted in W. Stephen Gilbert, op. cit., p.115.

13 Jonathan Aitken, *The Young Meteors* (Secker & Warburg, 1967), p.40.

14 Malcolm Muggeridge, 'Heroes of our time', *Observer*, 12 December 1965.

15 See 'Moravia dialoga con Antonioni' in *Antonioni/Cortázar: Blow-Up*, Daniel Mario Lopez and Alberto Eduard Ojam (eds), (Cine Club Núcleo, 1968), p.103.

16 *The surface of the world* is the subtitle of Seymour Chatman's monograph on Antonioni (University of California Press, 1985).

17 Robin Wood, *Hitchcock's Films Revisited*, revised edition (Columbia University Press, 2002), p.150.

18 Ibid., p.108.

19 Ibid., p.130.

20 Ibid., p.xi.

21 Pauline Kael, *I Lost it at the Movies* (Little, Brown, 1965), p.266.

22 Kingsley Amis, *Lucky Jim* (Victor Gollancz, 1954), p.174.

23 Kingsley Amis, *The James Bond Dossier* (Jonathan Cape, 1965), p.9.

24 Amis, Ibid, p.149.

25 See Zachary Leader, *The Life of Kingsley Amis* (Jonathan Cape, 2006), p.386, et passim.

26 Tony Benn, *The Benn Diaries, 1940–1990* (Hutchinson, 1995), p.132.

27 *Sun*, 14 June 1965.

28 Quoted in Philip Norman, *Shout* (Hamish Hamilton, 1981), p.239.

29 Ibid.

30 Ibid.

31 See http://www.beatlesbible.com/1965/06/12/press-conference-mbe-announcement/

32 Quoted in Norman, op. cit.

33 Quoted in the *New York Times*, 16 June 1965.

34 See *Newsweek*, 15 June 1965.

35   Quoted in *The Times*, 15 June 1965.
36   Robert Freeman, *The Beatles: A Private View* (Barnes and Noble, 1990), unnumbered page.
37   Philip Norman, *Lennon: The Life* (Harper Collins, 2008), p.160.
38   Tony Palmer, 'The Beatles' bull's-eye', *Observer*, 17 November 1968.
39   I have been unable to track down the essay in *High Fidelity* magazine in which Gould compares the Beatles unfavourably to Petula Clark. For more on this, though, see Jonathan Cott's *Conversations with Glenn Gould* (University of Chicago Press, 2005), p.106 et passim.

Epilogue

1   Quoted in Richard Williams, 'Now rest in peace, Albert Johanneson', *Guardian*, 3 October 1995.
2   Quoted in 'Atticus' (Hunter Davies), *Sunday Times*, 20 November 1966.
3   Quoted in Williams, op. cit.
4   Roy Jenkins, *The Labour Case* (Penguin, 1959), p.140.
5   See Roy Jenkins, *A Life at the Centre* (Macmillan, 1991), p.177.
6   Ibid., pp.136 and 137.

INDEX